The Vest-Pocket **Entrepreneur**

Everything You Need to Start and Run Your Own Business

David E. Rye

PRENTICE HALL
Englewood Cliffs, New Jersey 07632

Prentice-Hall International (UK) Limited, *London*
Prentice-Hall of Australia Pty. Limited, *Sydney*
Prentice-Hall Canada, Inc., *Toronto*
Prentice-Hall Hispanoamericana, S.A., *Mexico*
Prentice-Hall of India Private Limited, *New Delhi*
Prentice-Hall of Japan, Inc., *Tokyo*
Simon & Schuster Asia Pte. Ltd., *Singapore*
Editora Prentice-Hall do Brasil, Ltda., *Rio de Janeiro*

10 9 8 7 6 5 4 3 2

Library of Congress Cataloging-in-Publication Data

Rye, David E.
   The vest-pocket entrepreneur : everything you need to start
and run your own business / David E. Rye.
      p.   cm.
   Includes index.
   ISBN 0-13-158510-X
   1. New business enterprises—Handbooks, manuals, etc.
2. Small business—Management—Handbooks, manuals, etc.
I. Title.
HD62.5.R928   1994
658.02′2—dc20

94-34386
CIP

ISBN 0-13-158510-X

PRENTICE HALL
Career & Personal Development
Englewood Cliffs, NJ 07632

Simon & Schuster, A Paramount Communications Company

Printed in the United States of America

About the Author

David Rye's entrepreneurial experience ranges from starting a computer software company in the early 1980s to the management of several Fortune 100 start-up subsidiary companies. He is currently president of a recreational company based in Scottsdale, Arizona, that specializes in the marketing and promotion of recreational products. He has an MBA in marketing and is a Ph.D. candidate at the Fielding Institute. David teaches entrepreneurship and other related business courses at the University of Colorado. His other books on new business startups include *Two for the Money, The Corporate Game,* and *Winning the Entrepreneurial Game*. He is currently writing another book entitled *The Small Business Guide to Personal Computers*.

To my wife Cheri, and daughters Kristi and Kori, for their love, patience, and moral support in writing this book.

Acknowledgments

I wish to thank my literary agent Michael Snell, who over the years has given me invaluable guidance and advice in shaping my work. My thanks extend to the editors of Prentice-Hall and Karen Hansen for their input in the preparation of the manuscript.

Contents

Preface

An entrepreneurial wave is sweeping the United States. Each year, millions of entrepreneurs emerge out of our society to organize, manage, and assume the risk of starting new businesses — despite the overwhelming odds that 80 percent of them will fail. Although these modern day pioneers have high hopes and are not short on enthusiasm, most lack formal entrepreneurial training or education. *The Vest-Pocket Entrepreneur* is a step-by-step management tool that can be used to convert your entrepreneurial ideas into a successful business. The book's comprehensive table of contents offers quick access to hundreds of different personal business subjects you can use not only to start a business, but to keep it running.

This how-to book provides practical answers, examples, illustrations, sources of information, and advice for the variety of problems entrepreneurs face when they start a business. It's tailor made for people who want to master the fundamentals of becoming an entrepreneur and starting their own businesses without wasting time chasing "fly-by-night" schemes. *The Vest-Pocket Entrepreneur* will help you:

- Identify and qualify your entrepreneurial skills and ideas
- Discover viable business opportunities
- Obtain the financing you need
- Establish successful marketing, sales, and business plans
- Manage your business to assure its ongoing success and growth

The book guides you through the complete business startup process. It's easy to read and provides a comprehensive set of small business guidelines. Part One (Chapters 1–3) takes you through all of the startup elements you should consider before you begin to seriously investigate business opportunities. You'll learn how to appraise your personal entrepreneurial skills and prepare a business charter. We present compelling information about why many small businesses fail and what you can do to avoid failure. You'll also learn how to find and evaluate alternative business opportunities.

Part Two (Chapters 4–10) covers the three critical business disciplines — finance, marketing, and sales. We'll show you how to determine your financial requirements, develop investment strategies, and create a solid financial plan. You'll learn how to use your financial plan to establish a loan strategy. How to get loans and sources for loans are also covered. Marketing techniques are covered to set the stage for the chapters that follow on pricing and sales strategies.

Part Three (Chapters 11–14) takes you through all of the issues that are associated with the accounting of your business. We begin the section with a discussion about the insurance issues you should consider to protect your investment. Next, we cover the various types of accounting systems and reports that are important to any business. Many examples and illustrations are included to illustrate the accounting process. The organizational options for your business follow with a complete analysis of the advantages and disadvantages of each business form covered. You'll also learn how to acquire equipment for your business economically.

Part Four (Chapters 15–18) covers a variety of people, business planning and management issues. You'll learn how to find and hire the right people. The alternative of using contract employees is also covered along with state and federal employment regulations that can affect your business. You'll see how to apply copyrights, patents, and trademarks to protect your business assets. The importance of a formal business plan is covered, followed by a how-to-manage-your-business discussion that's filled with meaningful examples.

The Vest-Pocket Entrepreneur has been designed to be clear, concise, and to the point. It is a valuable reference tool that gives you hands-on techniques for developing and refining your entrepreneurial ideas. For the entrepreneur who wants the new business development process boiled down into commonsense words, there is no better book.

David E. Rye

PART ONE

EVALUATING YOUR OPTIONS

1

Evaluating Your Entrepreneurial Potential

Until recently, entrepreneurs were not widely understood. There was a general lack of knowledge and information about what made them successful and how
they operated. The recent interest in America's small
businesses has revitalized our interest in entrepreneurs. Most business universities and colleges now
offer courses in entrepreneurship. As a result, business professionals and management scientists have
learned a lot about what it takes to become a successful entrepreneur.

   If you think you want to be your own boss and
run your own business, but you're not sure you have
the right qualifications to be an entrepreneur, then
you will appreciate the material in this chapter. We
cover the important qualifications of successful entrepreneurs and profile their attributes.

   Do you have a personal profile that is similar to
a successful entrepreneur? We'll show you how to
analyze your entrepreneurial potential in the balance
of this chapter. The intent of the exercise is to help
you identify skill areas in which improvements can
be made. Toward the end of the chapter, we will show
you how to create a business charter, which is one of
the first essential steps to starting your own business.

PROFILE OF AN ENTREPRENEUR

Let's establish a definition for an entrepreneur before
we discuss profiles. An entrepreneur is one who orga-
nizes and directs a new business undertaking. The entrepreneur assumes the risks that are associated with
a startup process. Some entrepreneurs may appear to
have been born into the art — starting lemonade
stands in their youth and working up from there
but most learned to become entrepreneurs by following and studying successes of experienced entrepreneurs. In their subconscious minds, they may have
admired the entrepreneurial success of someone they

knew, such as a relative, friend, or even a parent. Here are some of the qualities that are typical of a winning entrepreneur's profile.

- Being a high achiever. Over the past 25 years, studies have shown that entrepreneurs are characterized by their high need for achievement. Because of their need for achievement, they prefer to work with experts when confronted with challenging problems. They tend to be long-range thinkers and will often focus on the long-range vision of their businesses rather than on immediate problems. This attribute can prove to be frustrating for people who work for entrepreneurs and are attempting to get their attention to help resolve near-term problems.

- Being a risk taker. Entrepreneurs are not afraid to take on tasks that are accompanied by some risk. However, they are neither low or high risk-takers. They prefer to take on intermediate risk and will avoid high risk whenever possible. Entrepreneurs recognize that higher levels of achievement are possible only if they are willing to accept risks to accomplish their goals.

- Being a problem solver. Entrepreneurs are natural leaders and are usually the first to identify problems to be overcome. If it is pointed out to them that their solution to a problem will not work for some valid reason, they will quickly identify an alternate problem-solving approach.

- Being a status seeker. Entrepreneurs find satisfaction in symbols of success that are external to themselves. They like the businesses they have built to be praised, but are often embarrassed by self-directed praise. You will often see highly successful entrepreneurs driving old cars.

- Having a high energy level. Entrepreneurs are physically resilient and in good health. They can work for extended periods of time when building their businesses. They almost refuse to get sick when they are in a "business-building" mode.

- Possessing self confidence. Entrepreneurs are highly confident individuals who believe in their skills and abilities. They think their actions can change events and believe they are the masters of their own lives. They refuse to believe that outside events can decisively influence their success and drive for achievement.

- Avoiding emotional attachments. Entrepreneurs frequently have difficulty forming close emotional attachments, which may result in developing poor relationships with friends and relatives. Because of the difficulty in forming close relationships, they will often become deeply involved in their work, and in the process transfer their feelings for others into their businesses. Some will subsequently treat their business as a living being and become emotionally involved with it. As a result, long hours of work are not considered burdensome to entrepreneurs.

- Needing personal satisfaction. Because entrepreneurs are motivated by a need for personal achievement, they often have little interest in any kind of organizational structure. They treat most of the traditional organizational activities of management with disdain and have a difficult time working for large corporations.

In summary, entrepreneurs are achievement oriented and believe they are masters of their own destiny. They are not dependent upon others for emotional support and are highly self-directed individuals. They tend to concentrate on the long-term vision of their businesses and ignore daily organizational problems. A summary profile of an entrepreneur is shown in Exhibit 1–1.

SUCCESS CHARACTERISTICS OF ENTREPRENEURS

Every year, thousands of businesses get started. Some will survive, but unfortunately, most will fail. The reason some businesses start with spectacular success isn't because their founders had a lot of money when

Exhibit 1-1. Profile of an Entrepreneur	
Profile Characteristics	**Distinctive Entrepreneurial Traits**
High Achievers	They prefer to work with experts to obtain achievement goals.
Risk Takers	They are not afraid to take on risks but will avoid high risk ventures whenever possible.
Problem Solvers	They are quick to identify and solve problems that may obstruct their ability to achieve their goals.
Status Seekers	They will not allow status needs to disrupt their business mission.
High Energy Levels	They are dedicated and are willing to work long hours to build their businesses.
Self Confidence	They rely on their high confidence levels to achieve success.
Emotional Attachments	They will not allow their emotional relationships to disrupt the success of their businesses.
Personal Satisfaction	They consider organizational structures as an obstacle to what they want to accomplish.

they started. Their success is attributed to the fact that they were put together by entrepreneurs who knew what they were doing.

In every instance, the founders either had, or acquired, the entrepreneurial experience and knowledge that were needed to startup the business. They recognized what their weak points were and acquired the skills they needed to assure the successful startup of their companies. They also understood how the various parts of a business fit together to form a total structure and knew that if one part was missing, their businesses would fail. For example, they knew that a successful sales plan is directly dependent upon support from the marketing and promotional plans, and that the strategic business plan acts as the glue that holds all of the sub-plans together so they work in concert with each other.

Entrepreneurs do not function well in structured organizations and do not like others to have authority over them. Most believe they can do the job better than anyone else and will strive for maximum responsibility and accountability. They enjoy creating business strategies and thrive on the process of achieving their goals. Once a goal is achieved, they'll quickly replace it with a greater goal. They strive

Exhibit 1-2. Success Characteristics of an Entrepreneur	
Success Characteristics	**Distinctive Success Traits**
Self Control	They like to be in control of everything they do.
Getting Things Done	They like activity that shows goal-oriented progress.
Self-Directed	They are self-motivated with a high desire to succeed.
Manage by Objective	They are quick to comprehend the detailed tasks that must be completed to achieve their objectives.
Opportunity Analyzers	They will analyze all options to assure their success and minimize risks.
Personal Controllers	They recognize the importance of their personal life over their business life.
Creative Thinkers	They are always looking for a better way of doing something.
Problem Solvers	They will always look at options to solve any problem that stands in their way.
Objective Thinkers	They are not afraid to admit if they are wrong.

to exert whatever influence they can over future events.

In large structured organizations, entrepreneurs are easy to recognize by the statements they make. You may hear them say "If they wanted that job done right, they should have given it to me." Entrepreneurs believe that they are smarter than their peers and superiors, which is a dominant characteristic in their behavior. They have a compelling need to do their own thing in their own way. They need the freedom to choose and to act according to their own perception of what actions will result in success. They generally display the following characteristics. (Other characteristics of entrepreneurs are summarized in Exhibit 1–2.)

- They need to control their work. Entrepreneurs are self-confident when they are in control of what they're doing and are working alone. They tackle problems immediately with confidence and are persistent in their pursuit of their objectives. Most are at their best in the face of adversity because they thrive on their own self-confidence.

- They enjoy getting things done. Entrepreneurs have a never-ending sense of urgency to develop their ideas. Inactivity makes them impatient, tense, and uneasy. They thrive on activity and are not likely to be found sitting on a bank fishing, unless the fish are biting. When they are in the entrepreneurial mode, they are more likely to be found getting things done instead of fishing.

- They are self-directed. They prefer individual sports over team sports. Entrepreneurs prefer games in which their brawn and brain directly influence the outcome and pace of the game. They have drive, display high energy levels, are achievement oriented, and are tireless in the pursuit of their goals.

- They manage by objectives. Entrepreneurs can comprehend complex situations that may include planning, making strategic decisions, and working on multiple business ideas simultaneously. They are always aware of important details and will continuously review all possibilities to achieve their business objectives. They believe in management by objective, or MBO principles.

- They are opportunity analyzers. Entrepreneurs will carefully analyze opportunities before they commit themselves. They will act only after they are convinced that little risk remains in the endeavor. These are traits that carry them on to success where others fail.

- They control their schedules. All successful entrepreneurs work long hours, which cuts into their personal life. Long working hours are not unique to entrepreneurs. Many corporate managers and executives work well beyond the average 40-hour work week. The primary difference between entrepreneurs and their corporate counterparts is schedule control. In the corporate world, you may not have control over your schedule. If some higher level manager calls a Saturday meeting, you've got no choice but to be there. Entrepreneurs don't mind working 60- to 70-hour weeks, but they will do everything they can to preserve their private time. They schedule important meetings during the week so they have weekends off for their personal lives whenever possible.

- They are creative thinkers. The opposite of creativity is rigidity. Entrepreneurs are not rigid in their thinking and become irritated with the person who says "We do it this way because that's the way it has always been done." They realize that if you cling to the old ways of doing things, you'll never come up with new solutions that are demanded by today's small businesses.

- They are problem solvers. Entrepreneurs have a clear understanding of what they want to achieve and can quickly resolve problems that stand in their way. They know how to evaluate alternatives when solving problems so that they are easier to resolve. For example, the problem may be that they need more space. They'll first challenge why they need more space and analyze all of the alternatives. The selection of an alternative may pose a new set of problems, but if it reduces the magnitude of the original problem, they will choose the alternative.

- They are objective thinkers. When entrepreneurs find a solution to a problem, they will brainstorm the solution with as many qualified people as they can find to avoid judging their own answers. They will accept solution modifications that make sense and will replace their solution with a totally new and better alternative. Entrepreneurs refuse to allow their egos to override their objectivity.

FAILURE CHARACTERISTICS OF ENTREPRENEURS

Stories about entrepreneurs tend to focus on why they succeed rather than on why they fail. However, their failure rate is significantly higher than their success rate. There are several reasons why entrepreneurs fail, which are summarized in Exhibit 1–3.

Exhibit 1-3 Failure Characteristics of an Entrepreneur	
Failure Characteristics	**Distinctive Failure Traits**
Management Experience	They lack a general understanding of the key management disciplines.
Financial Planning	They underestimate the capital needs for their business.
Location	They select a poor startup location for their company.
Business Controls	They fail to control key aspects of their business.
High Spenders	They incur high startup expenses that could have been deferred.
Receivable Management	They incur poor cash flow problems due to lack of attention to accounts receivable.
Dedication	They underestimate the personal time and dedication it takes to start a business.
Overexpand	They take on an expansion program before they are ready.

- They lack management experience. Many entrepreneurs do not fully understand the intricacies of running a business. Some entrepreneurs will enter lines of business they understand, but do not know how to manage. When business problems arise, they are not able to solve them. For example, an entrepreneur with an engineering background may have the skills to design valuable products, but know nothing about accounting, finance, marketing, sales, and personnel management. If these business disciplines are ignored, the business will fail.

- They are poor financial planners. Underestimating the capital needed to start a new business is one of the primary causes for failure. Entrepreneurs will often start a business thinking that they have enough capital to see them through the startup years only to discover that they are out of capital before the end of the first year.

- They are poor location analysts. Some entrepreneurs will attempt to save money by picking a poor location, only to find out that their clientele is not attracted to the location. The location may be unappealing or inconvenient to their customers. When location is critical, it is wise to spend the time and money to find the right one.

- They are ineffective business controllers. Another reason why entrepreneurs fail is because they use ineffective control procedures, such as inventory and accounting controls, to run the business. As a result, they will frequently not know the number of items they have in stock or how much they are spending. Poor business controls prevent effective business planning and can ultimately lead to the failure of the business.

- They are high spenders. Some entrepreneurs put too much of their capital into fixed assets, such as new, rather than used furniture and office equipment. This limits the working capital they have available to run their businesses, which can cause other problems. For example, a client may wish to double its regular orders, but the capital-constrained entrepreneur may not have the cash to increase inventories to accommodate the larger orders.

- They are poor receivable managers. Cash management problems can be compounded when entrepreneurs fail to manage accounts receivable. Credit-granting practices may be too liberal, which results in higher-than-expected bad debts and slow payments. If the accounts receivable problems are allowed to continue, the business may have to liquidate.

- They lack dedication. Entrepreneurs must be aware of the dedication to hard work that their business requires, especially in the formative years. They must work long and irregular hours, which may disrupt family life. Entrepreneurs must be willing to endure these difficulties until the business becomes sound. If prospective entrepreneurs are not willing to make these sacrifices, they should not start a business.

- They overexpand. Major problems may develop as a result of overexpansion. When the
  business expands, the quality of its products
  and services may decline, resulting in customer dissatisfaction and the loss of customers. In addition, the entrepreneur may be
  unable to generate enough new business to
  pay for the expansion.

  In summary, there are definite and clearly
  identifiable reasons as to why entrepreneurs
  fail. Potential entrepreneurs should be sensitive to the failure pitfalls they may encounter.
  All of the failure points discussed can be
  avoided — or minimize — through careful
  planning and the effective control of resources.

HOW SELF-ASSESSMENT WILL HELP YOU SUCCEED

Your success as an entrepreneur and a business owner
doesn't depend on any one factor, such as having a
perfect business location or an adequate source of
capital to get started. It depends on your ability to
provide excellent general management capabilities to
your business. Someone once asked me, "How do
you achieve excellence?" My answer: "In the race for
excellence, there is no finish line." As an entrepreneur, you will continue to develop excellence in
everything you do if you want to succeed.

In this section, you'll learn how to assess your
entrepreneurial strengths, weaknesses, and how to
satisfy your personal expectations. We'll show you
how to conduct a self-assessment exercise to help
you develop your strengths and eliminate or minimize your weaknesses. The exercise will conclude by
showing you how to relate your answers to the self-
assessment questionnaire to your personal expectations. In the process, you'll create a personal business
charter, which is a statement of what you really want
to do as an entrepreneur. The charter will become
your road map that you will use to get there.

Many of the questions and issues that you will
be asked to address are personal and self-probing.
They have been designed to assist you in evaluating
your strengths as well as your weaknesses.

OBJECTIVITY GUIDELINES

Here are some guidelines that you should consider to help maintain your objectivity.

1. Detach your ego from the evaluation questions and issues. That is a requisite qualification of a successful entrepreneur.

2. Be wary of achieving self-satisfaction in your answers because it will tend to drive you toward creating answers that you want to see, rather than valid answers.

3. A positive answer to a question should be based upon your demonstrated performance or expertise in the subject area that's presented in the question.

4. As you proceed through the exercise, remember that everybody makes mistakes. The smart entrepreneur knows how to correct mistakes and to learn from them so that they do not reoccur.

5. It is more important to acknowledge what you do not know than it is to acknowledge what you do know.

6. Ask your trusted friends and associates to answer the questions on your behalf. Do their answers agree with your answers? If not, don't aggressively challenge them to defend their answers. It is more important to find out about the reasoning behind their answers. They may be right!

Create your own questions to help you discover new knowledge and insights about yourself. Ask questions of yourself even if you know in advance that you don 't have an answer. Again, the intent of this exercise is to determine what you don't know, which is just as important as knowing what you do know.

ANSWERS GUIDELINES

1. Answer every question in writing. You may have more than one answer to a given question. If you don't honestly know the answer, state the reasons why.

2. If the question generates other questions in your mind, write them down, and attempt to answer each new question.

3. Keep asking yourself additional questions about a subject until you are satisfied that the collection of answers to the questions will tell you what you need to know about that subject. Always be aware of the fact that the more you learn about any one subject, the more questions will arise in your mind.

4. If your answer to a question demonstrates a limited knowledge about a subject, identify steps you can take to strengthen your expertise in that subject. For example, if you know nothing about accounting, is there a night-school course that you can take?

Your answers to the questionnaire should provide you with a profile of your personal strengths and weaknesses as an entrepreneur. Obviously, you will want to leverage your strengths to your maximum advantage when you start your business. But what about your weaknesses? It is human nature for people to play on their strengths and ignore their weak points. None of us want to admit that we have any weak points, but the fact of the matter is, we all do.

All successful entrepreneurs are not only willing to recognize their weak points, but they know how to correct their weaknesses as well. If they are weak in accounting, they will spend more, not less, time on the subject to improve their accounting strengths. In the process, they'll ask a lot of questions — including all of the "dumb" ones — until they know the subject.

APPRAISING YOUR PERSONAL SKILLS

One of the most important steps you must take to become a successful entrepreneur is to be honest with yourself. Four questionnaires are included here to help you evaluate your skills. The intent of all of the questions in this section is to answer one basic question: Are you the type of person who should run your own business? When you answer the questions, write down the reasons as to why you gave a "yes" or "no" answer. If you do not have an answer to a question, note why you cannot answer the question.

Entrepreneurial Qualification Questionnaire

1. Do you like to take charge of a given situation and make your own decisions?

2. Do you enjoy competing in competitive business environments?

3. Are you a self-directed individual with strong self-discipline?

4. Do you like to plan ahead and do you consistently meet your goals and objectives?

5. Are you good at time management and do you consistently get things done on time?

6. After you start your business, are you prepared to lower your standard of living until the business produces a solid income?

7. Are you in good health and do you have the physical stamina to consistently work long hours?

8. Can you admit when you are wrong and take advice from others?

9. If your business fails, are you prepared to lose everything you own?

10. Do you have the stability to withstand stress and strain?

11. Can you quickly adapt to changing situations and implement changes when necessary?

12. Are you a self-starter who can work on your own, independently of others?

13. Can you make decisions quickly and not regret bad decisions that you may make?

14. Do you trust people and do they trust you?

15. Do you know how to solve problems quickly, effectively, and with confidence?

16. Can you maintain a positive attitude even in the face of adversity?

17. Are you a good communicator and can you explain your ideas to others in words that they can understand?

Scoring the Questionnaire

If you answered "yes" to all seventeen questions, you achieved a perfect score. If you answered "no" to four or more of the questions, you may want to reconsider your interest in becoming an entrepreneur. For example, if you do not consider yourself a self-directed individual who likes to take charge of business situations, you may want to add another question to the list: Who will perform the "take charge" functions for you when you start your business? Scoring your responses to this questionnaire is relatively simple, as shown in the following example.

Total "Yes" Responses × Relative Weighting Factor
= Score
Assume 15 "yes" responses and 2 "no" responses
15 "Yes" Responses × 1.2 = Score
= 18 total points

The relative weighting factor is used to rank the "relative" importance of the answers in this questionnaire to the answers in the other questionnaires. We will show you how to evaluate your overall score to all the questionnaires at the end of the chapter. Any score below 14 may indicate that your profile does not match the profile of a successful entrepreneur. All scores are rounded to the nearest whole decimal. For example, a score of 8.4 would be rounded down to a score of 8.0, whereas a score of 8.5 or 8.6 would be rounded up to a score of 9.0.

Personal Skills Questionnaire

1. Can you list at least ten skills that will be critical to the success of your business?

2. Given the skills that you have listed, how do you rate your level of expertise in each skill area (high, medium, or low)?

3. How will your business effectively use each of the skills listed in question 1?

4. Can you acquire the skills or find people that have the skills and expertise that you need for your business?

5. Can you list at least five specific reasons as to why you want to become an entrepreneur and start a business?

Scoring the Questionnaire

Scoring this personal questionnaire is more involved than scoring the previous questionnaire because it involves some subjective judgment on your part. The following example will help you determine your overall score for this questionnaire. Your partial score for this questionnaire is the sum of your "yes" responses for questions 1,3,4, and 5.

For example, if you were able to list only seven skill areas in question 1, then this is equivalent to seven "yes" responses and three "no" responses for this question. Use the same procedure to score questions 3, 4, and 5. This example assumes 20 "yes" responses out of a possible 26 "yes" responses.

Partial Score = (yes responses to questions 1,3,4,
and 5)

= 20

In question 2, you should have assigned a high, medium, or low ranking to each of the ten skill areas that you listed in question 1. This example assumes that you assigned 4 highs, 3 mediums, and 3 lows to your critical skills.

Partial Score = (Highs × 3.0) + (Mediums × 2.0)
+ (Lows × .5)

= (4 × 3.0) + (3 × 2.0) + (3 × .50)

= 12 + 6 + 1.5

= 19.5 or 20 total points with rounding

The highest score you can achieve in question 2 is ten "highs" or 30 points (i.e., 10 × 3 = 30 points). To obtain your total score for this personal questionnaire, add the two partial scores together as we have show below. A perfect total score would be 56.

Total Score = 30 + 19.5

= 49.5 total points out of a possible score
of 56 maximum points.

Any score below 40 may indicate that you do not have the personal qualifications to start your own business.

Success Questionnaire

1. Can you list five success factors that you want to achieve within the first year of your new business?

2. Is the product or service that you are considering for your new business unique and in demand by the market you propose to serve?

3. Do you know who your competitors are and how you will successfully compete against them?

4. Do you know what your personal income expectations are and when you expect to achieve your desired income?

5. Do you know what you will do if you do not achieve your income expectations?

6. Do you know how much money you need to startup your business and where the money will come from?

7. Will you make more money in your own business than you could working for someone else?

8. Does your family support your new business idea and are they prepared to make the necessary sacrifices to help you get started?

Scoring the Questionnaire

There are several difficult questions to answer in this questionnaire. Do not be concerned if you answered "no" to several of the questions at this time. This book will help you find the answers that you need.

The sum of your "yes" responses to the eight questions represents your total score for this questionnaire. You must be able to list at least five solid success factors in question 1 to achieve a "yes" response on this important question. The example that follows assumes six "yes" responses were given out of a total of eight:

Total "Yes" Responses × Relative Weighting Factor
= Total Score
6 "Yes" Responses × 4.0 = 24 total points

Any score below 20 may indicate that you do not have a profile that matches that of a successful entrepreneur.

Partnership Questionnaire

If your business startup will involve the activities of more than one person, then each partner should independently answer all of the questions in this section. Compare your answers and consider the issues that are covered in the following questions:

1. Was each partner chosen on the basis of contribution to the business (i.e., not just friendship)?

2. Do the partners have complementary rather than conflicting goals for the business?

3. Do the partners acknowledge their limitations (i.e., the strengths and weaknesses they bring to the business)?

4. Do you know the skill and expertise qualifications of all your potential partners?

5. Do you have a compensation plan that is acceptable to all partners?

6. Are the decision-making and functional responsibilities of each partner clearly identified and acceptable to each partner?

7. If one of the partners fails to perform to the expectations of the other partners, is there a mechanism in place that allows for the removal of that partner?

8. Do you know what you will do if one of the partners decides to leave the business or dies?

Scoring the Questionnaire

If you do not get satisfactory answers to any of these questions, you may want to re-evaluate your partnership structure. If major partnership conflicts cannot be resolved, the partnership should probably be dissolved before you enter into the startup steps of the business. The scoring example that follows assumes six "yes" responses were given out of a total of eight possible "yes" responses:

Total "Yes" Responses × Relative Weighting Factor
= Total Score
6 "Yes" Responses × 2.0 = 12

Any score below 12 may indicate that you have a problem with the structure of your partnership. Partnership issues are covered in more detail in Chapter 13.

CREATING AN EXPERTISE WORKSHEET

Your business and technical expertise will be extremely important to assure the success of your busi-

Exhibit 1-4. Expertise Worksheet				
Expertise Categories	**High**	**Medium**	**Low**	**Business Rank**
Finance				
Marketing				
Product and Service Development				
Direct and Indirect Sales				
Advertising and Promotion				
Accounting				
Personnel Management				
Business Planning				

ness. The worksheet in Exhibit 1–4 has been designed to help you assess what expertise levels you need to achieve the goals and objectives of your business. The worksheet asks you to perform a self-assessment by indicating what you consider your level of expertise to be in each of the key skill areas — high, medium, or low.

For example, if you have formal training or practical experience in finance, you may rate yourself "high" in this area. On the other hand, if you feel that you do not understand the basic principles of financing, you may choose to rank your level of expertise as "low." We recommend that you complete the first part of the worksheet by rating your expertise levels first. Then, complete the second part of the worksheet by ranking the importance of each expertise category to the business.

Rank the skill categories in order of the importance you believe they have to your business by using a 1 through 8 numbering system, where 1 is most important, and 8 is least important. For example, if you assessed your financial expertise as "low," but you plan to use personal funds to finance the startup of your business, then you may decide that the finance "business rank" is an "8," relative to the importance of starting your business. However, if you know that you will need financial assistance before you can start your business, a "1" business rank for finance may be appropriate.

The worksheet will help you identify an expertise area for which you may need assistance. The intent of the worksheet is to help you identify your business strengths and areas of weakness.

Defining Skill Attributes

To help you determine your level of expertise in each skill category, we have summarized skill attributes in the list that follows.

- Finance. Finance includes the ability to manage money, interpret financial statements, and successfully seek out sources of funds for the business.
- Marketing. Marketing includes the ability to identify target markets for the products and services of your business.

- Sales. Sales includes the ability to initiate sales calls and to close sales for the business.

- Product and Service Development. Development includes the ability to create unique and competitive business offerings that consumers will buy.

- Advertising and Promotion. Advertising includes the ability to create advertising and promotional campaigns that successfully sell the offerings of your business.

- Accounting. Accounting includes the ability to accurately record and interpret the income and expenses of your business in a timely manner.

- Personnel Management. Personnel management includes the ability to hire good people and to supervise their work activities to achieve high productivity levels.

- Business Planning. Business planning includes the ability to maintain and achieve both the short and long-range planning goals of your business.

Scoring the Expertise Worksheet

Do not be concerned if you are lacking experience in some of the skill areas. We will help you develop your expertise in all of these areas in the later chapters. In the worksheet, you should have assigned a high, medium, or low ranking to each of the eight skill areas. This example assumes that you assigned 3 highs, 3 mediums, and 2 lows to the worksheet skill categories for the different weighting factors.

$$\begin{aligned} \text{Score} &= (\text{Highs} \times 3.0) + (\text{Mediums} \times 2.0) + (\text{Lows} \times .5) \\ &= (3 \times 3.0) + (3 \times 2.0) + (2 \times .5) \\ &= 9 + 6 + 1 \\ &= 16 \end{aligned}$$

The highest score you can achieve on the worksheet would be eight "highs" or 24 points (i.e., $8 \times 3 = 24$ points). Any score below 17 may be cause for concern.

Exhibit 1-5. Consolidated Score Worksheet			
Questionnaire/Worksheet	**Highest Possible Score**	**Your Score**	**Percent Score***
Qualification Questionnaire	20		
Personal Skills Questionnaire	56		
Success Questionnaire	32		
Partnership Questionnaire	16		
Expertise Worksheet	24		
Totals	148		

* To obtain your percent score, divide your score by the highest possible score.

CONSOLIDATING YOUR SCORES

The worksheet in Exhibit 1–5 consolidates the scores from all of the questionnaires and worksheets in this chapter. At a glance, it should show you where your strengths and weaknesses are relative to starting your own business.

The questionnaires and worksheet that were included in this chapter are listed in the left column. The maximum number of points that you could have scored in any questionnaire, or the worksheet, is shown in the "Highest Possible Score" column. Record your score in the next column and divide your score by the total possible points to obtain a percentage score. Any percentage score that is below 80 percent is an indication that you may have problems in one of the respective scoring categories.

Do not be concerned if your total score is lower than what you may have anticipated. As you proceed through this book, we encourage you to repeat the exercise of completing the questionnaires and worksheets to see if your score improves as a result of what you have learned.

CREATING A BUSINESS CHARTER

Clever product and service ideas are a dime a dozen. Everybody has one — and most of them never get implemented. The pseudo entrepreneurial itch often ends before the basic idea ever gets tested. Studies show that a high percentage of people open new businesses because they are frustrated with their current jobs. They'll jump into any business venture that comes along, without first checking it out. Ninety percent of this group will go out of business in their first year.

Those that make it are smart enough to recognize the symptoms of their emotional state. They are acutely aware of the fact that they may be in a vulnerable position. As a result, they will "hang on" to the security of their current job and may start a business on the side. They'll make their move to become a full-time entrepreneur when the time is right for them and after they have thoroughly checked out their business venture ideas.

To choose an entrepreneurial path that best meets your personal needs, first determine where there is a need for a product, service, or some combination of products and services. Start with a basic idea and carefully proceed through the qualification steps. Does your product or service idea have "staying power"? Can it be used to grow a customer base and will it be profitable?

For example, you may be considering a product that is in acute demand by a particular industry, or one that does not yet exist. The product may be unique, or a significant improvement over a competitive product. You may be able to produce or obtain the product at a lower cost than your competitors. Your product or service may not be available in the market you choose to serve. The first step you take toward starting a business is the analysis of your proposed product and service offerings.

To formalize the startup process, you need to create a business charter, which is the front end of your business plan (discussed in later chapters). The business charter defines the business you plan to start and addresses a number of specific questions that you may not be prepared to answer at this point in your startup process. For this reason, treat your charter as a dynamic document. As you learn more about what you want to do and refine your ideas, you can update your charter so that it reflects your current thinking. This business charter checklist will help you get started.

BUSINESS CHARTER CHECKLIST

1. What product or service do you plan to offer?
2. Who will be your primary customers?
3. What are the strengths of your product or service offerings?
4. What are the weaknesses of your product or service offerings?
5. What is the market demand for your business?
6. Where will your business be located, and what are the advantages and disadvantages of this location?
7. What facilities and levels of inventories will you need?
8. Who are your competitors and how will you compete against them?
9. What will make your business unique and why will customers want your offerings?
10. How will you advertise and promote your business?
11. How will you finance the startup and ongoing operations of your business?
12. Do you have all of the skills needed to start your business?

Do not be concerned if you lack the information needed to answer all of the questions and issues in the business charter checklist. You should be content if you can complete a working draft of a business charter at this time. Make modifications and refinements to your charter as you learn more about entrepreneurship.

SOURCES FOR ADDITIONAL INFORMATION

Two researchers (Baumback and Mancuso) have compiled an excellent set of readings on entrepreneurs in their book, *Entrepreneurship and Venture Management* (Prentice-Hall, 1975). Many of their conclusions are based upon extensive research that was conducted by the authors and other recognized experts in the field of entrepreneurship.

You may want to consider joining the American Entrepreneurs' Association. The association conducts annual seminars and publishes a monthly magazine. For further information, write or call:

American Entrepreneurs' Association
2392 Morse Avenue
Irvine, CA 92714
(714) 261-2325

Courtney Price has published a book entitled *Courtney Price Answers the Most Asked Questions from Entrepreneurs* (McGraw-Hill). As the title suggests, the book is filled with entrepreneurial questions and answers. She also offers a syndicated column, "Entrepreneurs Ask," which is featured in 350 newspapers nationwide.

2

Starting Your Own Business

In this chapter, you will learn more about what makes some businesses highly successful and why others fail. We 'll show you where you can find new business ideas that you can use to develop a business or build upon your current ideas. In the process, we encourage you to update and modify the business charter that you started in Chapter 1.

GETTING STARTED

Starting your own business includes opportunities as well as risks, which is true with any business. That is why the financial industry created profits as the reward for taking business risks. There are an infinite number of reasons why people want to start their own businesses. Two reasons always seem to stand out. First, it is possible to become wealthy from a well-managed business, even if it's a one-person operation. Second, and often the most satisfying reason, is the entrepreneurial feeling of "being your own boss" and "doing your own thing."

However, when you choose not to work for someone else, you lose the security of a regular paycheck, fringe benefits, and health coverage if you are sick. These are just a few of the obvious risks you incur in your own business. You may also be risking your personal estate if it has been used as collateral to finance the business, or your health, if excessive hours are required to launch the business.

REASONS FOR SMALL BUSINESS FAILURES

"Optimist" is the one word that best describes the person who starts a business. Unfortunately, it is a cold, hard fact that less than half of the businesses that are started this year will survive the first two years of operation. Only 20 percent will still be around five years from now. Over the past several

Exhibit 2-1. Primary Causes of Small Business Failures and What to Do About Them

Cause of Failure	Reason for Failure	How to Recognize	How to Resolve
Overcrowded market	Too many competitors offering the same products and services	Customers look but don't buy	Unique advertising and pricing discounts
No buyers	Poor location, high prices, or poor quality	Income statement shows declining profits or losses	Must resolve the specific buyer concerns. Survey customers.
Failure to change	Owner becomes complacent	Slow and progressive decline in sales	Implement recurring new programs
Lack of knowledge	Results in poor management performance	Continuous mistakes occur in the weak knowledge area	Implement a training program
Lack of capital	Poor financial planning	Always short of money	Reduce expenses and monitor cash flow
High interest rates	Poor economy	Financial news reports	Reduce borrowing and tighten credit policies
No business plan	Poor management	Always caught by business surprises	Develop and implement a business plan

years, the Small Business Administration has maintained elaborate data on the causes of business failures. Business owners may tell you their businesses failed because of too much competition, high interest rates, government regulation, a poor economy, or numerous other reasons. Although these factors may have contributed to their demise, mismanagement is the primary reason for most business failures. According to a study that was conducted by Dun and Bradstreet, mismanagement causes 90 percent of all business failures.

Most of the primary causes for business failures have been studied and documented over the past several decades. Exhibit 2–1 summarizes how to recognize the problems that cause business failures and covers the corrective action you can take to eliminate the problems before the failure occurs.

Overcrowded Market

There is an old story that brings to light the "overcrowded" market problem. If you are a dog watching other dogs chasing a car, and you decide to chase the same car, then you are just another dog. The story implies that there are a multitude of businesses in your market area that sell products and services similar to yours. If you have conducted an acceptable market analysis before you started your business, the overcrowded problems should have surfaced in the study.

Presumably, your decision to open a business in an overcrowded market would be based upon some solid evidence that you had relative to the superiority of your offerings over the competitions (e.g., price, quality, distributions, etc.). Be careful about opening a business in an overcrowded market even if you believe you have a decisive advantage over the competition. For example, let's assume that you can offer your product at a price that is 25 percent below the competition. Key questions to ask yourself in this scenario might include the following:

- Will the competitors match your price? Why or why not?
- If you start a price war, how long can you last?
- Given your lower price, are the other benefits of your offerings — such as location and quality — equal to or better than the competitors' offerings?

Make sure that you have solid answers to these and other relevant questions before you enter into an overcrowded market. As a general rule, the business owners that have the most money will be the ones who survive in an overcrowded market.

No Buyers

Your business may offer the perfect product and service, but if no one buys what you are offering, you're out of business. We have all heard the story about the Eskimo who tried to sell air conditioners in the Antarctic. As basic as this story seems, many startup business entrepreneurs ignore the fact that somebody must buy their products if they are to stay in business. The preplanning emphasis on marketing and sales will be critical to the success of your business. Your marketing analysis should tell you the number of prospective customers who reside in the market that you choose to serve. It should also identify the characteristics of your preferred customers, and which ones are most likely to buy. For example:

- Are they male or female, married or single?
- Is their age or income category a factor?
- Where do they live and how can you reach them?
- What do they like and dislike?

The chapters on marketing, sales, and promotion will help you qualify your sales and marketing strategies in detail. Nobody should ever open a business without thoroughly qualifying their marketing and sales strategies. You open the doors of your business after you know precisely who your top customer prospects are, what they want, and how you will sell to them.

Failure to Change

Every business must change to survive in the dynamic and economic climate of the 1990s. Successful entrepreneurs know this and recognize that small businesses can often implement changes faster than their large business counterparts. In a small business, you make the decision and the change occurs. In a large business, changes are often subjected to countless review meetings and executive level approvals before they can be implemented.

Lack of Knowledge

There are two aspects to the lack of knowledge issue. First, you are required to admit to the fact that you lack sufficient knowledge in a specific area. (Review your answers to the questionnaire that we developed on this subject in Chapter 1 when you identified your strengths and weaknesses.) Nobody, including entrepreneurs, likes to admit that they may not know something. But, the process is basic to assure the ongoing success of your business. The second step in the knowledge improvement process is to develop a plan that will allow you to acquire the knowledge you need. For example, if you know that you lack a basic understanding of marketing, perhaps there are courses at the local college you can take to develop your knowledge in this area.

Lack of Capital

At a minimum, all new businesses should know exactly how much capital they will need to run the business for its first three years of operation. As a part of the preplanning business phase, you should know what the capital requirements are for your business. The second part of the equation is to identify where the money will come from, such as from loans and sales. The accounting report that is used to determine the capital requirements of a business is called a cash flow analysis. A simplified version of the report is shown in Exhibit 2–2. (We show you how to prepare this document in Chapter 12 (Accounting).)

High Interest Rates

Every entrepreneur knows that interest rates will fluctuate over time. If you start your business when interest rates are low, they will undoubtedly go higher at some future point in time. Businesses with "staying power" know how to survive the peaks and valleys of interest rates by developing contingency plans. For example, during periods of low interest rates, they will develop a "plan of action" that they will implement when interest rates increase. The plan may include a reduction in equipment purchases and tighter customer credit policies.

Poor Economy

Every business that withstands the test of time will be subjected to poor economic conditions. Entrepreneurs consider economic fluctuations as one of the important "staying power" tests of a business. As a business

Exhibit 2-2. Simplified Cash Flow Statement

Accounting Category	First Quarter	Second Quarter	Third Quarter	Fourth Quarter	First Year
Source of Cash					
Sales					
Other Income					
Total Available Cash					
Business Expenses					
Payroll					
Other Expenses					
Total Expenses					
Total Available Cash					

owner, you must be able to anticipate and plan for poor economic conditions. Some key questions include:

- What are the key events that lead to poor economic conditions?
- Which economic events will have a direct and indirect effect on your business?
- What corrective action can you take to minimize the effect these events will have on your business?
- How will a downturn in the economy affect the income of your business?

Preplanning and anticipation are essential to your survival in good and bad economic times. If you wait for an economic event to occur before you start the planning process, the economic crisis may disrupt the objectivity of your plan to eliminate the crisis. The case study in Example 2–1 illustrates this point.

Example 2–1. Economic crisis case study

John Doe owned an electronic component store that specialized in the sale of high-end sound equipment (stereos, CDs, speakers, etc.). A majority of his customers charged their purchases to John's store charge card, which offered low interest rates. The low interest rates were possible because John could refinance the purchases through the local bank at a relatively low interest rate to maintain the store's cash flow. John was concerned about the effect that an adverse change in the economy (i.e., inflation, high interest rates, etc.) might have on his monthly sales. In anticipation of a downturn in the economy, he developed the following contingency plan:

- If interest rates increase by some percentage above current rates, offer customers a one percent discount if they pay with cash.
- Negotiate a long-term interest rate with the local bank to minimize the effect of short-term interest rate fluctuations.
- Offer free service packages to cash-paying customers.
- Self-finance customer credit loans to save on bank charges.

No Business Plan

The lack of a business plan is synonymous with mismanagement. A common and consistent attribute of poor managers is that they never seem to have a plan. They will all tell you that they have a plan, but if you ask to see the plan, they will either tell you they don't have it with them or that it's inside their heads. They simply don't have one. Without a plan, you will have no way of determining if your business is consistently making progress toward established goals. Your business will tend to "float along" on a daily basis on the hope that it will make it. Most will fail because of the lack of consistent and dynamic planning.

COMPONENTS OF A SUCCESSFUL BUSINESS

Having covered the failure points that are common to many small businesses, it is appropriate that we identify the primary reasons why many small businesses thrive and prosper. We will follow the same format that we followed in the previous section on business failures. One of your primary new business missions should be an "alert mission," where you are constantly on the alert to identify business failure warning signs. At the same time, you should be on the alert to reinforce the successful aspects of your business.

If you are satisfied that you have the entrepreneurial qualifications to start a business, and you have started to develop the business charter that we discussed in Chapter 1, you are now ready to qualify the viability of the type of business that you want to start. Many people will start a business in an area that they like. They like dogs, so they will start a grooming service, or they like electronics, so they will open a computer store. All of this is human nature and an important ingredient to the success of a new business. It is important that you like what you are doing. However, it is not the most important success factor.

Your business must sell what people want and not what you want to sell. (We will cover this subject in considerable detail in Chapter 7 (Marketing).) The intent of this section is to help you focus your attention on the proven success factors of small businesses, so that you can begin to incorporate those same success factors into your ideas for a business. Exhibit 2–3 includes a list of the most common success factors that will help you get started.

Exhibit 2-3. Reinforcing Business Success Points			
Cause of Success	**Reason for Success**	**How to Recognize**	**How to Develop**
Increased sales	Customers like your products and services	Increase in sales over the same period last year	Know what keeps your customer coming back and reinforce the program
Competitive prices	Key ingredient to attract referral business	A continuous flow of new customers	Always analyze ways to reduce costs
High quality	Customer "word of mouth" testimonials attract new business	Customer comments and opinion surveys	Implement a continuous improvement program

FINDING BUSINESS OPPORTUNITIES

The first step in determining the type of business that you want to start is to locate the market area that you want to serve and to begin to analyze the needs of the market. Start by preparing a list of product and service areas where people's needs are not being met, in your opinion. As you review your options, broaden your perspective to include as many products and services that are meaningful to you in a larger geographical area than you were originally prepared to consider. The more alternatives that you have to consider, the better opportunity you have to compare and choose the alternative that's right for you. As you begin to develop your list of alternatives, identify any problems and success points that are relevant to the alternative. Modify and update your business charter accordingly.

At this point in the alternative evaluation process, avoid judging the relative merit of each alternative or problem that you may have identified. One of the interesting things that occurs as you go through

Exhibit 2-4. Sources of New Business Ideas	
Periodical Name and Address	**Features**
Business Age, PO Box 11597, Milwaukee, WI 53211	Current events
Business Startups, 2392 Morse Ave., Irvine, CA 92714	Home based
Entrepreneur, 2392 Morse Ave., Irvine, CA 92714	Franchise opportunities
Fortune, Time Life Bldg., New York, NY 10020	Financing
BusinessWeek, P.O. Box 8829, Boulder, CO 80308	Business successes
Inc. Magazine, 38 Commercial Wharf, Boston, MA 02110	Entrepreneurs
Venture, 521 Fifth Ave., New York, NY 10175	New startups

the alternative listing process is that one alternative may cause you to think about another equally if not more viable alternative. There are a number of published sources that you can access to find new business ideas (see Exhibit 2–4).

In many cases, the problem that you may have identified could lead to the development of a business alternative. For example, personal computers are fast becoming common appliances in homes. The problem that may need to be confronted is based upon the fact that many people are reluctant to disconnect all of the cables connected to their personal computer in order to transport it to the repair shop. An in-home computer repair service may be what's needed to solve the problem. Expand on your new business ideas. If you are thinking about opening a business in your hometown, what would prevent you from simultaneously opening the same business in the adjacent towns or cities? This leads us to the next step in the analytical process. How do you determine whether each alternative and problem can be transformed into a business opportunity?

CREATING A BUSINESS OPTIONS WORKSHEET

Each alternative problem area needs to be expanded into its possible business opportunities. For example, we identified an in-home computer repair service as a possible business opportunity. This opportunity could logically be expanded to include in-office computer repair services as well. However, up to this point in the discussion, we have ignored a critical component in the evaluation process. Given the business options that you have listed, which ones can you do? The fact that you may know how to repair computers may not be sufficient. Can you do it well and do you like doing it? A triple "yes" answer is prerequisite to determining if the business opportunity is right for you. If the opportunity passes the "right for you" test, list it on a worksheet similar to the one we have prepared in Exhibit 2–5.

- Business Options. List your various options in order of importance (e.g., first, second, etc.).
- Market and Sales. Identify your primary market and where you believe most of your sales (i.e., customers) will come from for each option.

Exhibit 2-5. Expertise Worksheet

Business Option	Market and Sales	Viability Factor	Profitability Factor

- Viability Factor. How viable or conceivable is each option? Rank the options in order of viability (e.g., first, second, etc.).
- Profitability Factor. How profitable is each option? Rank the options in order of profitability (e.g., first, second, etc.).

ANALYZING STARTUP OPTIONS

Developing a set of viable business options that meet or exceed basic market needs criteria is important but, as discussed earlier, the personal expertise that you bring to the business can have a direct effect on the overall success of the business. Consider our previous computer repair service example. You may have a desire to become a computer repair person but have no expertise in this field. Does that mean that this business option is no longer valid for you? The answer is "no." You can acquire expertise in anything if you are willing to devote the level of effort that is required to obtain the expertise.

Home-study courses enable people to study a wide range of business and trade subjects ranging from accounting, marketing, and finance to computer repair and automobile maintenance. Home-study programs allow students to enroll in an educational institution that provides lesson materials prepared in a sequential and logical fashion so that students can study on their own time. Completed assignments are typically submitted to the school by the student, who in turn receives corrected assignments.

Home-study courses vary in scope, level of complexity, and length of course time. Some courses can be completed in a few weeks whereas others may require years to complete. Most of the accredited home study schools are listed by the National Home Study Council, which has served as a standard-setting agency for 75 years. For further information, contact:

National Home Study Council
1601 Eighteenth St., NW
Washington, DC 20009
(202) 234-5100

Exhibit 2-6. Expertise Worksheet			
Business Option	**Expertise Required**	**Your Level of Expertise**	**Importance Ranking**

The worksheet in Exhibit 2–6 will help you rank your level of expertise at running the various business options that you have developed. The ranking process requires subjective judgment on your part.

- Business Options. List your various options in order of importance (e.g., first, second, etc.).
- Expertise Required. List the major expertise categories (e.g., computer knowledge, sales, etc.) that are required to assure the success of each business option listed.
- Personal Level of Expertise. Rank your personal level (e.g., high, medium, or low) next to each of the expertise levels listed.
- Importance Ranking. Rank the level of importance (e.g., first, second, etc.) that each expertise has relative to the business options listed.

ESTIMATING FINANCIAL REQUIREMENTS

Up to this point in the opportunity analysis, you may have eliminated several opportunities that were on your original list for reasons that we have already discussed (e.g., lack of a market, expertise, etc.). This next qualification step involves projecting the level of sales, expenses, and profit for each business option. The intent of this process is to answer a basic question: Can you afford it and will it return a profit to you that justifies your investment? Most startup businesses take time before they are able to generate a profit. Until the profit point is achieved, your business will suffer from what accountants call "negative cash flow." A "positive cash flow" is generated by profits. Your "cash flow" answer is critical because many businesses run out of money before they are profitable and are subsequently forced to shut down.

ESTIMATING STARTUP COSTS

The worksheet in Exhibit 2–7 will help you eliminate business options that you cannot afford, or that do not generate sufficient profits to justify your time. This exercise illustrates the need for all entrepreneurs to have some level of expertise in finance and accounting. Whether you like it or not, accounting numbers tell you where your business is and where it is going at any one moment in time. If you do not know how to read and interpret the numbers, you will have no control over the financial direction of your business.

- Business Option. List your various options in order of importance (e.g., first, second, etc.).
- 1st/2nd/3rd Year Costs. Identify your estimated total costs per year to operate the business for the first three years.
- 1st/2nd/3rd Year Profits. Identify your estimated total profits or losses per year for the first three years.
- Ranking. Rank each option in order of importance to you (e.g., total profits, least cost, etc.).

When you consider the financial aspects of the business options that you listed in the worksheet,

Exhibit 2-7. Estimating Business Option Startup Costs			
Business Option	**1st/2nd/3rd Year Costs**	**1st/2nd/3rd Year Profits**	**Importance Ranking**

consider the controversial point of money. Many new entrepreneurs will often say that making money is not the primary reason they want to start their own business. Being their own boss and independent of the corporate bureaucracy may hold a higher meaning for them. In the interest of maintaining objectivity and preserving your reasons for owning a business, always remember that your business must make a profit to preserve whatever life-style you have set for yourself.

ESTIMATING OPERATING COSTS

The key consideration in establishing what it will cost to run your business over some period of time is how much money you and others (e.g., partners, investors, bank, etc.) are willing to invest in the business before it makes a profit. The amount of money required to start a business, and the point when profits will occur, vary between business types. Bankers and accountants are an excellent source of local financial information. Ask you local banker and accountant what are the preferred financial expectations from a startup business similar to yours. Ask the same question of existing business owners. If there is a trade association that covers businesses like the one you want to start, contact the association. Many associations maintain extensive cost and profit information for their respective industries. The names and addresses of associations are listed in the following publications, which are available in most public libraries:

- The Encyclopedia of Associations
- National Trade and Professional Associations of the United States

The U.S. Department of Commerce maintains a wealth of historical accounting and financial data on more than 200 industries, which is available free or for a minimal charge. Check your telephone directory to locate the office that is closest to you. Other sources of financial data that are available in a good public or college library include the following:

- Standard & Poor's Industry Surveys
- National Cash Register's Expenses in Retail Business

- Robert Morris Associates Annual Statement Studies
- Almanac of Business and Industrial Ratios
- Financial Studies of the Small Business
- Business Profitability Ratios
- U.S. Industrial Outlook

ESTIMATING YOUR PROFITS

Profit is not a dirty word, and as a business owner you should never apologize for making a profit. If you do not make a profit for some sustained period of time, you are out of business and your creditors will come after you without any hint of an apology. Any business that you start should have the potential to make a good and lasting profit. You may have many reasons for starting a business. Although profits may not be on the top of your list, profits are probably required to support every other reason on the list. It's a lot easier to handle normal business pressures if your business is making money. You can afford to hire people to ease your own workload, and your daily business activities aren't disrupted with creditor calls. If you decide to sell your business, profitable businesses are easier to sell and demand a higher price than losers.

RANKING YOUR OPTIONS

As part of the ranking process, eliminate the opportunities that do not appear to have the profit potential that you are looking for, or that require an investment beyond your means. We recognize that there may be opportunities you may want to keep "open" for a number of reasons. At this point in your evaluation, you may feel that you need access to more information before you can pass final judgment over a given opportunity. As you continue reading through the remaining chapters in the book, use the information that we provide to continue to refine your list down to the best possible choice for you.

SELECTING THE RIGHT BUSINESS

Up to this point in the evaluation process, your personal preferences have been largely ignored. As we alluded to earlier in the chapter, we wanted you to objectively evaluate various business options without regard to your personal preferences. If there was no profit potential in an opportunity that you liked, it should have been eliminated without regard to your preference. Remember, businesses make money. Activities that take up your time and cost you money are called "hobbies." New entrepreneurs can sometimes come up with excellent rationales for lowering their profit objectives because they are doing something they like doing. If your thinking follows this pattern, it is time to raise a red flag. Ask a starving artist if he or she is having any fun! At the same time, we do not want to discourage people from starting a business that they enjoy and that makes money. Those two components are an important part of the business success formula as long as you are able to exercise self-discipline. The business opportunities that remain on your list can now be subjected to a consolidated ranking score that best fits your requirements. The worksheet in Exhibit 2–8 will help you accomplish this task.

- Business Option. List your various options in order of importance (e.g., first, second, etc.).

- Personal Ranking. Rank your personal preferences on a first to last basis. Personal preferences can be totally subjective, relative to the business that you "really" want to start.

- Success Ranking. Rank your personal success criteria on a first to last basis. Your definition of success may be minimum risk, prestige, or some other criteria that is meaningful to you.

- Financial Ranking. Rank your financial criteria on a first to last basis. Your definition of financial success may be profitability, gross income, or some other criteria that is meaningful to you.

- Total Score. Total the score by row for each business option. For example, if a given business option was ranked first, second, and third in the three ranking categories, it would receive a total score of 6 (e.g., first = 1, second = 2, and third = 3 points). The lowest scoring business option should represent the best business option for you.

Exhibit 2-8. Selecting the Business That Is Right for You				
Business Option	Personal Ranking	Success Ranking	Financial Ranking	Total Score

At this point in the business options analysis process, you should have reduced your options list to one or possibly three options. If your list includes more than three options, you may want to repeat that analysis process as many times as it takes until you are able to arrive at a workable set of options. We recommend that you work on no more than three options at any one time, but if you are comfortable with five or even ten options, "go for it" as long as you don't spread yourself to thin. Make sure you have the time to adequately analyze each option.

Compare the business options that are on your list against the business criteria that you established in your business charter. Does your business charter track against your desired business options? If your thinking has been consistent up to this point, it probably does. If your business charter requires some modification to reflect your current thinking, now would be a good time to update your charter. If the business options analysis has completely reshaped your thinking about what you want to do, it may be appropriate to develop a new business charter.

ESTABLISHING DEVELOPMENT PHASES

The development of a business covers two distinct stages. The first development stage covers all of the steps, checks, and balances one must go through to create the business entity itself. This stage is considered complete on the first day the business opens. The second development stage cuts in at that point and covers all of the ongoing activities that are essential to the operations of the business.

SETTING GOALS AND OBJECTIVES

Like a finish line in a race, business goals have a defined and measurable purpose — be the first one at the finish line. There is typically some kind of score or reward that is associated with achieving a goal. Objectives reinforce goals in that they establish a purpose for achieving a goal, or a related set of goals. Examples of goals for a startup business are shown as follows:

1. Obtain the required startup capital needed by May 1.
2. Have all partnership agreements signed and approved by June 1.
3. Hire three additional sales people by July 1.

Each phase of the business development process will typically have its own defined set of goals and objectives. However, the achievement of initial goals and objectives can directly affect the activities of the next phase. For example, let's assume that the Phase 1 objective is to obtain a capital equipment loan. The loan is considered a requisite to starting the business (i.e., the business cannot produce a product without the equipment). For whatever reason, the loan cannot be secured. In this example, the second phase of the business plan cannot be started because it depends on the successful completion of Phase 1.

IMPLEMENTING A STARTUP PLAN

When a business startup project consists of many integrated steps, PERT (Program Evaluation and Review Technique) chart offers an easy way to plan. A

Exhibit 2-9. Milestones for a New Business Startup Project			
Milestone Identification	**Description**	**Expected Completion Time (weeks)**	**Preceding Milestone**
1	Obtain financing	2	None
2	Hire employees	3	1 must be completed
3	Create packaging	5	None
4	Order materials	1	3 must be completed
5	Secure location	3	None

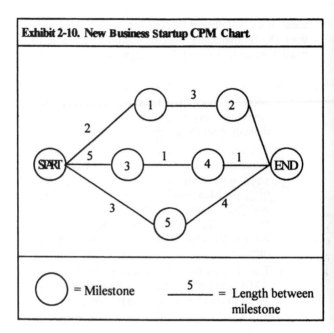

Exhibit 2-10. New Business Startup CPM Chart

○ = Milestone   ——⁵—— = Length between milestone

series of integrated steps or milestones are identified to complete a project similar to what we show in Exhibit 2–9. The five milestones that we identified in Exhibit 2–9 are plotted on a chart in such a way that you can see which one must be completed before others can be started (see Exhibit 2–10). It is not necessary for all milestones to be placed one after the other. Usually different parts of the startup process can be worked on at the same time. However, as the arrows indicate, some milestones cannot be started until another milestone is completed.

SOURCES FOR ADDITIONAL INFORMATION

THE AMERICAN MANAGEMENT ASSOCIATION

The American Management Association is the largest membership organization for professional managers who seek "a forum for personal development, sharing ideas and commitment to common goals." The more than 78,000 managers who are members are able to avail themselves of the following programs:

- AMA's Center for Management Development conducts more than 3,000 courses every year, covering every area of job training and career development for every level of employee.

- The Management Courses constitute a professional management education in four one-week sessions covering topics such as strategic planning, decision making, problem solving, team building, financial analysis, human resource management, and leadership. Attendance at all the above courses is open to members and nonmembers.

- The Management Information Service gives AMA members sources of information for answers to tough management problems.

- The AMA Library has more than 100,000 up-to-date resource materials including some 12,000 books and 250 periodicals.

- AMA publications include several periodicals, a newsletter, and a growing line of handbooks and reference materials.

- The Extension Institute trains supervisors, managers, and top executives through private, self-paced study at home or in the office under the guidance of a qualified AMA instructor.

AMA programs operate principally through its divisions, each offering a complete meeting schedule within its field. The divisions are Finance, General Management, General and Administrative Services, Insurance and Employee Benefits, International Management, Information Systems, Technology, Manufacturing, Packaging, Human Resources, Purchasing, Transportation and Physical Distribution, and Research and Development. There are four types of memberships: Individual, Affiliate, Corporate, and Limited Company. The last category, of special interest to small businesses, is available to organizations with fewer than 250 employees or less than $25 million in annual income. For further information, contact:

Membership Department
American Management Association
135 West 50 Street
New York, NY 10020
(212) 586-8100

LEARNING INTERNATIONAL

Another company that specializes in learning programs is Learning International (formerly Xerox
Learning Systems). Its mission is to help people maximize the return from all the work they perform. Cultivating productivity and a positive attitude is a basic
part of Learning International's mission. The titles of
a few programs and services follow: Professional
Selling Skills System, Account Development Strategies, Selling Against the Competition, Telephone
Prospecting, Customer Satisfaction Skills, and Inter-
personal. For further information, contact:

Learning International
200 First Stamford Place
Stamford, CT 06904
(203) 965-8400

CHAMBERS OF COMMERCE

Chambers of Commerce are found in more than
7,000 cities and towns throughout the United States.
In addition, there are many other chambers that represent foreign nations. Chambers are service-oriented
groups, providing all types of information to their
members, the public at large, travelers and tourists,
business interests, and those who request specialized
data. Thus they serve as an excellent research source
for all types of information about communities or areas. When data is needed about another city or town,
start your research by contracting that chamber of
commerce. If you do not know the address, consult
the World-Wide Chamber of Commerce Directory
that is published annually by:

Johnson Publishing Company
P.O. Box 1029
Loveland, CO 80539
(303) 663-6187

3

Buying a Business

This chapter is for entrepreneurs who are interested in buying an existing business rather than starting one from scratch. Even if you are a "die-hard" startup entrepreneur, we recommend that you read this chapter for several reasons. First, it will provide you with some valuable insights into what people are looking for when they buy businesses. You can use this information to leverage the value of your business as you build it. Second, you will gain some important insights into negotiation techniques and sources of franchise information that can be used to enhance your startup operation.

WHAT TO LOOK FOR

Up to this point, we have focused on starting a business from scratch and have taken you through a number of pre-qualifications steps to validate and qualify your ideas for a startup. One of the primary advantages of starting a business is to capitalize on a unique opportunity or idea that simply does not exist. Hence, purchasing a comparable business is not an option. The disadvantages of starting from scratch are that you will have to search out and find answers to countless questions before you can open the doors of your business. On top of that challenge, you must have concrete assurance that you can acquire customers for your products and services. These two critical obstacles represent a considerable challenge and risk as well.

Throughout this book, we stress the importance of preparing a complete business plan before you start your business. Although a thoroughly prepared business plan will reduce a number of the risks that are associated with new startups, like all plans, your business plan is based upon assumptions. Your assumption checklist should include answers to the following questions:

- Customer Profile. Where do they reside and what do they like?
- Advertising. What media and techniques will work for your business?

- Pricing. What strategies will you use to sell your offerings and produce a profit?
- Profit Point. When will your business begin to make a profit?

As with any assumptions, yours will be subjected to trial and error. Some will be right on target and others will miss the mark. If you're right most of the time, your startup will survive. An existing business has an established track record, which offers several advantages over startups. Many of the basic assumptions, such as advertising techniques and pricing strategies, have already been determined. A customer base has been established to reinforce the validity of a working business plan.

There are two basic ways to acquire an existing business. You can buy a business or acquire the rights to startup a franchise. The existing business may be a franchise where acquiring the rights means that you are starting a franchise from scratch. Both alternatives typically cost more than starting a business on your own, which is the price you pay to reduce your risks. In the next section, we'll cover the issues you need to address before you buy any business.

ADVANTAGES AND DISADVANTAGES OF BUYING A BUSINESS

One of the biggest advantages of buying a business is that it already exists. The seller can provide you with actual financial data that reflects the operation of the business over a period of time. You can visit the business during operating hours and witness the interchange between real customers. This process can eliminate much of the guess work that goes into a startup business plan. However, it does not eliminate the qualification issues that were addressed in the previous chapter. Does the business under consideration offer you a substantial and lasting opportunity? Does it fit with what you want to do and what you are qualified to do? Do the financial and profit projections satisfy your income requirements?

The answers to these and other key questions should be relatively easy to obtain if the business is worth buying, which again is an advantage of buying an existing business. If the seller cannot provide the documented answers to your probing questions, the opportunity may not be worth pursuing.

ADVANTAGES

The advantages of buying a business are summarized as follows:

1. Financial track record can be reviewed to analyze the success of the business.
2. Loan approvals are easier to obtain for an established business.
3. Owner consultation and training can usually be negotiated.
4. Unique features and assets can be identified (e.g., business name, location, etc.).
5. A customer base already exists.
6. If the business is profitable, then you do not need to calculate your break-even point.
7. Most of the preplanning time and expense of a startup business can be eliminated.
8. Supplier and vendor relationships are already established.
9. Current record keeping and accounting systems are already installed.
10. The business may already have a good set of employees.
11. The existing owner may be willing to finance all or a part of the business.
12. The inventory and equipment that you need may already exist, which will save you ordering and shipping time.

If you are thinking about buying a business, carefully consider the advantages that we have listed and add other advantages that may be important to you. Go back through the list and prioritize the advantages that are most important to you. What would it cost you to develop that same advantage in a startup operation? In some cases, it may be impossible to duplicate. For example, if the business under consideration has a long-term lease at a preferred location, then its location can not be duplicated.

DISADVANTAGES

The primary disadvantages of buying a business are financial. You will be asked to pay for every advantage that's offered by the business. There is also the nagging question that may beg for an answer. If it is such a great business, why is it for sale? Does the seller know something that is not disclosed in the financial statements? Possible disadvantages are summarized as follows:

1. The cost of an existing business is generally more than a startup.
2. The owner's real reason for selling may be hidden from you.
3. Actual condition of assets may be worse than what they appear.
4. Validity of financial statements may be questionable.
5. Customer satisfaction levels may be below what you have been led to believe.
6. You may be liable for contracts that are not in your best interest.
7. The business location may be a drawback.
8. If the business has a poor image, it may be costly to change.
9. The purchase price of the business may create a burden on the future cash flow of the business.

LOCATING BUSINESSES FOR SALE

There are more than 20 million small businesses in the United States, and according to the U.S. Department of Commerce, more than half of our population will be working for a small business by the year 2000. The number of small business entries will increase significantly through the 1990s. The average small business changes hands every three years. One only has to review the classified section of a metropolitan newspaper to grasp a feel for the number of businesses that are for sale at any moment. And that is only part of the sales story.

Exhibit 3-1. Where to Find Businesses for Sale	
Sources of Opportunity	**Types of Information**
Classified section of local and national newspapers	List businesses for sale in the business opportunity section.
Trade magazines	Some trade magazines feature both classified and display ad sections that cover businesses for sale.
Business brokers and real estate agents.	Both sources are listed in the yellow pages. Business brokers specialize in the sale of businesses.
Chambers of commerce	Some chambers maintain a buying and selling service for their members.
Trade sources	Ask trade sources such as suppliers, distributors, and associations if they know of businesses that are for sale.
Business owners	Go directly to the source and ask the owner of a business that you are interested in if they want to sell.
Professional sources	Professional sources such as bankers, attorneys, and accountants may be aware of clients who want to sell their businesses.

It has been estimated that more than 75 percent of small businesses are sold outside of the classified advertising channels. For example, business brokers are often asked to discretely list businesses for sale without the benefit of advertising so as not to alarm the employees, customers, or suppliers. Business owners will often entertain an offer for their business to enable them to track what they think the business is worth, or to leverage a change in their personal situation (e.g., pending divorce, retirement, etc.). Sources for finding businesses for sale are shown in Exhibit 3–1.

HOW TO SPOT OPPORTUNITIES

Before you can spot an opportunity, you first have to
know what one looks like. The business charter that
you created in Chapter 1 was the start of the opportunity definition process. The general terms of the charter were more specifically defined in Chapter 2. At
this point, you should have a clear idea as to the type
of business you want to start. Your opportunity
checklist should also include the following:

1. The amount of money you are willing to invest in a business.
2. What level of risk you are willing to accept.
3. What your return on investment expectations
   are.
4. The amount of time you must devote to learn
   all aspects of the business.

If you have developed a viable set of business
opportunity qualifiers, test your qualifiers by looking
at business opportunities that may not interest you.
This experience will afford you with an opportunity
to modify and adjust your qualifiers before you begin
your search for the real thing. Exhibit 3–2 shows how
to qualify different business opportunities.

As a basic rule, don't be in a rush when you start
looking for a business to buy. Resist any temptation to
buy the first thing you see and avoid the impetuous
seller who tells you to make an offer today or some
other interested person will buy the business tomorrow (particularly if the business has been on the market for several months). There are a lot of businesses
for sale, but only a few are worth buying. Look for
businesses that have been operating for at least two
years. The first year of a startup is usually the most
difficult year to survive and the subsequent years
should show trends of sales growth and expense re-
ductions. If the business is not making a profit by the
end of the second year, find out why. Even if it is
making a profit, make sure that the profits are real. For
example, if you discover that the owner is working
twelve hours a day without the benefit of a salary, then
the owner's salary is buried in the profit, which may
grossly overstate the profitability of the business. In
the final analysis and before you buy a business, ask

Exhibit 3-2. How to Identify Business Opportunities	
Type of Opportunity	**Opportunity Qualifier**
Success with prospect to continue.	Consistent increase in sales since the conception of the business indicate its continued success.
Has been successful with diminishing prospects.	Products or services are becoming obsolete or are being replaced by cheaper products.
Moderately successful with potential to be very successful.	Gradual increase in sales.Limited market coverage indicates expanded market opportunities.
Business has difficulties but can be recovered.	Over a period of time, poor management has disrupted the business.
Moderately successful but sales are flat.	Indicates an ineffective advertising and marketing program.
Moderately successful but destined to fail without major overhaul.	The business cannot compete against its larger and more efficient competitors.

yourself a basic but critical question: Can I sell this business for at least what I am paying for it at any time after I buy it? To get a partial answer to your question, find out how long the business has been for sale.

ANALYZING OPPORTUNITIES

If you find a business that appears to match your personal objectives and satisfies your business charter, then it is time to conduct an in-depth analysis of the business. In an in-depth analysis, you look at every aspect of the business that you and others can think of to determine its real merit and value. Involve other qualified people in the analysis, such as your friends, partners, accountants, and attorneys. Review with the seller or, if applicable, the seller's broker the following basic issues to screen a business opportunity.

- Purchase price. Make sure you understand the exact purchase price of the business. In many cases, there may be several price options for you to consider such as a cash buyout and various inventory considerations. Always explore for different purchase price options and terms of the sale.

- Seller financing. Will the seller carry a loan on the business? In some cases, this is "seller qualification" issue. If the seller is not willing to finance a part of his or her own "perfect" business, can they offer you a solid reason why? Obtaining seller financing is a good way to assure that the seller maintains an active interest in the success of the business after you take over.

- Assets and Liabilities. What are the specific assets and liabilities of the business? Can the seller provide you with a list of each business asset and liability that you will take over when you own the business? Can the list be certified as "accurate" by a certified public accountant? Include the purchased assets and limits of your liabilities in the final purchase contract papers.

- Certification. Are the financial statements of the business prepared by a certified public accountant? Can they be made available to your account for review and certification? If the answers are "no," make sure that the seller's answer is acceptable to you and your accountant.

- Sales history. Since its conception, can the seller show you what the sales performance of the business has been on a monthly basis? Can these sales records be validated by your accountant? Do the records indicate that the business is progressively growing? If the seller does not have, or will not show you, established sales information, you have a clear warning signal that there may be problems with this business opportunity.

- Banking relationships. Where is the banking for the business performed? Who are the bank officers that are responsible for the business' accounts? If the business relies on a significant relationship with a bank, ask for permission to talk to the bank's officers to verify banking relationships. If you are denied access to the bank officers, you have a clear warning signal that there may be banking relationship problems.

- Inventory control. If you are buying a business that includes the acquisition of inventory, make sure that the value of the inventory is identified as a separate line item in the purchase price agreement. Establish mutually acceptable terms with the seller to determine a value and inventory counts just before the sale of the business. In addition, make sure that you have a complete list of all inventory items that are part of the sales price, and that you agree with the total unit counts and inventory value.

- Accounts receivable. If the purchase price of the business includes accounts receivable, can the seller provide you with an aged accounts receivable list? Any account that is over 45 days past due may represent a collection problem. Can the seller verify over a period of time the percent of collections the business has been able to achieve to your satisfaction and the satisfaction of your accountant? How will the value of accounts receivable be established before you purchase the business?

- Contracts. Is the business bound by any contracts that will be transferred to you when you become the new owner? Do you understand the practical and legal contents of every contract that you will inherit? Are the relevant contracts acceptable to you and your attorney? Are the key contracts that you want to inherit as a part of the purchase price of the business (i.e., location lease, etc.) in place, and will they be covered under your name after the sale of the business is consummated?

- Competition. Do you feel you know everything that the current owner knows about the competitors of the business? If not, you may want to establish a competitor dialog with the owner before you close the sale. If appropriate, add a condition in the sales contract that allows you to receive free consultations with the seller in regard to competitive questions, or any other questions that may arise after you take over the business.

- Franchises. If you are buying a franchise, make sure you understand and are satisfied with transferability conditions of the franchise. Look for any special transfer and renewal fees that you may have to pay that were not disclosed to you in the purchase price. Make sure your attorney reviews this section of the contract.

- Personnel. Are there any key personnel that you must rely upon when you take over the business? Who are they and why do you need them? How long have they been with the company and what would happen if they were to suddenly leave the company on the day you took over the ownership? You need to obtain acceptable answers to all of these questions, or have a contingency plan that can be implemented if key employee problems occur.

- Suppliers. Do you know who your suppliers are and has the business developed a good relationship with its suppliers? What are the payment terms and conditions of your major suppliers? Are they acceptable to you? Ask the seller for permission to contact the key suppliers. If permission is not granted, this may be an indication of supplier problems.

- Market share. Is the market that is being served by the business growing or leveling off? What has the current owner done to successfully increase the business' market share? Are their any future events such as the construction of a new shopping mall across the street that could affect your market?

- Proprietary items. Proprietary items cover the copyrights, trademarks, and patents of the business. Have all of the proprietary items of the business been transferred over to you? Are you legally protected from any proprietary legal action that could result from the prior owner's misuse of the proprietary items of the business? Make sure your attorney reviews this section of the contract.

- Business location. Do all aspects of the location of the business satisfy your needs? Are the terms and conditions of the location lease acceptable to you? If you are not satisfied with the terms of the current lease agreements, can they be changed? If you are not satisfied with the current location of the business, can you break the lease? What will it cost you to move the business?

- Economic stability. Historically, how has the business performed over periods of economic fluctuations? For example, what has happened to sales when interest rates changed over time? Have changes in the unemployment rates affected the business? Is the business affected by seasonal changes or any other economic event?

- Special requirements. Are there any special licenses, permits, or other legal requirements for the business? In some cases, "old grandfather laws" do not apply to new business owners. Will all "special requirement" issues be transferred over to you as the new owner to your satisfaction? Make sure your attorney reviews this section of the contract.

Some owners will ask for an initial offer and earnest money deposit before they will divulge proprietary information about their business. You may also be asked to sign a nondisclosure statement, in which you agree not to disclose to anyone — without the seller's approval — the information you are shown. All of these precautions are fair and justified to protect the seller from casual inquiries and even competitors who may be posing as a buyer.

ESTIMATING BUSINESS VALUES

In deciding how much a business is worth and how much you should pay, you must rely on all of the information, and answers to questions we have posed

about buying a business. Unfortunately, there are no
universally accepted ways to establish the value of a
business. The most common approach is to determine
what accountants call the book value of the assets and
then determine a goodwill value. These two values
are added together to determine the total value of the
business.

ASSET VALUE

Asset book value represents the assumed market
value of all the assets that are owned by the business,
after all business debts have been paid. Asset value
can be determined by reviewing a report called a balance sheet (see Exhibit 3–3).

Balance sheet reports are prepared at the end of
each month and are explained in Chapter 12 (Accounting). For the purposes of this exercise, you will
note that Exhibit 3–3 list two types of assets — current and fixed. As the name implies, current assets are
assets that can be converted over to cash in a relatively short period of time (i.e., less than 30 days).
Cash in a bank account is about as current as you can
get. Accounts receivable are not as current as cash,

Exhibit 3-3. Balance Sheet for ABC Company

Balance Sheet

End of February

Current Assets		Liabilities	
Cash in Checking Account	$21,000	Accounts Payable	$25,000
Cash in Savings Account	$20,000	Notes Payable	$30,000
Accounts Receivable	$10,000	Total Liabilities	$55,000
Total Current Assets	$51,000		
Fixed Assets			
Raw Materials Inventory	$8,000	**Owner's Equity**	
Plant & Equipment	$24,000	Retained Earnings	$18,000
LESS: Depreciation	($10,000)		
Total Fixed Assets	$22,000		
Total Assets	$73,000	Liability & Owner's Equity	$73,000

because they are dependent upon customer payment schedules.

Fixed assets are sometimes referred to as long-term assets in that they require more time to liquidate into cash than current assets. Examples of fixed assets in Exhibit 3–3 include plant (i.e., land and buildings) and equipment. The total asset values for the ABC Company are $73,000. The total liabilities for the company are $55,000. If the ABC Company were to be liquidated (i.e., went out of business) and in the process sold off all company assets and used the asset sales money to pay off company liabilities, then $18,000 would be left over after the transaction occurred. This is shown as owner's equity or retained earnings on the balance sheet. If you assume that all of the numbers in Exhibit 3–3 are accurate, then the retained earnings figure represents the minimum cash or asset value of the ABC Company (i.e., at a minimum, the business is worth $18,000).

GOODWILL VALUE

Goodwill represents the intangible side of the business and covers such things as an established name, the existing customer base, established banking relations, and other intangible business advantages. Goodwill is the part of the sales price that you will pay to acquire an ongoing business to reduce your risks. The value of goodwill is difficult to measure in terms of dollars. Sellers tend to place a premium on the value of goodwill because it represents their contributions and the excess of money they expect to get out of their businesses.

In some businesses, the value of goodwill will be significantly higher than the book value of its assets. For example, customers are often the most valuable component of a service business. The assets of the business may be insignificant when compared to the value of the hundreds of customers who faithfully buy products and services from the business. The employees of the business could also be considered a part of the company's goodwill value.

In the final analysis, goodwill is worth whatever you estimate it would cost to duplicate if you were to start the business on your own. If the goodwill value covers a customer base, find out how many customers are in the base. How much would it cost you in advertising and promotional activities to build a similar customer base from scratch? If you determine that the startup cost is equal to, or greater than, the goodwill value of the business you are thinking of buying, then the asking price may be acceptable. The following example illustrates this approach:

Example 3–1. How to estimate the values of goodwill

Let's assume that the following information is available for the ABC Company:

Average annual profits are $15,000
Estimated value of assets are $73,000
The average rate of return is 10%

Goodwill can now be calculated as follows:

Total implied value of assets ($15,000/10%)	$150,000
Less: fair market value of assets	$73,000
Estimated goodwill	$77,000

In our example, the value of goodwill reflects the ability of the assets of the company to make more money for the business than what could be made at the prevailing return on investment interest rate of 10 percent. For example, I could initiate an offer to purchase the business for the fair market value of its assets ($73,000) or elect to invest my $73,000 at the prevailing interest rate of 10 percent. If I choose the investment option, I would make approximately $7,300 a year or $73,000 over ten years from my investment.

However, if I buy the ABC Company, I can realize a higher interest rate of return on the assets of the business due to goodwill (i.e., efficient operations, customer base, etc.). The business makes approximately $7,700 a year or will make $77,000 over the next ten years. If I elect to buy the business for its estimated goodwill value of $77,000 the profits from the business will pay for the business in ten years.

EARNINGS VALUE

In the previous section, we estimated the value of a business based upon the value of tangible and intangible assets. Another approach is called the capitalization of earnings approach. This approach establishes the value of a business based upon its current and future profit potential and addresses the profit potential of the business. The purchase price is then based on the profit generating capability of the business.

On the surface, the capitalization of earning approach seems to be delightfully logical. If all of the numbers are accurate, you know from a financial viewpoint exactly what you are buying. The valuation process is dependent upon determining two key numbers that go into the capitalization formula. Let's assume you want to buy a business that makes $30,000 a year in profits. If the current capitalization rate for money is 12 percent (i.e., average interest rate), then our formula follows:

$$\text{True profitability rate} \times \text{capitalization rate} = \text{value of business}$$
$$\$30,000 \times 12 = \$360,000$$

Let's first address what is meant by the true profit component in the formula. Most new entrepreneurs assume that profit is whatever is left over at the end of a month after all expenses have been deducted from net sales. Technically, this is true; but the definition is open to different interpretations that may not be consistent with your definition of true profit. Exhibit 3–4 illustrates how two different "true profit" figures could be calculated for the same business.

Exhibit 3–4 shows what happens to profits based on two different accounting scenarios. In our example, the profits of the business were higher if the owner chooses to work for free. That is perhaps an acceptable scenario if you assume that the owner's donated hours did not contribute to the welfare of the business (e.g., the owner was sleeping on the job). Our intent here is not to be facetious because in most instances, one can logically assume that the owner's hours contributed to the operation of the business.

This example may be oversimplified, but it illustrates the complexity of determining the actual level of profits and the true value of a business. Even if you consider yourself an excellent accountant, seek out the advice and services of another accountant who has a background in business acquisitions to help you quantify the true profits of the business you are considering.

Exhibit 3-4. True Profit Calculations for the ABC Company in the Same Month

Account Description	Method #1	Method #2	Explanation of Variance
Sales	$125,000	$120,000	Method #1 includes sales for services that have not been performed.
Less: Discounts and allowances	$10,000	$15,000	Method #2 is more conservative than Method #1 in its allowances for bad debts.
Total Net Sales	$115,000	$105,000	The $10,000 variance between the two methods is due to discounts and early sales bookings.

Expenses

Direct Expenses	$75,000	$70,000	Method #1 depreciates assets faster than Method #2, resulting in higher depreciation expense.
Indirect Expenses	$25,000	$30,000	Method #2 is retiring its loan obligations at a faster rate than Method #1.
Total Expenses	$100,000	$100,000	Although the total expenses are the same for both methods, Method #2 is more conservative.
Gross Profit	$15,000	$5,000	The $10,000 variance in profits for the same company reflect aggressive sales and expense bookings.

The second component in the capitalization formula is based on the rate-of-return concept. How much money are you willing to pay to buy an anticipated level of earnings (i.e., profits)? The following example will show you how to compute the capitalization rate. Assume that the purchase price for a business is $360,000 and that the current profits are $30,000 per year. Our capitalization rate formula follows:

$$\frac{\text{Price of the business}}{\text{Current annual profits}} = \text{Capitalization rate}$$

$$\frac{\$360,000}{\$30,000} = 12.0 \text{ capitalization rate}$$

The capitalization rate of 12 indicates that in 12 years, the annual profits from the business would cover your $360,000 investment in the business. The return rate is based upon time and the subsequent answer to a basic investment question. If you invested $360,000 into a given venture, and you get $360,000 back in 12 years, what is the rate of return on your money? Any simple business calculator or personal computer will provide you with the answer to the question when you enter the appropriate variables.

The Rule of 72

The "rule of 72" is another way to illustrate how you can quickly determine the rate of return from the capitalization rate. If you divide 72 by the capitalization rate, the resulting quotient will be the annual interest rate that your original investment (e.g., $360,000) will earn. The following example illustrates this principle:

Example 3–5. Applying the rule of 72 to the purchase of a business.

(72) / (Capitalization rate)
= Return on investment
(72) / (12) = 6 percent return on investment

The return on investment (ROI) measurement is widely used by investors to determine the financial viability of making a particular investment. They will often compare multiple investment ROI options to determine which option offers the greatest return potential for their investment. Hence, ROIs can be effectively used to compare the financial viability of alternative businesses to buy.

ANALYZING FINANCIAL STATEMENTS

The income statement can reveal a lot about a business that you are thinking of buying. If properly analyzed, it can tell you where the business has been and where it is potentially going. Let's assume that you are interested in buying the ABC Company which has provided you with the income statement in Exhibit 3–5. Here is how you might want to analyze the company's income statement.

The statement covers the end of February and includes a year-to-date column. The ABC company's annual reporting period is the calendar year (January through December), so we know that this income statement covers the months of January and February. Total sales in February were considerably higher than the January sales figure ($30,000 in February versus $24,475 in January). We were able to determine January's sales figure by subtracting February's sales from year-to-date sales (e.g., $54,784 − $30,000 = $24,475). Product sales were up in February, but service sales were down when compared to the comparable January sales figures.

Let's now turn our attention to the expense side of the income statement. Note that total expenses were higher in February ($25,000), than they were in January ($19,635). This makes sense because sales were higher in February. However, it raises the question of whether or not the increases in sales were in line with the increase in total expenses between the two months. The February percentage increase in

Exhibit 3-5. Income Statement for ABC Company

Income Statement

End of February

Sales	Current $	YTD $
Service Sales	$9,500	$16,500
Product Sales	20,500	37,975
Total Sales	**$30,000**	**$54,475**
Cost of Goods Sold		
Product Materials	$9,200	$17,110
Direct Service Labor	2,400	2,605
Total Cost of Goods Sold	**$11,600**	**$19,715**
Operating Expenses		
Utilities	$650	$1,210
Salaries	7,200	13,390
Payroll Taxes & Benefits	1,475	2,740
Advertising	400	745
Office Supplies	325	605
Insurance	490	910
Legal & Accounting Services	125	235
Telephone	165	305
Depreciation Expense	1,010	1,880
Travel & Distribution	460	855
Total Operating Expenses	**$12,300**	**$22,875**
Other Expenses	$400	$745
Notes Payable Interest	700	1,300
Total Expenses	**$25,000**	**$44,635**
Net Profit	**$5,000**	**$9,840**

sales and expenses can be quickly calculated as follows:

$$\text{Percent increase in February sales} = \frac{\text{February sales}}{\text{January sales}}$$

$$= \frac{\$30,000}{\$24,475}$$

$$= 123\%$$

$$\text{Percent increase in February costs} = \frac{\text{February costs}}{\text{January costs}}$$

$$= \frac{\$25,000}{\$19,635}$$

$$= 127\%$$

One could raise several questions from this oversimplified analysis. For example, why were sales down in January? Why did expenses increase at a faster rate in February than sales? These are just two basic questions that resulted from our analysis of the income statement for the ABC Company. The owner of the company may be able to offer you rational answers to your questions: January sales were lower because of severe winter weather conditions, or expenses increased in February to cover payroll raises.

NEGOTIATING THE PURCHASE

Negotiating for the purchase of a business demands that you consider and apply all of the information you have learned about the business to arrive at an acceptable price. Some businesses have special formulas for calculating a sales price based upon industry standards. For example, a multiple of the annual net profits of the business can be used to establish a price. If the average net profits of the business are $20,000 a year and the industry standard multiple is 5 years, then the business would potentially be worth $100,000 (5 years × $20,000). Check with business brokers or associations to find out if there are standard buying formulas. The 11 essential rules of "smart" negotiating procedures are summarized as follows:

1. Check to see if there are any liens against the assets of the business.

2. Verify that there are no outstanding lawsuits against the business and that all local, state, and federal taxes have been paid.

3. Draft a non-compete statement for the seller to sign.

4. Have the seller set-up an escrow account to cover all claims that the seller has agreed to cover.

5. Verify that the seller has notified all creditors of the pending sale.

6. Draft an agreement in which the seller guarantees all accounts receivable.

7. Make sure that you have possession of all warranties, license agreements, contracts, sales agreements, and distribution agreements.

8. Verify that all leases can be assumed when you take over the business.

9. Obtain a list of all assets including the serial numbers that will be included in the sale of the business.

10. Request a certified verification of all inventories that are included as a part of the sale.

11. Verify that all zoning requirements and permits are current and in order.

Your attorney and accountant will probably have a number of additional items to add to our checklist. Add your own items as you consider them appropriate. The basic premise of the checklist is to maintain goodwill with customers, suppliers, employees, and creditors.

MAKING THE OFFER

You must know what the business is worth before you can make an offer. This statement assumes that you know exactly what the assets are worth, what liability you will inherit as the new owner, and what the sales and profit performance of the business has been since its conception. Other important considerations include the level of skills and expertise that you bring to the business. Somewhere in your analysis, you have determined that this company that you are about to buy is right for you. You also know how you will be able to progressively grow the business.

You are now ready to make an offer. Most of us have made offers on a home or new car. Before you made the offer, you probably knew within a 10 percent range what the home or car was really worth. You may have initiated an offer at 15 percent below the asking price and ultimately settled on a price that was halfway between that and the original asking price. The asking price of a business can vary by significantly higher percentages than cars and houses. This is because, in most instances, no two businesses are even remotely alike, which makes it difficult to compare business selling prices.

Let's assume that the ABC Company is for sale at $100,000. Based upon your analysis, you believe that the company is worth $150,000. How much should you offer? The logical answer would be $100,000 and close the deal as quickly as possible. The more appropriate response might be to offer the seller something less than the asking price. How much less should you offer? If you know that there are other buyers standing in line to buy the company, your offer may be very close to the asking price. If this is not the situation, you may want to entertain an offer that may be as much as 25 percent below the asking price. How do you make a "low ball" offer for a business without insulting the seller? Again, the answer to the question falls back to what you discovered about the business during your analysis. You back your "low ball" offer with the negative aspects of the business that you discovered.

USING ESCROW SERVICES

The process by which money and documents are held by a neutral third party until the satisfaction of the terms and conditions of a sales contract have been met is called escrow. When the terms and conditions of the sales contract have been satisfied, a transfer of funds, documents, and ownership occurs. Most homeowners are familiar with how escrow services work if they bought a home that was processed through escrow. Escrow can also be used to acquire the ownership of a business. In some states, a real estate broker is authorized to handle an escrow. The common practice is to employ the services of a licensed escrow company, title company, or lending institution to carry out the escrow functions.

An escrow service can eliminate short- and long-term problems for any business you buy. The business sales contract serves as the basis for the escrow instructions for both the seller and buyer, because it should contain the agreement of the buyer and seller as to who will pay for what, to meet the closing requirements of the contract. In most cases, buying a business involves complications that are considerably more complex than buying a house. Using an escrow service can help eliminate many of the traditional problems that are associated with buying a business.

FRANCHISING ALTERNATIVES

Franchising offers a way to buy into a part of an existing business to minimize many of the trial-and-error steps that are an inherent part of starting a business from scratch. There are more than 3,000 franchise opportunities in the United States. Franchises cover nearly every type of business imaginable and have consistently grown over the past ten years. They currently control over 50 percent of all retail sales in the United States.

There are two basic types of franchises. "Trade name" franchises cover the auto dealerships, gasoline service stations, and soft drink dealerships. Franchise holders typically have the right to sell brand name products by using their own marketing and selling techniques.

The second type of franchise is referred to as a "business format" franchise. The franchiser establishes a fully integrated relationship with the franchise owner by providing all marketing, operating manuals, training, and quality control standards. Most of the franchise companies are small.

FRANCHISE ADVANTAGES

One of the primary advantages of buying a franchise is that they enjoy a higher success rate, or lower failure rate, than their startup counterparts. Less than 5 percent of new franchises fail in their first year as compared to 40 percent of independent startups. This is due to the fact that most franchises have already been subjected to the test of durability. They have an established "track record" that is a testimonial to their survival. Additional advantages of franchises include the following:

1. They offer a proven formula for success.
2. They provide training programs and other forms of management assistance for new business owners.
3. Many franchise programs offer expert assistance in starting the business.
4. Franchises offer volume discounts on group and national purchases.
5. Accounting systems are pre-tested and established.
6. Advertising and promotional programs are initiated by the franchise.
7. Brand and trade names are already established.
8. Some franchises offer financial assistance to qualified franchisees.

FRANCHISE DISADVANTAGES

Most "name brand" franchises cost a considerable amount of money to start. If you buy a franchise, you must abide by the rules and regulations of the franchise. This can present a difficult adjustment for some entrepreneurs. Additional disadvantages of franchises include the following:

1. Most franchises charge an "up front" franchise fee and annual fees.
2. The startup cost for a franchise is usually higher than it is for a startup business.

3. Franchise owners must abide by the operating restrictions mandated by the franchise.

4. Some franchises require a renewal fee after a specified period of time.

5. The growth of your franchise may be limited if you want to expand into an area that is already controlled by another franchiser.

LOCATING FRANCHISES

The process of locating a franchise that is right for you goes back to our earlier discussion about determining the business that is right for you. The business analysis process doesn't go away just because it's a franchise. A new pizza franchise that opens in a market that is saturated with pizza parlors will have less chance of being successful than an emerging franchise in a new market. The business opportunity has to be there before any business can make it, even if it's an international franchise. A franchise may have a good track record but none can guarantee success.

Before you begin to search out a franchise, first determine what are the best business opportunities. When you have qualified the best opportunities, find a franchise that will help you capitalize on the opportunity. A complete directory of all national and international franchises is available in most good public libraries. For additional information, contact:

International Franchise Association
1350 New York Avenue, NW
Suite 900
Washington, DC 20005
(202) 628-8000

WHAT TO EXPECT FROM A FRANCHISE

One of the legal advantages of buying a franchise, as opposed to buying an existing business, is that state and federal laws require franchisers to provide disclosure statements to franchisees. A disclosure statement must contain information about the franchiser, such as the names of the officers and principal owner, along with a description of their business experience. In addition, the statement must describe the terms of the licensing agreement, all fees to be paid, the types of assistance the franchiser will provide, and the territory covered by the franchise. An audited copy of the franchiser's income statement and balance sheet must be included in the disclosure statement. Some states require the franchiser to provide prospective buyers with additional information. Contact the attorney general's office in your state to find out what the state requires.

If you are considering a franchise, review the sales and profit figures in the disclosure statement for a cross section of the franchisees. Select a group of franchisees that reside in the section of the country that you are interested in and pay them a visit. A legitimate franchiser will help you set-up the meetings. Questions that you should be prepared to ask are summarized as follows:

1. Knowing what you now know, are you pleased with your decision to buy the franchise?

2. If a second franchise became available in your market, would you buy it?

3. Has the franchiser been responsive to the needs of your business?

4. What is your opinion of the franchiser's training program?

5. Were there any surprises in your first year of operation?

6. Do the franchise owners have an association and is it helpful?

7. How long are your average work days and do you take vacations?

8. Are the sales patterns in your business seasonal?

9. What were your annual sales over the past three years?

10. Do you believe this franchise has a strong future?

Meet with several franchise owners, selected at random. Don't let the franchiser choose the people you should meet with. When you talk to the different franchise owners, take note and carefully weigh the advantages and disadvantages of the investment. Only by asking the right questions will you get the facts you need to make an informed decision.

SOURCES FOR ADDITIONAL INFORMATION

Although almost 10,000 businesses are bought and sold every day of the week, most buyers have few, if any, guidelines to help them come up with the right price when they decide to buy a business. Although the traditional yardstick of real business worth is the value of net assets plus profit, there are other factors such as goodwill that should be taken into account. Business brokers specialize in both buying and selling businesses for a fee. Most brokers work for a percentage fee of up to 15 percent of the selling price. Fees are negotiable and many will work on a flat fee or hourly basis as a consultant. The Institute of Certified Business Counselors is a nonprofit trade association comprised of professional brokers who have expertise at buying and selling businesses. If you are interested in locating business brokers in your area, contact the association at the following address:

Institute of Certified Business Counselors
P.O. Box 70326
Eugene, OR 97401
(503) 345-8064

PART TWO

FINANCE, MARKETING, AND SALES TECHNIQUES

4

Insuring Your Success with Financial Planning

Financial management lies at the heart of your company's success. Whatever your academic or professional background, you must understand the basic principles of financial management, even if you choose to hire outside experts to consult with you on financial matters. As we stated earlier, poor general management is the number one cause of new business failures. Insufficient capital and poor financial management rank second.

The financial strategies and plans that you develop for your company will become an important part of your overall business plan. The success of your business requires having the right amount of capital at the key times when you need it. A good financial plan allows you to determine your cash requirements before you start your business.

THE FINANCIAL PLAN

Most new entrepreneurs either fail to prepare a financial estimate, or underestimate the amount of money they need to start their business. The beliefs that a few thousand dollars, a prayer, and hard work will carry the business, until it can carry itself, are the ingredients for failure. There are several ways to determine the amount of money you need to start a business. During the startup stage, cash disbursements to cover the daily operation of the business usually exceed the cash receipts from sales. If you don't have enough money to cover your obligations to suppliers, loans, employees, and advertising, your business may fail, just as you are about to realize the marketing opportunities you anticipated. We'll walk you through the essential steps that are required to prepare a financial plan to make sure your business starts off on a solid financial footing. Typical financial problems that are common to startup businesses are summarized in Exhibit 4–1.

Exhibit 4-1. Most Common Financial Problems and Solutions

Financial Problem	Typical Cause of Problem	Solution
No profits	Total costs are out-of-line with total sales when compared to industry standards.	Increase sales and reduce costs.
No cash	Incoming cash from sales is less than the cash needed to run the business.	Tighten credit policies and convert accounts receivable to cash.
Sales are sporadic	Sales are affected by changes in the seasons and inconsistent advertising.	Add nonseasonal items to your offerings and implement a consistent advertising program.

High liabilities	Liability expenses are excessive when compared to the assets of the business.	Reduce your debt obligations and seek out better credit terms.
High asset costs	The return on the company's assets are below an acceptable investment level.	Increase asset productivity and sell off marginally efficient assets.
Unexpected bills	Available cash is suddenly reduced to pay for unexpected invoices.	Implement a monthly and, if necessary, weekly cash flow statement.
High labor cost	Labor costs exceed the standard for the industry.	Increase the productivity of your labor force and consider using contract labor where appropriate.

The first step in preparing a financial plan is to estimate your first year's sales. The sales estimate is important because it is used as the basis for projecting various sales-related expenses, such as inventory levels and service-related salaries. You may feel that you are not prepared to accurately estimate sales at this time. For the purposes of this exercise, estimate your sales based upon what you now know. It is more important that you understand the mechanics of what is required to prepare the financial plan than it is to prepare a sales forecast at this time. You can always adjust your sales estimates later, after you have completed the chapters on sales and marketing.

When you complete the sales estimates, you will be able to estimate the cash outlay part of your financial plan. Initially, you will estimate the month-to-month expenses for the first year. Monthly expenses are then deducted from monthly sales to complete what accountants call a cash flow schedule. The cash flow schedule represents the "bottom line" of the financial plan. It tells you if your business is generating a surplus or deficit of cash at the end of each month. Sources of funding are discussed in the next chapter to assist you in covering deficit funding periods.

PREPARING FINANCIAL FORECASTS

Financial goals and plans are premised upon assumptions and projections about what you think will happen in the future. Most forecasts focus on specific factors affecting a company's revenues and expenditures. You cannot begin to develop a business plan without first forecasting the key financial components of the business, such as sales and cash requirements. Sales are what brings cash into the business. Cash requirements are what cash is taken out of the business to meet its debt obligations.

FORECASTING SALES

The accurate forecasting of sales is critical to the overall financial planning process. Sales forecasts are needed so that you can forecast the other key parts of the plan that are dependent upon the sales estimates. For example, the sales forecast will determine the levels of inventory you must stock, staffing requirements, and other sales- related expenses. There are three popular methods that are used to forecast sales: the survey, historical, and statistical methods.

The Survey Method

The survey method is based upon estimates that result from questionnaires and interviews. Questions may be directed at customers, suppliers, the company's sales force, or any other source that can provide qualified information about the future of your sales. This method usually relies on sampling a portion of your customer base and could include questions such as:

1. Do you intend to buy more or less of our products next year?
2. How would you rate the general economic conditions of the country over the next 12 months (i.e., high, medium, or low)?
3. Do you expect inflation to increase or decrease?
4. Are prices a major consideration when you buy our products?
5. Why do you buy our products and services?

The intent of the survey method is to measure the future mood of your customers. Are they likely to buy more or less of your product over some future time period? The questions should be structured to allow you to determine if you should increase or decrease your sales forecast. The same basic approach could be used to establish a forecast for a new business.

For example, let's assume that you are about to open a business in a market that includes three competitive companies. Based upon your competitive analysis, you have been able to determine that the three competitors have annual sales of $3 million. Since you will be the fourth competitor in the market, you could simply determine that you will control 25 percent of the market or $750,000 (e.g., $3,000,000 divided by 4). Is this a valid assumption? The assumption would hold more credence if you surveyed customer prospects to determine if their buying patterns will remain stable in the future. In addition, you could ask questions that would help you determine if you will, in fact, be able to capture 25 percent of the market when you start your business.

The Historical Method

The historical method is based upon gathering data from available sales records, plotting the data chronologically, and based on the trend lines, projecting future sales. This method assumes that historical sales trends will persist in the future. The drawback of this method is that the forecaster must make a prediction of whether the trend will continue, accelerate, or slow down, as we illustrate in Exhibit 4–2.

All three sales trends in Exhibit 4–2 would require analysis before you could determine if the trend could be used to forecast future sales. The "stable grow" trend line is perhaps the easiest of the three trend lines to follow, because it shows a consistent and progressive growth of sales over an established period of time. One could simply extend the trend line out over the next twelve months to complete the sales forecast exercise. No upward trend can continue forever, so it might be appropriate to use the survey method to help qualify the trend levels.

The accelerated growth line offers some interesting opportunities as well as dilemmas for the forecaster. For some reason, the sales of the business are accelerating at a rapid rate. One would assume that the business owner knows exactly why sales are accelerating. Are the sales increasing because of a special promotional or sales discount program? If the sales are accelerating because of a special program that cannot be sustained over the forecast period, then the sales forecast would be overstated, if it were based on an extension of the accelerated trend line. On the other hand, if sales are accelerating because one of your major competitors went out of business, you may have justification to use the accelerated trend line in your forecast. If sales are declining, one would again assume that the owner knows why sales are down and can initiate a program that will either

Exhibit 4-2. Historical Sales Graphically Illustrated.

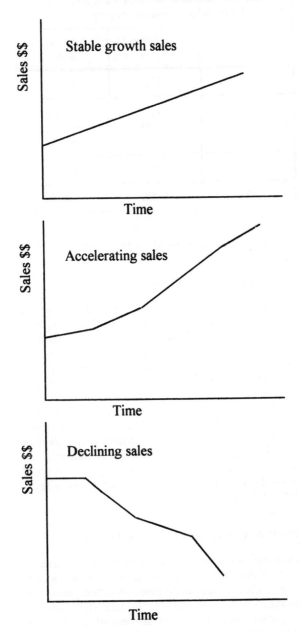

Exhibit 4-3. Increase in Sales That Are Attributable to New Housing Starts

Time Period	% Increase in Housing Starts	% Increase in Sales
1	.2%	1.0%
2	.4%	2.0%
3	.6%	2.5%
4	.8%	4.0%
5	1.0%	5.0%

flatten the downward trend, or turn it into a positive trend.

The Statistical Method

Statistical forecasting methods rely on mathematical analysis to establish a sales forecast. For example, a company that sells home furnishings may discover that when there is a 1 percent rise in the construction of new homes, store sales increase by 5 percent. This statistical method and approach is illustrated in Exhibit 4–3.

All sales are affected by something whether it be economic conditions, population growth, or changes in the seasons. As a business owner, it is important that you understand what events affect your sales. In the process, you will need to develop your own set of statistical techniques that you can rely upon to accurately forecast sales.

PREPARING A CASH FLOW STATEMENT

Up to this point, we have shown you how to estimate sales. Now we will show you how to prepare a cash flow statement, the single most important part of the financial plan. Although the balance sheet and income statement projection are important, the cash flow statement is indispensable in managing your business on a day-by-day basis. Cash runs the business. It pays the rent, pays suppliers, pays employees, and only cash keeps the doors of your business open. The basic concept of cash flow is quite simple to illustrate.

Let's assume that your company had a combined beginning cash balance it its savings and checking accounts of $25,000. The company expected to receive $50,000 in cash from the sale of its products and services. A total of $65,000 was forecast to cover projected cash expenses in the first month. Our cash flow equation follows:

$$(\text{Beginning cash} + \text{Cash receipts}) - (\text{Cash disbursements}) = \text{Cash surplus or shortage}$$
$$(\$25,000 + \$50,000) - (\$65,000) = \$10,000$$

If total cash disbursements exceed the total available cash, then you will need to seek funds from another source to cover the shortfall. In this next example, let's assume that your company generated a "cash surplus" of $10,000 and that you deposited the $10,000 into your checking account. Our cash flow equation for Month 2 follows:

$$(\text{Beginning cash} + \text{Cash receipts}) - (\text{Cash disbursements}) = \text{Cash surplus or shortage}$$
$$(\$10,000 + \$50,000) - (\$75,000) = (\$15,000)$$

As you can see from our equation, the business showed a deficit or negative cash flow in Month 2. You would need to cover the $15,000 deficit with funds that you obtained from another source such as a credit line with a bank, or your personal checking account. The next step in the process of creating a cash flow statement is to identify the elements that are used to construct the statement. As the name implies, the cash flow statement includes only those elements that have a cash impact on the business. The cash side of the equation is concerned with the following:

Beginning cash (e.g., checking account)
Cash sales
Collections from accounts receivable
Other sources of cash (e.g., bank loans, investor money, etc.)

Exhibit 4-4. Three Months Cash Flow Projection	Jan	Feb	Mar
Cash in:			
Cash Sales			
Credit Sales			
Other			
Total Cash In			
Cash out:			
Inventory			
Rent			
Utilities			
Loans			
Total Cash Out			
Monthly Cash Flow*			
*Monthly Cash Flow = Total Cash In - Total Cash Out			

The disbursement side of the equation includes cash outflows required to support the operating activities of the business such as:

Payroll
Equipment payments
Supplies
Inventory and raw materials
Rent and utilities
Selling expenses such as commissions
Loan payments
Transportation and distribution expenses
Overhead cost and miscellaneous expenses

When you prepare your cash flow schedule, start with beginning cash balances from checking and savings accounts (see Exhibit 4–4). Add credit sales that you expect to be paid for in the forecast periods and sources of other cash such as the sale of assets. Total all cash that you expect will come into the business for each of the forecast months.

Next, forecast the cash that you will need by month to cover operating expenses. The "total cash out" is subtracted from "total cash in" to determine the cash flow per month. A positive dollar amount indicates that you have forecast more cash than will be necessary to cover your forecast for operating expenses. The reverse is true if the dollar amount is negative.

PROJECTING THE INCOME STATEMENT

The projected income statement reflects what you anticipate will happen to the profitability of your business over a period of time. It indicates the level of expected sales, cost of goods sold, operating expenses, and the resulting profits. In many respects, the income statement resembles the cash flow statement format. However, there are several important differences between these two statements. The income statement projects profits, which are not included on the cash flow statement. Gross sales and expenses are also projected on the income statement. These elements may or may not be recorded on the cash flow statement. The cash flow statement is only concerned with cash receipt and cash disbursement items.

For example, assume that your business sold $25,000 in products and services to customers on credit. According to the company's credit terms, customers are allowed to pay for purchased products and services in 60 days, without interest. If you assume that all of your customers will elect to pay you on the 60th day, how would you estimate your cash receipts and sales on each statement for Month 1?

Answer

Cash flow statement for Month 1 = $00.00
Income statement for Month 1 = $25,000

The cash flow statement estimate reflects the fact that no customers will in all probability elect to pay cash until the end of Month 2. Hence, no anticipated receipt of cash is recorded for these accounts receivable transactions in Month 1. The cash flow statement for Month 2 would logically include the receipt of $25,000. Conversely, the income statement generally records sales when they occur, or in Month 1 in this example.

Now assume that your business purchases $10,000 of merchandise in Month 1. According to the terms that you have established with your supplier, the payment for the merchandise is not due for 60 days. If we assume that you elect to pay for the merchandise on the 60th day, how would you estimate your cash disbursements and expenses on each statement for Month 1?

Answer

Cash flow statement for Month 1 = $00.00
Income statement for Month 1 = $10,000

Again, the cash flow statement estimate reflects the fact that no outlay of cash will be required for the merchandise until the end of Month 2. The cash flow statement for Month 2 would logically include the anticipated balance due payment of $10,000. Conversely, the income statement generally records expenses when they occur, or in Month 1 in this example.

The projected income statement is important because it attempts to match actual sales against all costs to arrive at a projected profit for a given period of time (i.e., usually monthly). Accurate profit projections are extremely important because they can be used to fund the growth of your business, reduce debt obligations, and provide a return to investors. The basic concept of the income statement is quite simple. The income statement profit or loss equation includes the following elements:

(Total sales – Discounts & Allowances) –
(Total expenses + taxes) = Net profit
($75,000) – ($65,000) = $10,000

Since total sales exceeded total expenses in our example, the business made a net profit of $10,000. Most financial plans include two income statement projections — one for the first twelve months of the business, and a consolidated statement that covers the first three years. The twelve-month projection will serve to help you evaluate how well your business is trending toward achieving profit objectives. The three-year projections are particularly important in establishing the projected growth of your business. Lending institutions are often more interested in the long-term prospects of a business before they will consider loan requests.

Your sales estimate represents the most important part of your projected income statement. A dynamic startup business should show a continuous growth in sales, as you build a customer base and begin to realize growth from referrals. All line item estimates that you insert into the income statement, or any of the statements that we cover in this chapter, should be backed by your analysis that shows how you arrived at each respective number. That is important for two basic reasons. First, it will allow you to refer back to your business charter to determine if your original assumptions were valid, or if modifications are required. Second, if you apply for a loan, most investors will not accept the aggregate numbers that you may have "plugged" into your projections. You must be prepared to answer the question: How did you arrive at this number? If you can not come up with a qualified answer, your loan request will be denied. In Exhibit 4–5, we have included a summarized explanation of how each number in the statement was calculated.

A three-year income statement projection is important because it should indicate whether you expect your business to continue growing or level off. Everybody expects growth, although leveling off is not necessarily a bad scenario, which we will comment on in a moment. If your statement is showing growth, your financial plan should explain how you are going to achieve the projected growth. Does it involve opening additional outlets, offering additional goods and services, expanding sales territories, or other business opportunities. Your three-year projection

Exhibit 4-5. First Year Income Statement Forecast

ABC Company

Income Statement

Sales	Year 1 Forecast	Explanation
Service Sales	$95,000	Last year's actual plus 2% increase
Product Sales	205,000	Forecast based on customer survey
Total Sales	**$300,000**	
Cost of Goods Sold		
Product Materials	$92,000	45% of product sales
Direct Service Labor	24,000	25% of service sales
Total Cost of Goods Sold	**$116,000**	
Operating Expenses		
Utilities	$6,500	Last year's rate plus 5% increase
Salaries	72,000	Indirect management salaries
Payroll Taxes & Benefits	14,750	FICA and insurance benefits
Advertising	4,000	Covers our newspaper display ads
Office Supplies	3,250	Includes postage
Insurance	4,900	Reflects premium quote
Legal & Accounting Services	1,250	Covers annual tax return
Telephone	1,605	Monthly average projected
Depreciation Expense	10,100	Straight line method used
Travel & Distribution	4,600	Covers two annual trade shows
Total Operating Expenses	**$123,000**	
Other Expenses	$4,000	Petty cash account
Notes Payable Interest	7,000	First Bank note for equipment
Total Expenses	**$250,000**	Expenses are 7% below industry
Net Profit	**$50,000**	17% net profit projected

should reflect these anticipated events, as shown in Exhibit 4–6.

PROJECTING THE BALANCE SHEET

The projected balance sheet reflects the overall financial condition of your business at any one moment in

Exhibit 4-6. Three-Year Income Statement Projection

ABC Company
Income Statement

Sales	Year 1	Year 2	Year 3
Service Sales	$95,000	$105,000	$95,000
Product Sales	205,000	215,000	255,000
Total Sales	**$300,000**	**$320,000**	**$350,000**
Cost of Goods Sold			
Product Materials	$92,000	$98,440	$100,280
Direct Service Labor	24,000	25,680	26,160
Total Cost of Goods Sold	**$116,000**	**$124,120**	**$126,440**
Operating Expenses			
Utilities	$6,500	$6,955	$7,085
Salaries	72,000	77,040	78,480
Payroll Taxes & Benefits	14,750	15,782	16,077
Advertising	4,000	4,280	4,360
Office Supplies	3,205	3,478	3,543
Insurance	4,900	5,243	5,341
Legal & Accounting Services	1,250	1,337	1,362
Telephone	1,605	1,717	1,749
Depreciation Expense	10,100	10,807	11,009
Travel & Distribution	4,600	4,922	5,014
Total Operating Expenses	**$123,000**	**$131,561**	**$134,020**
Other Expenses	$4,000	$4,280	$4,360
Notes Payable Interest	7,000	7,490	7,630
Total Expenses	**$250,000**	**$267,451**	**$272,450**
Net Profit	**$50,000**	**$52,549**	**$77,550**

time. The basic concept of the balance sheet is quite simple and can be explained in the balance sheet equation that follows:

$$(\text{Total Assets}) - (\text{Total Liabilities}) = \text{Owner's equity}$$
$$(\$175,000) - (\$100,000) = \$75,000$$

In our example, the total assets of the business exceed the total liabilities of the business, which resulted in a positive owner equity or book value of $75,000 in our example. As we explained earlier, the balance sheet is a simple statement of what would happen to a business if it were to abruptly go out of business. The example shows that our business owned $175,000 in assets and owed $100,000 to creditors. If the business folded, sold its assets, and paid off its creditors, then $75,000 would be left over as surplus money to the owners. On the basis of this balance sheet, a lending institution should be willing to finance the business for $75,000, or the net value of the assets.

Profitable businesses are expected to have a positive cash flow, increase their assets, and to retire debt. Hence, your projected balance sheet should consistently track any growth shown in your income statement (i.e., corresponding growth in equity). In the first year, it may be reasonable to show a negative owner's equity number as your business acquires the assets it needs to grow. The liability side of the projected balance sheet would show the debt that was incurred to acquire the necessary assets. This is illustrated in Exhibit 4–7.

Projecting the second and third years of your balance sheet is particularly important not only to yourself but to investors. The balance sheet more than the income statement is the indicator of how successful your business will be at retiring debt — a major concern to creditors. The balance sheets represent an overall financial picture of what your business looks like at the end of a time period. It is closely integrated into the financial activities that occur in your income statement. The example below illustrates this point.

There is a close relationship between the income statement and the balance sheet. Assume that at the end of Month 1, your business produced a profit of $10,000 and you used the profit to retire a portion of

Exhibit 4-7. Two-Year Balance Sheet Comparison				
	Year 1	% Assets	Year 2	% Assets
Assets				
Cash	$50,000	20%	$60,000	21%
Accounts Receivable	$125,000	49%	$137,500	48%
Inventory	35,000	14%	38,500	13%
Fixed Assets	43,000	17%	52,300	18%
Total Assets	$253,000	100%	$288,300	100%
Liabilities		% Liab.		% Liab.
Accounts Payable	$75,000	51%	$78,750	50%
Notes Payable	22,500	15%	23,625	15%
Long-term Debt	36,400	25%	42,900	27%
Other Liabilities	12,800	9%	13,440	8%
Total Liabilities	$146,700	100%	$158,715	100%
Owner's Equity	$106,300	72%	$129,585	82%
Total Liabilities & Equity	$253,000		$288,300	

a $100,000 balance sheet debt in Month 2. What would be the effect of this transaction on the owner's equity side of the balance sheet between Months 1 and 2? Total assets and liabilities in Month 1 were $200,000 and $125,000 respectively.

Answer

Owner's equity in Month 1
= Total assets – total liabilities
= $200,000 – $125,000
= $75,000

Owner's equity in Month 2
= Total assets – total liabilities
= $200,000 – ($125,000 – $10,000)
= $85,000

Owner's equity increased by $10,000, or the exact amount that was applied from income statement profits to reduce the liabilities of the business.

BREAK-EVEN ANALYSIS

As we have stated earlier, one of the cardinal rules of a business is that it should endeavor to make a profit. To determine when your business will be profitable, you must gather all of the elements of your cost and compare costs to projected sales. This analysis is known as the break-even analysis and is used to determine whether or not a viable sales-cost relationship exists. The break-even point is established when you determine the sales-cost combination point where total sales equal total costs. There are five elements in the break-even point equation that are used to calculate the break-even point:

1. Price (P). The price at which a unit of product or service will be sold.

2. Quantity (Q). This is the amount of product or service units that will be sold.

3. Fixed Cost (F). Fixed costs are present regardless of the number of units produced. Fixed cost includes such items as rent, indirect labor, and the cost of equipment.

4. Variable Costs (V). These costs are directly related to each unit of production. The costs are incurred when an item is produced and sold. Variable costs typically include direct labor expenses, raw materials, and sales commissions.

5. Profit (PR). Profit is the difference between total sales and total expenses. Profit at the break-even point is zero.

The graph in Exhibit 4–8 presents the break-even analysis concept. Your business makes a profit as it moves above the break-even point — and it loses money when it moves below this point.

The horizontal axis on the graph represents the price of a product or service unit. The vertical axis represents the total quantities of product or service units sold. The total cost line is the summation of total fixed and variable costs. The revenue line represents total sales at different unit sales prices and quantities. The break-even point occurs when sales revenues equal total costs.

Exhibit 4-8. Break-Even Graph

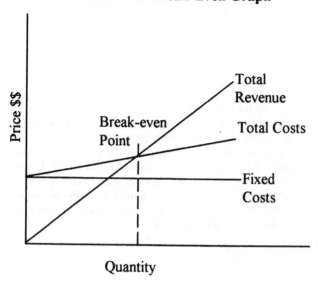

DETERMINING BREAK-EVEN POINTS

Now that the elements of the break-even point have been defined, the basic break-even point equation can be shown as follows:

Profit = (Price × Quantity) –
(Fixed Cost + Variable Costs)
Abbreviated form: PR = QP – F – QV

Profit was inserted into the equation to allow you to determine the level of sales needed to achieve different profit levels. However, our general equation includes a term for profit (PR).

Let's adjust the equation to solve a break-even pricing problem to answer the question: What price must I charge to break-even? Assume that the fixed costs for the ABC Company are $20,000 and that variable cost for product A are $4 per unit. The company believes it can produce and sell 2,000 units of product A. The break-even price can be calculated as follows:

$$P = \frac{(F + QV)}{Q}$$

$$P = \frac{(\$20,000) + (2,000 \times \$4)}{2,000}$$

$$P = \$14$$

In this example, we would need to obtain a price of $14 for every product A unit sold to break-even, given our cost and quantity assumptions. Suppose we knew how much we wanted to charge for a product (e.g., $20 each) and subsequently wanted to know what quantity we would have to sell to break-even. If we use the same cost assumptions from the previous example, we can again apply the break-even formula to find the answer we need.

$$Q = \frac{(F)}{(P - V)}$$

$$Q = \frac{(\$20,000)}{(\$20 - \$4)}$$

$$Q = 1,250$$

PERFORMING BREAK-EVEN PRICING ANALYSIS

A number of important "what if" business scenarios can be played out by applying different parts of the break-even equation. Let's assume that your business can sell everything it produces. It is currently producing at its capacity level of 50,000 units. Your annual fixed costs are $25,000 per year and variable costs are $5 per unit. If your business produces and sells at maximum output, what is the break-even price? Because you are looking for the break-even price, you apply the break-even price equation.

$$P = \frac{(F + QV)}{(Q)}$$

$$P = \frac{(\$25,000) + (50,000 \times \$5)}{50,000}$$

$$P = \$5.50 \text{ per unit}$$

Now, let's assume the same set of cost and volume assumptions in this next example. However, if each unit is sold for $7.50 per unit, what is the new break-even quantity? Because you are looking for the break-even quantity, you apply the break-even quantity equation.

$$Q = \frac{(F)}{(P-V)}$$

$$Q = \frac{(\$25,000)}{(\$7.50 - \$5)}$$

$$Q = 10,000 \text{ units}$$

The use of the break-even analysis equations provides you with a great deal of latitude in the analysis of your financial strategies. It allows you to manipulate many variations, or combinations of variables, to find the answers to important financial questions, and ultimately the point above which you will create a profit. Knowledge of where the point is located is extremely important in that it will help you to identify products and services that are profitable.

Although the examples presented in this chapter have been for a product company, the break-even principles work equally well for service businesses. Instead of product units, you'll use service hours or some other appropriate unit factor for your business.

FUNDING THE OPERATION

The basis for financing your business depends upon the amount of money that you need to cover the cash flow deficit periods. Although many entrepreneurs fund their companies with their own or the bank's money, there are a growing number of entrepreneurs who are discovering the advantages of equity funding. Equity funding is where you grant part ownership in the company in exchange for something that is needed by the company. For example, some startup companies pay for professional and contract services in stock. Low employee salaries are supplemented with stock.

If the company is successful, equity can be an expensive way to raise capital, since stock that is issued during the startup period for $1 a share could someday be worth many times that much. However, the benefits of aligning the interest of investors and employees in the effort to build a viable company can offer a significant advantage to a startup business. Lending institutions are often more willing to accommodate loan requests to companies that can show internal equity investment.

SELECTING THE MANAGEMENT TEAM

Management weakness is a risk in the eyes of investors. Putting together a management team that knows the business you are in will, in all probability, fit well with investors. For example, if you can assemble a team that has been involved with successful startups in the same industry as yours, you can substantially raise the comfort level of investors. Even better, if you can assemble a management team that has worked together on a previous venture, you can further improve upon your odds of getting a loan. Investors know that management teams can disintegrate under stress. A team that has worked together before demonstrates staying power.

CREATING A BOARD OF DIRECTORS

Many entrepreneurs think that only corporations have boards of directors. Any company can establish a board of directors. Boards are created to bring outside experience and expertise into a company. A qualified board of directors offers an excellent business credential when you apply for a loan. Avoid appointing friends or associates who do not have the expertise you need.

USING PROFESSIONAL ADVISORS

The creation of an established group of professional advisors can also strengthen your financial plan. Initially, your advisors list might include an accounting and a law firm. Your financial plan should show why you picked this particular accounting or law firm. For example, your accounting firm may specialize in accounting for other companies in your industry. Other advisors might include an advertising agency that knows your product, or technical consultants that specialize in your primary areas of research. Expert backing always adds credibility to the financial credentials of any business.

DEVELOPING A PRESENTATION

Developing a top-quality financial presentation does not just happen overnight. It takes time to develop a "first class" presentation that can attract the interest of sophisticated investors. Take time now, while you have the time, to prepare a financial presentation complete with charts and appropriate copy material. Then, if you receive a call from a prospective investor, you will be prepared to make a good presentation.

PREPARING A FINANCIAL PLAN

The financial plan is one section in your overall business plan and it serves several purposes. First, it provides insights into the financial viability of your business venture. This issue is important to you and it is vitally important to anybody who may be interested in investing in your company. It also serves to attract and convince talented people to join your company. Nobody wants to join a company that is not financial viable.

A significant part of your plan will be composed of financial projections. Keep in mind that financial projections do not stand on their own. Anybody who reviews your projections will expect to read a discussion that supports your projections. Keep your projections conservative and back them up with actual numbers whenever possible.

STARTUP COSTS

The startup section of the plan identifies the anticipated costs for initially establishing the business. The list in the plan can be a summary description of your startup cost and the dollar amount need per item. For example, you may show that you need $10,000 for inventory. However, if you are asked to further quantify your inventory needs, you should be prepared to show exactly how the $10,000 will be applied to acquire inventory. Your list may include such items as:

Inventory
Equipment
Fixtures
Rent deposits
Remodeling
Utilities
Legal and professional fees
Advertising

USE OF FUNDS

If the purpose of your financial plan is to secure funding, then it is important to show how you will use your investor's money. The following example illustrates the words that might be appropriate for this part of the plan.

The ABC Company has developed a line of products that are superior to all other products that exist in the market today. In order to penetrate the identified target markets with its superior products, significant capital infusion is required. Specifically, the company needs $100,000 that will be allocated as follows:

Marketing and advertising — $23,000
Salaries — $10,000
Research and development — $28,000
Packaging — $9,000
Operating expenses — $30,000

FINANCIAL PROJECTIONS

Your financial projections can appear in the back of the plan. The discussion in the body of the plan can refer to the numbers in the various projections. If you use a lot of projections, you may want to assign exhibit numbers to each projection. For example, let's assume that you have assigned Exhibit 1 to your income statement. In the plan, you could use the following words to explain some part of the income statement: "In reference to our income statement that is shown in Exhibit 1, our sales increased by 25 percent over the past two years." At a minimum, your financial plan should be supplemented with the following projections:

Income Statement (three years)
Cash Flow Statement and Forecast
Balance Sheet
Break-even Analysis

Conclude your financial plan by restating your capital needs. Emphasize why you believe it will be a safe investment. Cover the expected profits you will make and the time period when they will be made.

SOURCES FOR ADDITIONAL INFORMATION

There are a number of periodicals and newspapers that publish financial information and articles for startup businesses. Since editorial policies differ widely, read several issues before subscribing. If your local library or magazine store does not have copies of magazines of possible interest, write the publisher and ask for a sample copy. A select list of publications follows:

Barrons National Business and Financial Weekly
22 Cortlandt Street
New York, NY 10007

Financial World
1328 Broadway
New York, NY 10018

Forbes
60 Fifth Avenue
New York, NY 10011

5

Financing Your Business

Armed with the financial plan that you prepared in the previous chapter, you are now ready to go forward and apply for a loan. Borrowing money is one of the facts of life when starting a business. In some instances, it may be advisable to borrow money even if you believe you have enough money to get your venture started. If never hurts to have some additional cash on deposit just in case you need it. It also helps to establish a professional relationship with lending institutions for future growth and expansion needs. In this chapter, we will review several loan sources and show you how to apply for a loan.

LOAN PLANNING

In the perfect world, it would be nice if a lender financed most of your business. This would limit the amount of personal money you would have to invest in the business. When your business paid off all of its debts, you would get all the profits and own the assets. Unfortunately, most lenders are not that generous because they are acutely aware of the fact that the lack of capital is a major reason behind small business failures.

The terms and the amount that a lender will loan you will be directly dependent upon the quality of your financial plan. Your strategy needs to be thorough and reflect the potential for success that will justify the financial risk others will have to take, if they invest in your business. Your plan should include checking with as many lending sources as you can think of to find the best loan. Some lending institutions are more receptive to startup loans than others, and loan terms can vary significantly between institutions. If you have to settle for a loan that is less than what you originally needed, be prepared to scale down your business idea to fit the amount of money you can raise to get started.

WHAT LENDERS WANT TO KNOW

No matter how receptive the market may be to the offerings of your business, it takes outstanding people
to startup and manage a business into a profitable
growth position. Investors know this and they will be
looking for a well-rounded management team that
has all of the ingredients for success. Is there a vi-
sionary CEO running the company who is backed by
financial, marketing, and sales experts? Does the
management team have prior experience in the business that they are about to enter?

Astute investors will spend as much time examin-
ing the members of your startup team as they will evaluating your projected income statement and balance
sheet. Your character and past business associations
will be carefully reviewed before your loan will be approved. Therefore, make sure that you provide enough
background information, client names, and previous
lending sources to augment your loan request.

Describe how the key credentials of your startup
team meet the needs of the business. Fancy titles do
not compensate for experience and background qualifications. Anybody can be a vice-president of something, but what do they offer to the business? Project
your staffing needs over the first year of the business.
If you are in a highly competitive industry, show how
you will attract, hire, and keep the best people. Describe the career path and potential for key members
of your staff. Consider using competitive salaries that
are supplemented with stock options, profit sharing,
and other compensation methods to further encourage
"buy-in" from key employees.

Beyond the human side of your loan application,
investors will want to see precisely how much capital
you need to raise, when you will need it, and when
you can pay it back. You'll be asked to show how you
plan to use the funds and to identify what your personal investment is in the business. Lenders will also
view your financial package by analyzing key financial ratios before they will approve your loan.

FINANCIAL RATIOS

Potential investors will want to see financial ratios
that show how well the cash cycle blends in with the

operational cycle of your business. The key ratios that they will be primarily interested in reviewing are the current ratio, debt-to-equity ratio, and the accounts receivable turnover ratio. The three ratios are illustrated in the examples that follow:

Current Ratio

Let's assume that your current assets are $80,000 and current liabilities are $31,000. The current ratio can be calculated by using the following formula:

$$\text{Current ratio} = \frac{\text{Current assets}}{\text{Current liabilities}}$$

$$= \frac{\$80,000}{\$31,000}$$

$$= 2.58$$

The current ratio indicates the number of times current assets will pay off current liabilities. Historically, a 2:1 or higher ratio is considered a good financial indicator. This ratio indicates how well your business can meet its current liabilities when they come due. Companies that can maintain low inventories and tight credit policies usually have high current ratios.

Current Debt-to-Equity Ratio

Let's assume that owner's equity is $55,000 and current liabilities are $31,000. The current ratio can be calculated by using the following formula:

$$\text{Debt - equity-ratio} = \frac{\text{Current liabilities}}{\text{Owners equity}}$$

$$= \frac{\$31,000}{\$55,000}$$

$$= .56$$

The current debt-to-equity ratio compares what is owed against what is owned. It measures the financial leverage of the business. The lower the ratio, the greater are the profits from sales. Determining a favorable ratio is difficult to determine because it depends on a number of factors, such as accounts receivable and inventory turnover.

Accounts Receivable Turnover Ratio

The receivable turnover is the ratio of total credit sales to receivables. It is also known as the sales-to-receivable ratio. Assume that total net sales on account are $250,000 and that the receivable balance is $1,000,000. The receivable turnover is calculated by using the following formula:

$$\text{Receivable turnover ratio} = \frac{\text{(Net sales on account)}}{\text{(Receivable balance)}}$$

$$= \frac{\$250,000}{\$1,000,000}$$

$$= .25 \text{ or } 25\%$$

The receivable turnover ratio is an indication of how efficient your company is at collecting credit account money. In our example, 25 percent of the total accounts receivable balance was collected over some designated time period. The typical time period is monthly. Therefore, the company in our example is averaging four months to complete the collection of receivable balances (i.e., $1,000,000 divided by $250,000 is 4 months).

A receivable turnover ratio of two months or lower is considered a preferred ratio. Lenders use this ratio to determine the relationship between the volume of credit business and average outstanding receivables. A higher turnover ratio indicates a shorter collection period.

FINANCIAL PROJECTIONS

Most investor want to see your financial projections for three to five years out, including your balance sheet, cash flow, and income statements. At a minimum, they also want to see your monthly projections for the first year of operation. Pay particular attention to your cash flow projections, which indicate how well your financing is timed and tracks the repayment terms of your loans.

Financial projection checklist

1. Three-year balance sheet projection.
2. Three to five year income statement projection.
3. Three years of previous tax returns.
4. Break-even analysis.
5. Cash flow analysis.

Your projections should include three scenarios for the company's performance; strong, neutral, and weak. Identify what your assumptions are for each scenario given and clearly identify the break-even point for each scenario.

TYPES OF LOANS

The savings and loan crisis, and the billions of dollars it took to bail out the banking industry, led to increased government regulation of banks. Bankers found themselves constrained by the mounds of costly paperwork that had to accompany every loan they made. Consequently, getting a loan to expand or improve a small business can be a difficult process.

Finding a lender isn't a scientific task, but there are several steps you should take when you start looking for lender. Find out in advance who's lending and who's getting what types of loans by talking with your business associates. Look for a lender who knows your industry and has done business with companies like yours in the past. Seek out a loan officer who has the authority to make a loan decision on your behalf.

There are a number of different types of loan sources that you may want to consider for your business, including *unsecured* and *secured* loan options. An *unsecured loan* is one in which collateral is not required to secure the loan. This type of loan is generally short-term in nature (less than one year) and is only granted to creditworthy customers. These types of loans are generally made for specific purposes, such as the purchase of inventory and supplies. *Secured loans* are secured by collateral, such as fixed assets or real property. Automobiles, trucks, fixtures, and leasehold improvements are examples of secured collateral loans. The length of time allowed to pay back secured loans can be several years.

ACCOUNTS RECEIVABLE LOANS

Accounts receivable financing is a type of loan that is also known as a secured line of credit loan. These lines are generally short term in nature and are periodically reviewed by the lending institution granting the loan. The purpose of the loan is to fund the investment a business has in its accounts receivable. The lending institution will advance a certain amount, based upon what it believes is an acceptable value of your accounts receivable. The value of your accounts receivable is based on your past collection's history, bad debt write-offs, and the average age of your past due accounts.

Many banks and finance companies will lend money on the basis of your accounts receivable. Generally, you can get as much as 80 percent of the value of your receivables, depending on the payment patterns of your customers. In most cases, you continue to handle customer billings. Some lenders may take on this task.

Although most banks will not loan based on a contract you may hold, finance companies will. Financing is based on a contract yet to be performed. They will need assurances that you will perform satisfactorily and that the firm granting the contract is reliable. Interest rates for contract loans are very high.

BANK LOANS

Commercial banks are one of the best sources of capital for small businesses. Most banks offer three general types of loans: short-term loans (30 to 90 days), intermediate loans (1 to 5 years), and long-term loans (over 5 years). Lending institutions look for borrowers with good credit ratings, experience in the business they propose to enter, and business plans that demonstrate an ability to repay the loans. Interest rates and repayment schedules will vary between banks.

Unless you are an established business person

with a good credit rating, banks usually expect you to
have raised as much as 50 percent of the money you
need. They are more willing to supply financing after
your business is established. A line of credit may be
extended to a business to be used as the owner sees
fit. Lines of credit extend from 30 days to as long as
several years. The interest on a credit line is computed on the amount actually used. Fees are sometimes charged for keeping credit line funds in reserve.
Some banks have special loan programs aimed at
helping small business in general and minority entrepreneurs in particular. Check with business associates to find banks with special programs.

COMMON STOCK FINANCING

If your business is a corporation, you may elect to issue common stock to finance the company. This type
of arrangement allows the investing public to receive
a share of the profits, yet permits the officers of the
corporation to retain control over the management of
the company. The advantages and disadvantages of financing with common stock are summarized as follows:

Advantages

1. The corporation is not legally obligated to
   make payments to stockholders, so long as
   the board of directors acts in the best interest
   of the corporation.
2. Stock improves the credit rating of the company because it increases the amount of capital in the company, which is more attractive
   to creditors.
3. Stock are attractive to some investors who
   prefer this type of investment, because it often offers a hedge against inflation.

Disadvantages

1. Common stock owners have corporate voting
   rights and control can be transferred to the
   new stockholders.
2. Shareholders share in the profits of the company through dividend disbursements.

PREFERRED STOCK FINANCING

Corporations can issue preferred stock as a means of financing the business, which has certain advantages over common stock. Preferred stockholders have priority over common stockholders in the distribution of dividends. Dividends must be paid to preferred stockholders first, before they can be paid to common stock holders. In the event of a dissolution of the corporation, the claims of the preferred stockholders must be satisfied first, before distribution can be made to the common stockholders.

Preferred stock has either a par value, stated value, or liquidated value. These values are used to establish the amount due to the preferred stockholders in the event of liquidation as well as the amount of dividends each preferred shareholder will receive. Preferred stockholders do not have corporate voting rights.

CREDIT CARDS

Many entrepreneurs overlook the credit card loan source. Credit cards — such as VISA and Master Card — offer competitive interest rates to anybody who can qualify with a good credit rating. Credit cards are easy to get and require a minimum amount of paper work to obtain. Make sure you shop for the best credit terms that are available because credit card interest rates vary significantly.

FINANCE COMPANIES

Finance companies will normally assume a greater amount of risk in a startup loan than will banks, but they typically charge higher interest rates than banks. For example, commercial finance companies will make loans based upon the strength of your collateral, rather than your track record or the potential of the business. Consider a finance company only if you can't find another lender source and can afford the high interest payments. Commercial finance companies are listed in the yellow pages.

SELLER LOANS

If you are buying an existing business, you may be able to get financial help from the seller. If the seller does not participate in the financing, you may have trouble getting money from lending institutions who may feel that the seller does not have the confidence in either you, or the future of the business.

Normally, you would be expected to pay between 20 and 40 percent of the purchase price and get financing to cover the rest. Ask the seller to consider financing the balance as a loan at low interest rate. Don't accept the argument that interest rates will never go down again. Try to get the repayment terms extended with an agreement that you have the right to prepay without penalty. You can then approach conventional lenders for the rest of your financing requirements. You will have the expressed confidence of the seller and the past track record of the company to support your request.

EQUITY FINANCING

Exchanging cash for partial ownership in the business is called equity financing, which is another method for generating capital. To raise equity dollars, you may persuade friends and relatives to participate in the ownership of the new enterprise. The agreements can be in the form of joint ventures, partnerships, limited partnerships, or other equity arrangements, where private investors can also share in the ownership of the new company. Negotiated equity terms include profit and loss distribution, percent ownership over time, and other payment considerations.

LOANS FROM FRIENDS

Friends and family are often a logical source for a loan, and for many this may be their only alternative. Friends and family are the second most popular source for business startup capital after personal financing. However, taking money from people you know has its own risks and can threaten the relationship if your business fails. A bad loan to a family member or friend, can result in lingering hostility. There are ways to control this delicate loan process without upsetting anybody, if you handle the situation in a professional manner.

"I'll just pay you back when I can" is the wrong

approach. Many business owners erroneously assume a personal loan from a friend means they can take their time paying it back, which is wrong. Treat a loan from a friend exactly as you would treat a loan from the bank. Document everything in writing and set-up a repayment schedule at the prevailing market interest rates.

Some people are willing to put up money to get your business going and assume the investment gives them authorization to assist you in running your business. If the person who's lending you money has some business expertise that you can use, you may want to include that person as a partner in your business. However, if you're looking for a straight investment as opposed to a partner, make it clear from the start that the loan doesn't entitle them to dictate how you run your business.

Before you ask friends for a loan, hold an informal investment meeting to qualify their interests. Tell them about the business and your need for capital to see if they are receptive to the idea. Don't pressure someone to give you money. Give people an out and let them know your relationship won't be affected if they don't invest. Avoid friends who are too willing to help, or who may offer you a loan they can't afford.

Once you've assessed a person's willingness and ability to make an investment, arrange a more formal meeting, to hammer out the details of the agreement and prepare a brief contract outlining the terms of the loan. Show them how you plan to make your business profitable enough to repay the loan in the prescribed time period. During your meeting, try to separate your personal relationship from the business transaction.

Writing the contract yourself saves you costly attorney's fees. If you don't feel comfortable drafting the final document, take what you've written to a lawyer to make sure you've included all the essential points. With a loan in hand, your association with your friends isn't over. When people have invested money in a business, they take a marked interest in its progress. Make an effort to keep your investors informed about your business's progress to prevent investors from becoming anxious about what's happening to their money.

Guarantee Loans

Lending cash isn't the only way friends and family can help finance your business. Loans come in other forms as well. A friend may sign a bank loan guarantee, or put up assets as collateral for a loan on your behalf. Although this is not a direct cash loan, the person is still liable for the loan, so this is not something to enter into lightly. Finding someone who is willing to put their house up as collateral and cosign a loan, may be easier than finding someone who has the money to loan you. Keep this option in mind as an alternative to cash loans from friends.

Insurance Company Loans

Many insurance companies will loan money to small businesses at competitive rates. Many people are not aware of this fact. Contact insurance companies to find out which ones would be interested in considering your business for a loan.

Inventory Loans

Inventory loans are similar to accounts receivable loans. Inventory financing is a secured line of credit. Advances are made based on a formula established by the bank as to the acceptability and marketability of the inventory being offered. Many banks will not lend on inventory, since control is both difficult and expensive. Typical inventory loan rates rarely exceed 50 percent of the inventory value.

Loans from Mergers

Merging with another business can have the same effect as getting a loan, depending upon how the terms of the merger are negotiated. In a merger transaction, one company typically takes over another company for a variety of reasons. Usually the merger offers benefits to the two companies involved in the merger. For example, if one company has a cash surplus that is needed by another company with expansion needs, then a merger may be a practical way of financing the growth of a business.

SELF-FINANCE LOANS

In many cases, self-financing is required. Even if you are successful at negotiating a loan with a lending institution, you may be required to self-finance a certain percent of the business by the lending institution. They do this to assure that you also have a stake in the company. Home equity loans are a popular and inexpensive way to finance a business.

BONDS AND SECURITY LOANS

Bonds, which are also known as securities, are usually long-term loan contracts in which the company issuing the bonds agrees to make principal and interest payments on specific dates to the bond holders. There are three basic types of bonds that are issued to secure money for a business: mortgage bonds, debenture bonds, and convertible bonds.

Mortgage Bonds

These are bonds that are back by fixed assets. The company issuing the bond pledges certain assets as security for the bond. If the company defaults on bond payments, the bond holder can foreclose on the assets to satisfy the bond.

Debenture Bonds

Unsecured bonds are called debenture bonds. The bond holder is a general creditor of the company. In the event of a liquidation, the debenture bond holder must wait until the secured creditor's claims are satisfied before they can receive their share of the remaining assets.

Convertible Bonds

Convertible bonds can be converted into common stock at the option of the bond holder. The conversion is usually at a fixed price per share of common stock.

Startup corporations will usually sell common stock, while established companies that are earning consistent profits may choose to issue bonds. One of the advantages of issuing bonds over common stock is that you can deduct the interest you pay to the bond holders, while you use their capital to finance the business.

THE SMALL BUSINESS ADMINISTRATION (SBA)

The SBA was started in 1953 to help small businesses start, grow, and prosper. Included in that pledge was a loan program to make low-interest and long-term loans available to businesses that would otherwise have a hard time finding capital. Today, the SBA has loan funds that are distributed both as direct loans and through loan guarantees administered by local banks. In its 40 years, the SBA loan program has helped more than a million small-business owners get the money they need to develop products, hire employees, purchase equipment, and make building improvements. The SBA focuses less on the business owner's collateral and more on their repayment ability. They want to see a detailed cash flow projection showing how the loan will be paid back.

The SBA makes several different types of loans. Understanding the different programs, before you start your search, puts you that much closer to getting the money you need. Most people think of SBA loans as money going straight from the government's coffers into an entrepreneur's hands, which rarely happens.

Direct loans are a small percent of the SBA loan programs. Direct loans are given to applicants who are unable to secure a loan from another source. The SBA's most active lending arena is the Guaranteed Loan Program. Based on a working partnership with local banks and other lending institutions, the program guarantees small business loans issued by qualified lenders.

Business owners gain significant advantages from SBA guarantee loans, such as longer terms. At least 50 percent of traditional business loans by banks are for less than one year. The average maturity for most working capital SBA loans is between five and seven years. Because payments are amortized over a longer period of time, they are smaller and more manageable. Another advantage is that applying for an SBA-guaranteed loan helps build the relationship between bankers and business owners.

APPLYING FOR AN SBA-GUARANTEED LOAN

First, the SBA must consider you a small business. Size standard eligibility is based on the average number of employees for the proceeding twelve months, or the sales volume over a three-year period. If you are a manufacturing company, the SBA has different employee head count qualifications that they place on different industries. Additional qualifications include the following:

- Your company cannot be dominant in its field.
- Your company must comply will all federal employment laws.
- Your company must pursue traditional lending sources first. If you cannot obtain financing at reasonable terms, you may qualify for an SBA guaranteed loan.

In addition, your company cannot be involved in the creation or distribution of ideas or opinions, which includes newspapers, magazines, and academic schools. Businesses that are engaged in the speculation or investments in rental real-estate are also excluded. You must be able to demonstrate that you have a reasonable investment in your business and can provide sufficient collateral for the loan. The best way to initiate an SBA loan is to contact the commercial banks in your area to determine if an SBA guaranteed loan would be an appropriate approach for your business.

If you satisfy the basic requirements, you can begin the application process, which involves a considerable amount of paperwork. Both the bank and the SBA will want a detailed analysis of your business with cash flow numbers and research data to back up your sales projections and cash flow needs. Here are some of the application elements you'll need to provide:

- A business description and strategy
- Management capability summary
- Capital requirements
- Personal financial statement
- Financial plan and cash flow

- Investment statement
- Loan application

The entire process can take as little as 60 days, depending on the bank's backlog and your own preparation. Any complications or incomplete information takes additional time. It's not easy to get financing through the SBA. If your business doesn't qualify for a loan now, keep trying. In the meantime, learn as much as you can about the many non-financial resources the SBA has to offer. Then when it's time to grow your business, you'll be ready. For further information about the services of the SBA, contact:

Small Business Administration
Office of Public Communications
1441 L Street, NW
Washington, DC 20416
(202) 653-6832

Your regional SBA office can tell you what SBA loan programs are available and how to apply. There is no central clearinghouse of information on SBA loans. The best way to find these programs is to ask around at business events, chambers of commerce, or business group meetings.

For businesses planning to expand their market, the SBA offers several financial programs through its affiliation with the Office of International Trade. Although its primary purpose is to educate small business owners on the benefits of exporting, the SBA's Export Financing Program also provides partnership financing programs, as well as exporting revolving lines of credit.

Before you contact the SBA, be aware that certain enterprises are not eligible for SBA loans. These include magazines, newspapers, religious bookstores, most live entertainment, nonprofit ventures, and multilevel marketing businesses. You can't use an SBA loan to make speculative investments, or to pay off non-business related debt. The SBA also imposes certain limits on annual revenues and number of employees.

In summary, the SBA exists solely to support and make loans to small businesses. Like banks, the

SBA may limit the loan amount to 50 percent of the capital needed. In some cases, they will consider ventures with less capitalization, if they are convinced of the favorable prospects of your business. A list of regional SBA offices is available in a good public library.

SMALL BUSINESS INVESTMENT COMPANIES (SBICs)

SBICs are private investment companies that supply small businesses with equity capital and long-term financing. They are private companies that are not directly connected with the SBA. Like investment bankers, they take an ownership position and a strong hand in the management of their sponsored ventures. There are hundreds of SBICs in the United States. Many of them are subsidiaries of banks and other financial firms. For more information, contact:

National Association of Small Business Investment
  Companies
1119 N. Fairfax Street, Suite 200
Alexandria, VA 22314
(703) 683-1601

TRADE CREDIT

Trade credit is sometimes referred to as "supplier loans," in which the payments for delivered goods and services are not due until sometime after the delivery date. The supplier who is extending the credit is essentially lending its buyer the amount of the invoice. Suppliers will often use trade credit as an incentive to increase sales and attract new customers. Trade credit terms can vary from very strict, such as cash before delivery, to very lenient, such as "net 90 days."

In some businesses where trade credit can represent as much as 40 percent of current liabilities, keeping trade creditors happy is an essential element of doing business. There are times when cash flow delays may necessitate delaying payments to suppliers. Most suppliers are sensitive to industry trends and will modify their trade terms to accommodate their preferred customers.

At the other extreme, suppliers may offer terms that will motivate companies to borrow the money from another source to pay their invoices early. For example, assume that a supplier has offered you payment terms of "2/10 net 30." These industry terms mean that if you pay the invoice within 10 days of the invoice date, you may deduct 2 percent from the invoice amount. Let's say you have just received goods and an invoice for $10,000. If you pay by the tenth day after the invoice date, you would owe:

$$\$10,000 \times .98 = \$9,800$$

If you elect to pay after the tenth day, the total payment of $10,000 is due in 30 days, which would cost you an additional $200 by not taking the discount. Let's assume that you must borrow the money to pay off the $10,000 on the tenth day. Is the supplier's "2/10 net 30" terms a good investment? To determine whether or not you should take the discount, you need to perform a cost benefit analysis. The following formula can be used to convert supplier discounts into annual interest rates:

C = Cost of credit expressed as an annual percentage if discount taken.
D = Cash discount expressed as a decimal.
   = .02 or 2%
T = Number of days earlier you must pay to get the discount.
   = 20 days
365 = Number of days in a year.
$C = (D/1-D) \times (365/T)$
$C = 37\%$

Trade discounts can amount to an outstanding annual interest rate that exceeds most borrowing rates as we demonstrated in this example (i.e., 37%). By completing this simple computation, one can quickly determine if the terms of a trade discount should be financed. Trade credit is a fragile relationship and great care should be taken to cultivate a relationship with suppliers. Treat them as though they were your bank for trade transactions and take advantage of trade discounts that offer significant dollar savings to your business.

VENTURE CAPITAL FINANCING

Venture capitalists are professional investors who give advice and money in return for stock and ownership in companies. They look for business ideas that may ultimately grow into multimillion dollar companies. Venture capitalists are usually investment bankers, private capitalists, and syndicates. Most have a minimum size venture that they will consider and charge relatively high interest rates. Less than 1 percent of venture capital proposals get funded, so be prepared for an aggressive sales campaign if you want to obtain venture capital financing. For more information about venture capital sources, obtain a copy of *The Guide to Venture Capital Sources,* published by the Capital Publishing Company, 10 South LaSalle Street, Chicago, IL 60603.

FINANCING WITH LEASES

In times of tight capital, companies may choose to lease equipment rather than borrow the money they need to purchase equipment. According to the Equipment Leasing Association, equipment leasing has tripled since 1980 and exceeds $125 billion a year. Even if banks are willing to make loans, they require a large down payment for capital purchases. Leasing companies can usually find money, because they can use the equipment as collateral for their loans.

There are many advantages of leasing, in spite of the fact that leasing is more expensive than buying. Companies that lease can bypass down payment requirements and finance 100 percent of the purchase over several years. If the equipment becomes outdated during the term of the lease, they can upgrade the asset with little or no penalty.

Before you consider leasing, you need to understand leasing options. Capital leases generally require a company to purchase the equipment at the end of the lease term at a percentage of the original price. Operating or open-ended leases allow you three options after the term expires: (1) purchase the equipment at its fair market value; (2) negotiate and extend the lease; or (3) simply terminate the agreement. For tax purposes, operating lease payments are treated as operating expenses with no capital investments and can be deducted from revenues to reduce tax liabilities. If you elect to buy the equipment at the end of the lease, the purchase becomes a capital expense.

If your business uses assets that have a substantial value, it may be possible to lease them to help preserve your working capital. If you already own key assets, consider selling them to a leasing firm and leasing them back. This method of financing is often used with office buildings, trucks, land, office equipment, and machinery.

Leasing is like any installment purchase. You pay for the privilege of buying over time. To calculate the monthly cost of a lease, lessors figure a rate factor into the purchase price. For example, a three-year operating lease valued at $100,000 is calculated at approximately $35 per $1,000. Using an industry-wide rule of thumb of $35, the monthly payments would be $3,500 ($35 × 100).

Leasing is not an option for every company. Most equipment lessors want to do business with established companies with credit histories. Unfortunately, this can make leasing difficult for startups, the companies that can benefit most from the cash-flow advantages.

ADVERTISING FOR A LOAN

Thousands of potential investors can be cost-effectively reached by advertising for the investment dollars you need. The two best places to advertise for a loan are newspapers and magazines. Newspapers reach thousands of people every day. If you place a good advertisement, you can achieve excellent results.

NEWSPAPERS

If you're looking for a small number of investors, try the classified section of your local paper under the heading business opportunities, where you'll see many companies advertising for investors. Classified ads in local newspapers work well if you want to raise $100,000 or less. If you want to reach an even larger audience, place a classified ad in a national newspaper such as *The Wall Street Journal* or *USA Today*. These publications have specific sections for investment ads.

If you need more money, consider placing a display advertisement in the business section of your local or national newspapers. This type of advertisement is more expensive, but it is seen by a wider audience. To be effective, display ads may require help from an advertising professional to create an effective message.

MAGAZINES AND TRADE JOURNALS

Magazines are also a good medium for investment advertising because they are read over an extended period of time. Consider placing a classified advertisement in a trade magazine, or journal that covers your industry. Magazines have a long publication "lead time," so your ad must be placed well in advance of the publication dates.

There are three basic parts to an investment ad: The heading, the copy, and the close. Here's an example of an ad that is aggressively looking for qualified investors:

> Investors Wanted. Growing and dynamic manufacturer needs investors who want to make double digit returns on their money. Retailers can't keep our products in stock and we don't have the capacity to meet their demands. Investors needed to help us expand and take company national. Exceptionally big return on your investment. For further information, call or write. . . . . .

How you handle responses to investor queries is just as important as how you attract investors. Designate someone with sales expertise and the ability to encourage excitement about the investment to handle prospect calls. Once you have mailed any requested information, follow-up with a phone call to answer any questions. Whenever possible, arrange for a personal meeting to discuss your opportunity.

LOAN REQUEST STRATEGIES

Be prepared before you approach a lender for a business loan. Have solid cash flow and financial statement projections in hand that show where your company is going financially over the next several years. Customize your loan request approach depending upon the nature of the lender. For example, banks focus heavily on cash flow lending rather than straight asset-based lending. Be sure your marketing strategies are outlined in detail to lend credence to your financial projections.

Loan Application Checklist

1. What is the exact amount of your loan request and the desired terms of the loan?
2. What is the purpose of the loan? State specifically how the money will be used.
3. How and when will you repay the loan?
4. What collateral does the company have to back the loan?
5. What will happen to your business if you do not get the loan?

In addition to numbers, be prepared to give your lenders other insights into your business that will help them become effective advocates for your business.

LOAN APPROVALS

There comes a point when you've shown your lending institution everything you've got and told them everything you can think of to get your loan approved. Now it's simply a matter of waiting for an answer. Once a bank turns you down, it's almost impossible to get the powers to change their minds, unless you can point to some error that prevented you from getting the loan.

One of the most important parts of the loan process is what happens after your loan is approved. Maintaining a good relationship with your lender is essential to making sure things go smoothly. It's important to negotiate an agreement you can live with.

When you sign the loan agreement, you are signing a covenant with the lender that can carry serious consequences for default. If you agree to unrealistic repayment terms and fail to meet them, the lender can call the loan.

Strategy Checklist

1. Describe your business in 25 words or less.
2. Project the major changes that your business will go through over the next 2 to 5 years.
3. Summarize the experience and education of your key personnel.
4. What outside advisors do you plan to use to support your business and why?
5. Provide a brief description of your products and services.
6. How will you market, sell, and distribute the offerings of your business?
7. Who are your customers and how will you meet their needs?
8. Who are you competitors and how will you effectively compete against them?

NEGOTIATING STRATEGIES

When entrepreneurs talk to lenders about financing, they usually try to negotiate better terms on interest rates and collateral. One aspect that few try to negotiate is how long they'll have use of the funds and the schedule for paying them back. Usually, a borrower starts paying off the principal right away. However, the longer you can use the full amount of the loan, the more flexibility you'll have.

Many loans are written for one-year periods, so the potential for extending the average life of capital is limited. Slowing down the principal payments can reduce the pressure of thinking about the next round of financing. Lenders want to get their money back sooner rather than later, so don't expect them to offer suggestions. Here are some negotiating points to consider:

Longer Maturity

If you need money to buy equipment, or assets you'll be using over a long time, negotiate for the longest loan term possible.

Less Frequent Principal Payments

Once the loan maturity date has been set, negotiate for as few regular principal payments as possible (e.g., quarterly or semiannually payments).

Principal Payments Moratoriums

An attractive alternative is to press for interest only payments for some period of the loan.

Balloon Payments

If possible, negotiate to make a single principal payment or at least as much of the principal as possible when the loan matures.

SOURCES FOR ADDITIONAL INFORMATION

Financing for Small and Medium-Sized Businesses, Harry Gross (Prentice-Hall, Englewood Cliffs, NJ 07632)

Going Public, Daniel Berman (Prentice-Hall, Englewood Cliffs, NJ 07632)

Anatomy of a Merger, Robert Parsons and John Baumgartner (Prentice-Hall, Englewood Cliffs, NJ 07632)

6

Introducing Products and Services

Now that you have developed a financial plan for your business, you can begin to develop business strategies to introduce your products and services. This chapter is directly linked to the next three chapters on marketing, pricing, and sales. In fact, one could make a case for starting with marketing first, before we introduced the material on products and services. We choose to introduce the offerings of your business first to set the stage for the next three chapters, because product and service strategies are directly dependent upon marketing, pricing, and sales strategies. You can refine your overall strategies as you proceed through the next three chapters.

There are several advantages to introducing new offerings. The new product may reduce your overhead by allowing you to spread your fixed cost, such as administrative costs, over a larger base of products. New products and services may open new, and more profitable markets, than your current markets. The new market may also allow you to sell more of your old products, as well as the new product. And, new offerings are simply needed to replace old, obsolete products and services.

INFLUENCING CUSTOMER PERCEPTION

One of the basic principles of business success is that you must be able to offer something that is better than your competition to stay in business. You must be different in a manner that is perceived to be better by your target market (e.g., your preferred customers). The distinction here is that anybody can be different, but if your customers do not like the difference, you're out of business. The second part of the better formula assumes that your customers are willing to pay for your "better" offerings. Both parts of the equation must be achieved to succeed. The example that follows emphasizes what we mean by "successful" differences.

Let's assume that you want to open a restaurant in the midwestern town where you live. To be different from the other restaurants in town, and based on the market research that you have conducted, you have decided to open a seafood restaurant. The questionnaire that you sent to your target market customers, confirms that a seafood restaurant would be a positive improvement to the restaurant cuisine of the area.

However, you have discovered that the cost of shipping seafood into your midwest town, will escalate your average price per meal by 50 percent above the average restaurant meal price in your target market. A follow-up survey of your potential customers indicates that they would not be willing to pay a 50 percent premium for a seafood meal.

What are your options relative to the customers' perception of your new restaurant idea? You believe they would patronize the restaurant if you could offer competitive prices. Alternatives for you to consider might include exploring the cost advantages of shipping in bulk and storing frozen seafood in a local warehouse. As a supplemental business, perhaps you could supply seafood to the grocery market.

CUSTOMER ACCEPTANCE

New businesses must be tailored to meet the needs, desires, and preferences of your target market. The customers in your target market will be the ultimate judge and jury of your business. Their preferences can sway the success or failure of your business. They may elect to pay a higher price, as long as they believe that your business offers a quality level that matches your price. If you are not on top of your customers' running opinions of your business, and for whatever reason they determine that your quality has deteriorated, you could instantly lose your customer base.

PRODUCT CONSIDERATIONS

Discovering a new product that has all of the potential to attract customers and increase your sales, is the first half of the introduction process. Is the new idea right for you and your business? Do you have the background and knowledge of the new market to assure the success of the new product? The checklist that follows will help you make this determination:

New Product Checklist

1. Does the new product fit within the needs, interests, and capabilities of your company?
2. What will the new product do for your business (e.g., increase sales, reduce costs, etc.)?
3. What are your chances that the new product will succeed?
4. Do you have capable people already in place to help you introduce the product?
5. Is there a profitable market for the product that has been thoroughly analyzed?
6. Do you need to acquire additional people and equipment before you can introduce the product?
7. What is the break-even point for the product?

Your answers to these and other relevant questions that you may develop, will help you screen different new-product alternatives. The same set of questions could also be applied to new service offerings. The important point to remember as you go through the screening exercise is to focus your attention on what must happen to be successful.

DETERMINING MARKET CLASSIFICATIONS

Before you can begin to develop the introductory strategies of your products and services, you need to determine where the new offerings of your business fit in the market, which we will refer to as market classification. There are four basic market classifications that you should consider—shopping, specialty, convenience, and impulse. Although our description of each classification implies a unique set of boundaries around each, you may have a product or service that is covered by more than one classification. Consider the overlap issue when you classify the offerings of your business.

SHOPPING CLASSIFICATION

Products and services are considered shopping items if consumers purchase the items based on their comparative price and quality relative to competitive items. Customers may prefer an established brand, but if they are shopping they will always look for a better buy based on quality and price. They will check multiple stores and newspaper advertisements before they will make a decision to buy.

If your marketing analysis indicates a wide disparity of offerings (i.e., quality and price), and you believe that you have a shopping product that offers distinct advantages, then you may have an opportunity to compete in the competitive shopping market. Initially a competitive price usually offers a more distinct advantage over quality. That is because price offers an immediate benefit to the consumer, whereas quality offerings take time to establish.

SPECIALTY CLASSIFICATION

Specialty products and services have a distinct appeal to consumers who typically associate them with brand names. Product examples include food and clothing brands. Service examples include rental car services and repair shops. Consumers tend not to be price sensitive to specialty products and services and tend to ignore competitive ads since they believe in the ultimate quality of the specialty outlet they have selected.

Specialty outlets have a partial lock on their target markets. But because they are usually highly successful, new competitors are constantly evaluating ways to break into the market. If they do not change, other businesses will ultimately develop a better product and take over their market. Specialty businesses must change their offerings to meet the changing needs of their target markets to remain competitive. Astute entrepreneurs never assume that customers will always buy whatever they choose to sell.

CONVENIENCE CLASSIFICATION

Convenience customers place a preference on how easy it is to purchase certain items, regardless of costs or brand names. The huge growth in convenience stores illustrates this principle. The homeward-bound worker who needs to pick up a quart of milk will, in all probability, stop at the local convenience store to avoid the crowds at the supermarket. With the advent of working couples, convenience shopping has grown significantly, with drive-through windows for fast-food chains and food marts attached to every corner gas station. As the name implies, convenience must be important to customers. They will place the premium of convenient shopping above brand loyalty and price. Convenient store locations and hours are the most important part of the convenience industry.

IMPULSE CLASSIFICATION

Impulse items are products and services that are purchased by customers who initially had no intention of buying the item. They are typically enticed into the purchase when they are shopping for some other item that they need. In order for impulse items to sell, they must be located and displayed in such a way as to attract the attention of a passing customer prospect. The message on the product or the display, features benefits that are designed to catch the attention of passing customers.

IDENTIFYING NEW PRODUCTS AND SERVICE SOURCES

The first part of the process of determining the potential uniqueness of the offerings of your business is to find out what is currently being offered. The oldest and best known products directory is *The Thomas Register of American Manufacturers,* which consists of several volumes that are updated and published each year. The directory lists over 115,000 American manufacturers, and a supplemental product index. It includes instructions on how to get manufacturer's catalogs, flyers, and brochures.

A number of startup periodicals are published monthly that feature new product and service startup ideas. For example, *Entrepreneur Magazine* publishes the *Small Business Development Catalog,* which lists hundreds of startup guides for different products and services. We have listed the names and addresses of several new idea sources in this section. Most of the directories and periodicals are available in a good public library.

CATALOGS

Small Business Development Catalog
Entrepreneur Group
P.O. Box 2072
Knoxville, IA 50198-2072
1-800-421-2300

MAGAZINES

Entrepreneur Magazine
2392 Morse Avenue
Irvine, CA 92714

NEWSPAPERS (BUSINESS OPPORTUNITY SECTION)

Wall Street Journal
200 Burnett Road
Chicopee, MA 01021

INVENTOR SHOWS

Office of Inventions and Innovations
National Bureau of Standards
Washington, DC 20234

FOREIGN PRODUCTS

International Commerce Magazine Weekly
U.S. Department of Commerce
Herbert Clark Hoover Bldg.
14th Street N.W.
Washington, DC 20230

INVENTIONS

The Official Gazette of the U.S. Patent Office
Superintendent of Documents
Government Printing Office
Washington, DC 20402

TRADE SHOWS

Directory of U.S. Trade Shows, Expositions, and
    Conventions
United States Travel Service
U.S. Department of Commerce
Washington, D.C. 20230

MANUFACTURERS

The Thomas Register of Manufacturers
Thomas Publishing Company
5 Penn Plaza
New York, NY 10001

IMPORTING

If you plan to import products, you may need to hire
the services of a customs broker to help you get
through the complex import process. Almost all entries of foreign goods into the United States are controlled by customs brokers, who work on behalf of
their importer clients. Some brokers are sole proprietors, whereas others are large corporations with
branches in many countries. All are licensed and regulated by the U.S. Treasury Department.

The customs broker is the agent of the employing importer and often the only point of contact with
the U.S. Customs Service. The broker's duties may
include advising you on the technical requirements of
importing, preparing key entry documents, obtaining
bonds, paying import duties, arranging for the release
of goods, and coordinating the transportation of
goods to your warehouse. Most customs brokers belong to the National Customs Brokers Association.
The association publishes a membership directory

and lists the U.S. Customs regional offices, which is available in a good public library, or contact:

National Customs Brokers and Forwarders
    Association of America
5 World Trade Center
New York, NY 10048
(212) 432-0050

U.S. Customs Service
1301 Constitution Avenue, NW
Washington, DC 20229
(202) 566-8195

DEVELOPING MARKETING STRATEGIES

Developing product and service marketing mix strategies reflects how you will exploit your competitive advantages to penetrate the market. Each component of the marketing mix plays an integral role in your effort to find and satisfy customers. The development of a product-service strategy begins by identifying the products and services your business offers. How many product brands and models will you offer? How many service options and variations will you offer? What are your customers looking for in a particular type of product or service that is not currently offered? The market analysis that you will complete in the next chapter will help you refine your market mix. Some businesses may offer very limited product and service mixes, whereas others may offer expanded mixes.

The sporting shoe market offers an excellent example to illustrate how an industry implemented a highly effective marketing mix strategy. If you wanted to buy tennis shoes a few years ago, there were few brands to choose from, and the colors were limited to either white or black. Now tennis shoes are called athletic shoes, and they cover every sport imaginable, in numerous brands and colors. By mixing products (e.g., tennis shoes) to match the needs of different market segments (e.g., joggers, hikers, etc), tennis shoe sales increased ten-fold over the past five years.

The service business has expanded significantly as the United States has progressively moved into a service economy. Although service businesses sell labor, the process of developing a service strategy is not much different from developing a product strategy. The primary difference is that the potential customer may be able to perform the service you are offering. In a sense, the customer is your competitor. Although price is a factor, you have to be able to convince customers that you can perform the service better, quicker, and more conveniently than they can. If you cannot offer these benefits, then why would anybody want to buy your services?

Many product-oriented businesses also offer services, and many service businesses offer products. The two offerings could be combined to the customer's advantage. For example, today's supermarket offers postal, video rental, and banking services to supplement their food products business. The important point to keep in mind, is that you want to offer whatever combination of products and services it takes to keep your customers coming back.

Be careful of the fact that success can breed complacency. You may have the best products, prices, quality, and service combination in the market you choose to serve. However, your competitors will quickly replicate whatever it is you are doing right. To stay ahead of the pack, constantly review and improve upon your overall business strategies.

SEGMENTING THE MARKET

According to a recent study, companies that controlled more than 30 percent of a market segment were consistently profitable. Those that controlled less than 15 percent were invariably unprofitable. The percentages will vary between businesses and industries, but the study does point out the importance of establishing a segment of the market that you can control.

We saw a classic example of this situation in the early 1980s, when hundreds of small businesses entered the personal computer industry without any regard for market segmentation. They all offered personal computers, word processors, and spread sheet software. Only a few survived — Microsoft segmented its market by offering operating systems for personal computers. Today, Microsoft is a multi-billion dollar corporation.

SERVING UNFILLED MARKETS

How do you discover a market need for a new product or service? Established companies rely on market research techniques to identify new markets. Market research is great, if you can afford to hire a professional market research firm to assist you. One way to get around the cost problem is to use marketing information that already exists. Sometimes called secondary information, it is information that is available from a variety of sources including the following:

- Federal government information. There is an abundance of government information that is available for little or no cost, if you know what you want and where to find it.

- Specialized information. Specialized information is available in a vast variety of different directories and other publications. Visit the research desk at your local or university library and tell the research librarian what information you need. You may be pleasantly surprised at what the librarian will tell you already exists.

- State and local governments. Many state and local governments maintain extensive marketing information to attract out-of-state businesses. Much of this information is available for little or no charge.

- Annual reports. If your competitors publish an annual report, obtain a copy. Annual reports can reveal interesting competitive and marketing information.

- Advertising media reports. Advertising media such as the local newspaper or national trade magazines, offer extensive marketing information that covers their distribution areas. Contact media sources and ask them to send you their display advertising package, which usually includes market demographic information.

These are just a few of the available sources of secondary marketing information that can be used to help you introduce new products and services. The subject will be covered in more detail in the next chapter.

QUALITY STRATEGIES

Why is it necessary to enter a market with a superior, rather than just a slightly better, product or service? One reason is that consumers may already be attached to a competitive product. They feel comfortable with what they have and must be substantially motivated before they will switch over to a new product. They may feel that it is not worth the trouble to switch over to something that is perhaps just "slightly" better.

In addition to quality, there are other product and service attributes that you will want to develop. If your offering is the first of its kind in the market, and you are successful, you will become the standard that new competitors will try to dislodge. If you are the first to announce the new product, you become established, which means that it is more difficult for competitors to convince your customers to switch over to their competitive product. To maintain your competitive position, initiate a research and development program that will obsolete your existing product by replacing it with a better product on a recurring basis. Perpetually replacing it with a better product will outmaneuver your competitors. Don't wait for your competitors to obsolete you.

VisiCalc is a classic example of a company that allowed its competitor to make its product obsolete. The company developed the first superior spreadsheet program for personal computers in the early 1980s. VisiCalc became complacent with its program and subsequently made no significant improvements to their spreadsheet product. A new startup company called Lotus Development Corporation was formed to introduce an upgraded spreadsheet product called Lotus 1•2•3. The product became the 'new" spreadsheet standard and VisiCalc subsequently went out of business.

SALES STRATEGIES

Implementing a winning sales strategy is critical to the introduction of new products and services. Anyone who says 'this product will sell itself' is asking for trouble. Very few products or services sell themselves. A good sales strategy can catapult your product into instant success. It involves advertising, pricing, packaging, and creating a constant appeal for your product. Communication and timing substrategies are essential to the startup of an effective sales strategy.

COMMUNICATION STRATEGIES

In the past, business communication strategies involved nothing more than informing customers about products and services. While that was important, communications in today's volatile market must cover a broader range of issues. For example, your customer prospects may want assurance that you will still be in business five years from now. No one is interested in buying a superior product from a company that they believe will go out of business. Public relations techniques are often used as an inexpensive way to build the stature of a business. Articles that you may write for the local newspaper, or a speech that you make at a Chamber of Commerce meeting, can enhance your business faster than advertising.

Communication is also important in helping you establish a desired position for your products and services. For example, let's assume that you are about to open an appliance store. You have discovered that the market perceives your store as 'just another appliance store." However, your store is the only store in the area that offers 'in store" service on everything you sell. By applying effective communication techniques, you could reposition the image of your store as an important service center for appliances.

TIMING STRATEGIES

The timing of the introduction of your offering is critical to the success of your sales strategy. Execute everything you say you will do on time, every time.

Missed schedules and procrastination can cause even the best of sales strategies to fail. Meeting timely commitments will set the tone for the professionalism of your company.

If your sales are influenced by holidays and seasons, you should maintain a rolling twelve-month schedule that identifies the precise time and strategies you will employ to enhance sales. For example, if Father's Day draws customers to your new product, you should know in advance how you will advertise during the Father's Day event. The timing of your program should be so well organized that it almost becomes automatic. This is an important consideration so that you can devote more of your time to analyzing the success of the program — and what you can do to make it better next year.

SOURCES FOR ADDITIONAL INFORMATION

Purchasing has attained a high state of the art in entrepreneurial businesses. Wise and careful buying is imperative to the successful introduction of new products and services. For further information, contact:

The National Association of Purchasing Management
2055 E. Centennial Circle
P.O. Box 22160
Tempe, AZ 85285-2160
(602) 752-6276

7

Marketing Your Business

Good marketing can mean the difference between success and failure for your business. For many businesses, the cost of hiring the services of a professional market research firm to assist you in developing a marketing program can be prohibitive. The alternative is to do your own market research. In this chapter, we walk you through each step necessary to collect marketing data, interpret the results, and develop a market plan. We do not want to discourage you from seeking the services of a professional firm if you can afford it. We'll cover professional service options later in the chapter.

DEVELOPING A MARKETING PLAN

A marketing plan relies on market research techniques to help solve marketing problems. Almost every business is constantly doing some level of marketing research to answer marketing questions. What line of products should you stock? What optimal price should you charge to assure that you capture your share of the market? Guessing the correct answers to these and other relevant marketing questions can be a costly mistake if your decision is wrong. If you apply modern market research methods to the problem, you have a much better chance of finding the right answers to your marketing questions.

Market research is the foundation of the market plan and is an organized effort to gather market knowledge to help make better marketing decisions. Facts, opinions, and attitudes are sought from a number of sources, until the most logical answer to your marketing question is found and can be acted upon. Setting up clear objectives, organizing the search for information, and interpreting the information to help answer your marketing questions are all part of the market planning process. There are six basic steps that you must complete to create a marketing plan:

1. Understand your market.
2. Conduct market research.

3. Collect and analyze secondary marketing information.

4. Collect and analyze primary marketing information.

5. Segment the market.

6. Establish market niches.

Once you select a business opportunity, you need to learn everything you can about all marketing aspects of the business. Your goal is to seek out perceived needs that are not being met to help you determine how you will serve the market. The following two lists illustrate competitive marketing opportunities for a new business.

COMPETITIVE MARKET OPPORTUNITIES
FOR A SERVICE BUSINESS

- The personality of the people providing the service is arrogant or antagonistic.
- The overall quality of the service is poor.
- The service is slow and limited.
- The service is either overpriced, of poor quality, or is not guaranteed.

COMPETITIVE MARKET OPPORTUNITIES
FOR A PRODUCT BUSINESS

- The product does not come in all popular colors or sizes.
- The product is overpriced or is not made well.
- It is difficult to find service outlets for the product.
- Delivery of the product is slow.

Initially, these problems could be perceived problems on your part that may be based on some marketing information you have obtained by reading articles or asking questions. To determine if there really is a problem that represents an opportunity to you, additional market research must be conducted. The following checklist will help you develop your marketing plan before you begin your search for information.

Market Research Checklist

1. State the purpose of the research and compose the marketing questions that need to be answered.

2. Identify research sources to be covered and the extent of coverage.

3. Project possible findings and the action you would take based upon different findings.

4. Establish a schedule and budget for the project.

CONDUCTING MARKET RESEARCH

Market research is the process used to gather information needed to complete the market analysis. The research effort focuses on understanding the customer. It may involve asking prospective customers questions, researching existing customer data, and collecting and interpreting the information. The research findings should identify your potential customers and answer important marketing questions. What do your customers like and dislike? How can your business best satisfy their needs? Fundamental market research projects must invariably answer four basic marketing questions:

1. What do you need to know to make a correct marketing decision?

2. What sources are likely to have the information that you need?

3. What research must you conduct to collect information that is not already available?

4. How important will the answers to the market research questions be to the overall success of your business?

The market information that you collect is used to help you identify the needs of your market. Market needs could include new products and services, pricing considerations, and other consumer preferences. In a tough competitive environment, market appeal is extremely important. Your business must be able to focus its product and service offerings on the specific

needs and preferences of your customers. The following examples illustrate the types of problems market
research addresses.

Example 7–1. Percent of market share

You have just introduced a new product (e.g., product A)
and are delighted with initial retail sales, which are averaging $10,000 per month. However, you can only guess at
what your market share is, because there is no market information available that covers the sales levels of your competitors. You need access to this information to determine
how well your business is performing against the competition. Based upon the market research that you have conducted, you have discovered the following information:

According to your industry's statistics, the average retail
store sells $100 of product A per square foot of retail space
that is allocated to product A each month.

Based upon your personal survey, you have estimated that
your competitors currently allocate 1,000 total square feet
of retail space to product A.

Market share calculations for product A

Estimated
competitors
sales per $= \$100/\text{Month} \times 1{,}000$ square feet
month

$= \$100{,}000/\text{Month}$

$= \dfrac{\text{Your monthly sales}}{\text{Total sales}}$

Your estimated
market share $= \dfrac{\$10{,}000}{\$100{,}000}$
per month

$= .10$ or 10 percent

Example 7–2. Market attitude analysis

Your distributors are critical to the success of your business. You believe your relationship will all of your distributors is excellent, but how can you qualify their attitudes toward your business? What specific actions can you take to
improve the relations with your distributors?

Solution:

You create a direct mail survey that you send to all of your
distributors. The survey includes a number of questions that
have been designed to measure their opinion of your business and asks them to suggest areas for improvement.

Example 7–3. Introduction of a new product or service

You are about to introduce a new product, which will be a costly experiment for your business. What market research steps can you take before the planned introduction date to give you confidence that you will succeed?

Solution:

You create a prototype of your new product and introduce it at a trade show where you demonstrate the features and benefits of your product. The comments from the potential consumers are carefully documented.

Example 7–4. Testing the success of your advertising campaign

You are uncertain about the effectiveness of your display advertising program in the local newspaper. Are your costly ads increasing sales and profits? Are they improving the image of your business? How can your advertising program be improved?

Solution:

You decide to insert the following words at the bottom of your display ad: "Mention this ad and receive a 10 percent discount off our normal service price." When customers mention the ad, you ask them what they liked and disliked about your advertising program.

COLLECTING SECONDARY MARKETING INFORMATION

The two basic types of marketing information are primary and secondary information. Primary marketing information is information that either does not already exist, or is not in a form that you can use. Therefore, if you need primary information to answer a marketing question, you will have to collect it on your own. For example, if nobody has ever conducted a market survey that asked the same questions you need answers to, then you may have to conduct your own survey to collect the primary information you need.

Secondary market information is information that already exists in a format that you can use. Census data and published statistical data are two examples of secondary information. Most secondary marketing information is easier, and less expensive to obtain, than primary marketing information. Since it already exists, it's usually readily available at minimal or no cost. It therefore makes sense to exhaust all secondary sources first, before you develop a primary information collection program. In the sections that follow, we cover several sources for secondary marketing information.

PUBLIC LIBRARIES

Without exception, a good public or college library is the best place to obtain secondary information. Modern library information search techniques enable you to locate books, periodicals, articles, magnetic, and digital media of all types simply by scanning computerized data bases, by entering the name of the author or title of the information source. If the material that you are looking for is available in the library, the terminal will respond by identifying its location.

As is true with most research projects, you may not know the name of the author or title of the material you are trying to locate. All you may know is the general subject category of the material that you are trying to locate. One of the major advantages of computerized library data bases is that you can enter what are known as "search words" to locate sources of material that "match" your search criteria.

For example, let's assume that you are interested in starting a "high-end" men's clothing store featuring work suits in Boulder, Colorado. You have formulated the following marketing questions:

1. What is the average profile of a man who buys a suit that costs more than $500?
2. Given the average customer profile, how many men fit this profile in Boulder?

The library terminal offers you a search word option. Assume that you elect to use the search word option since you are looking for information on a given subject. When you enter the search words (e.g., men's suits) the terminal will display every source of material, from books to periodicals, that are available in the library covering men's suits. You could narrow your search parameters by adding the word "expensive" to your search parameters.

At some point in the secondary search process, you will discover several sources of information that address the profile of men who wear expensive suits (e.g., average age, income, family status, etc.). The second marketing question becomes relatively easy to answer — how many men in Colorado fit this profile and where do they live by entering the search words "Colorado men."

Using On-Line Data Bases

There are hundreds of specialized data bases that cover all types of research data, articles, and marketing-related data. Once you find what you are looking for, the information can either be printed or "downloaded" onto a disk. Many libraries, colleges, and universities have direct access to research data bases through their computer terminal networks. If you have access to a personal computer that is equipped with a communications device called a modem, and communications software, you can access these data bases directly from your computer. Telephone companies such as U.S. Sprint, MCI, and AT&T offer line access into most of the research databases. Call your local phone company for more information. Two of the most popular directories that list on-line resources are: (1) Directory of On-Line Resources, and (2) The Data Base Catalog.

Library Reference Departments

All good libraries have a reference department that is staffed by research librarians who are trained to find material on just about any subject and are familiar with the library's information resources. Don't hesitate to ask a reference librarian for help. They are available to show you how to use research catalogs, indexes, and other library tools. If a book or periodical that you need is not available at your library, it may be possible for your librarian to obtain the document through an inter-library loan program. The reference section of the library is filled with specialized reference sources including paper and electronic media that cover all types of subjects. Most reference material can not be checked out of the library, but it is available for review in the library. Photo copying of the material is usually permitted.

Newspapers

Back issues of newspapers and periodicals are stored in a special periodical room of most libraries. Subject indexes are maintained on computer data bases by journal name (e.g., Wall Street Journal) and in hard copy directories. Special subject periodicals are an important source of marketing information.

Periodicals

More than 7,000 periodicals are published in the United States alone. Current and recent periodicals often provide a valuable source of secondary marketing information. There are a number of useful indexes that you can use to find specific articles, or several related articles on a given subject. *The Reader's Guide to Periodical Literature* indexes over 200 of the more popular magazines. *The Business Periodical Index* indexes over 300 periodicals in the fields of accounting, advertising, banking, communications, computers, economics, industrial relations, international business, marketing, and real estate.

U.S. DEPARTMENT OF COMMERCE

The Department of Commerce publishes a Standard Industrial Classification manual that assigns classification numbers to all types of businesses in the country. If you know the SIC number for your type of business, you can quickly isolate specific statistics for your type of business. For example, a 275 SIC code denotes commercial printing businesses, whereas an extended SIC code of 2751 denotes commercial letterpress printers.

The department also publishes an annual document entitled Statistical Abstracts of the United States. It is the basic starting point for statistical data about the country and includes thousands of tables, census information, and data about national characteristics. The Survey of Current Business is another department information source that is published monthly. This publication covers important information such as gross national product, national income, personal income, employment, and other current business statistics. If these directories are not available in your local library, contact the U.S. Department of Commerce.

U.S. CENSUS BUREAU

The Census Bureau provides statistical data that covers a broad range of marketing information that is useful to small businesses. The offerings of the Bureau are so numerous and varied that it would be impossible to list them all in this book. The Bureau maintains regional offices in the major cities, or you can contact the national office at the following address for further information:

Bureau of the Census
Washington, DC 20233
(301) 763-4100

The constitution authorizes the Bureau to take a census of the population every ten years. Here is an example of how census data can be used to qualify a location for a business: Let's assume you wanted to open a travel agency that would cater to seniors. By using census data, you could identify metropolitan areas that had a sufficient senior population to support your travel agency. You could also access other information that might be important to your agency such as average income by age and location.

STATE INFORMATION SOURCES

State and local government agencies can provide you with a variety of secondary market information. Some of the sources to consider include the following:

State Department of Commerce
Department of Development
State and local Chambers of Commerce
State Controller's Office
State Tourism Office

All of these agencies are interested in supporting businesses. The agencies in your state may be listed under a different title than what is shown in our list. The Book of States is the standard reference volume on state government, and it is available in public libraries. This comprehensive book includes almost anything you need to know about any state, including the names of top state officials. Subjects covered include the names, functions, addresses, and key contacts of state agencies. The book also contains a variety of information and statistics about each state.

BUSINESS AND PROFESSIONAL ASSOCIATIONS

Business and professional associations can be an excellent source for marketing information. Many associations publish current market information for their members that is also available to non-members for a reasonable fee. There are thousands of associations in the United States that cover almost every industry or professional group. To find associations that might match your needs, review the following directory, which should be available in your local library:

The Encyclopedia of Associations
Gale Research Company
835 Pendoscot
Detroit, MI 48226-4094

DIRECTORIES

Most directories are composed of specific lists, such as the names of businesses, people, products, and services that are organized in logical groups. They provide easy access to specific marketing and other business-related information. All of the directories listed in this section are available in a good public library.

State Industrial Directory. Lists most state firms by location and product.

The Dun & Bradstreet Directory. A listing by firm size, industry, sales volume, products, services, trade names, parent company if applicable, and the names of the key executives.

Moody's Manual. Lists industries, public utilities, and transportation companies.

Thomas Register of American Manufacturers. Lists more than 100,000 manufacturers in the United States by products and trademarks, and identifies who to contact for information.

Advertising Age. Publishes a monthly magazine and an annual directory that lists most advertising agencies, their annual sales, key contacts, and clients.

Directory of Industrial Data. Provides detailed information by industry.

Sales Management Annual Survey of Buying Power. Provides useful local information about population demographics including individual income, certain types of retail sales, and an index of market potential.

Editor and Publisher Market Guide. Provides information on household incomes, retail sales, and other marketing data for readerships of more than 1,500 newspapers.

Encyclopedia of Business Information. Contains basic information sources covering more than a thousand business topics and industries.

PUBLISHED INDEXES

There are a number of indexes that are published monthly, quarterly, and annually that identify sources of marketing information. The indexes listed in this section are available in a good public library.

Business Index. Indexes books and hundreds of periodicals including the New York Times Financial Section.

Art Index. Indexes periodicals that specialize in subjects such as architecture, city planning, graphic arts, industrial design, interior design, and photography.

Public Affairs Information Service Bulletin. An international index that covers an enormous range of materials on business, economics, finance, law, trade, political science, and much more. Reference books are also included in the index.

Specialized Indexes. Various trade magazines offer indexes for their own magazines. Examples include American Druggist, Consumer News, and Motel Management.

   In conclusion, it is impossible to list every source of secondary market information is this book, or any book, for that matter. We hope that the sources listed will point you in the right direction and impress upon you the fact that there is a significant amount of secondary marketing information available to anybody who is willing to do some market research.

COLLECTING PRIMARY MARKETING INFORMATION

Secondary marketing information may not tell you everything you need to know about your market. You may have to collect your own marketing information first hand, before you can make an intelligent marketing decision. Marketing people refer to this category of information as primary market information. In this section, we will describe some of the general techniques that are used to acquire primary information.

FORMAL MARKET SURVEILLANCE

Market surveillance refers to a process in which one conducts an observation to learn about some marketing event that is occurring. The physical observation could cover the events at a competitor's location, the marketing patterns of consumers, or other types of observation studies.

For example, let's assume that you are interested in opening a retail store in your hometown that will specialize in selling country home decorating products. There is only one competitor store that sells similar products, and it is located in a mall at the south end of town. You want to locate your store in a comparable mall at the north end of town. Before you commit to opening your store, you need information about two aspects of your competitor's business:

1. What foot traffic is your competitor experiencing at their south mall location?

2. What are your competitor's average daily sales?

To obtain the marketing information you need, you establish an observation point on a mall bench outside of the entrance into your competitor's store. Over a period of days, you count the people entering the store and you count the people who purchase items as they exit the store. Because you are familiar with the retail prices of the store's product, you estimate the purchase price of each cash register transaction. At the conclusion of the observation period, you have collected the information shown in Exhibit 7–1.

If we expand upon the retail store scenario, let's assume that you are also interested in knowing something about the demographics of the customers that shop at your competitor's store. Because your store will be located at the north end of town, you are specifically interested in knowing how many customers reside in the north end of town and frequent your competitor's store, because there is no comparable north end store. To collect the primary marketing information you need, you ask customers who exit the store two questions:

1. Do you live at the north or south end of town?
2. If there was a comparable store that was located at the north end of town, would you prefer to buy from that store?

As a result of your interview questions, you discover that 60 percent live on the north end of town, and 65 percent indicated that they would prefer to shop in a comparable store, if it were located on the north end of town. We can now calculate the estimated average daily sales for our proposed north end store, by using the primary information we have collected.

Although the example may be oversimplified, our intent was to illustrate how the observation process can be used to obtain primary marketing information. The data collected could open up additional questions. For example, our observation showed that 60 percent of the population lived in the north end of town, and yet 65 percent of the country store customers indicated a preference for shopping in a comparable store, if it was located at the north end of town. Where did the other 5 percent come from? The search for additional primary information in many cases continues, as you constantly seek to find

Exhibit 7-1. Primary Market Information Collected by Surveillance

Observation Category	Day of Week						
	M	T	W	T	F	S	S
Customers Entering Store	125	225	300	285	430	687	98
Estimated Sales Per Day	$885	$1.250	$1.980	$1.760	$2.600	$3.400	$600
Average Customer Sale	$7.08	$5.50	$6.60	$6.18	$6.05	$4.95	$6.12

answers that will improve your marketing knowledge.

INFORMAL MARKET SURVEILLANCE

The formal market surveillance approach that we have been discussing was designed to answer specific marketing questions. The informal approach is basically a "listening approach," where you are tuned into what is happening within your business domain. By listening, you may learn about significant events that could represent advantages, or disadvantages, to your business. For example, you could be attending a Chamber of Commerce meeting where a business associate casually mentions the fact that one of your major competitors is about to go out of business. If it is used effectively, informal primary market information can enhance the position of your business. Imagination is the catalyst to develop informal primary market information.

PERSONAL INTERVIEWS

The personal interview is a technique favored by many marketing professionals to gather primary information. Primary information refers to marketing information that is not available through secondary or existing sources. The interview process allows face-to-face interaction between the interviewer and the respondent. The interviewer can explain complex questions, and use audiovisual aids, pictures, and diagrams to further clarify questions directed at the respondent.

On the negative side, personal interviews require more time than other survey techniques. They can be expensive and the presence of the interviewer can bias the survey. Some respondents may alter their responses to be positive, in an attempt to placate the interviewer. The way in which a question is presented by the interviewer, such as their tone of voice can influence the answer received. Interviewing is an art that requires training to minimize these problems.

In the past, interviews used to be conducted in the home but with more working couples, home interviews are no longer popular. They have been replaced by shopping mall "intercept interviews." Interviewers approach people in a mall and solicit their responses to questions. Focus groups are another popular interview technique. Groups of eight to twelve people are brought together to offer their answers and views on a set of marketing questions. The sessions are informal, and a moderator controls the discussion by asking questions.

TELEPHONE SURVEYS

Telephone surveys are the most frequently used interview method. They are fast, easy to conduct, and the response rate tends to be high. People are more willing to respond to a stranger on the telephone, than they are in a face-to-face situation. Telephone interviews are cost effective, even for national surveys when WATS lines are used. Interviewing by telephone allows the interviewer to probe for a response. On the other hand, they do not allow for observation or the use of visual aids, such as product pictures to supplement the interview.

DIRECT MAIL SURVEYS

Direct mail questionnaires are the least flexible of the market survey techniques. The foundation to the survey is a standardized questionnaire. Questionnaires must be short and easy to complete (in five minutes or less if you expect a good response rate.) Interview bias is eliminated in direct mail surveys. Questionnaires can be returned anonymously, which can result in more honest responses. Direct mail surveys generally cost less than personal and telephone interviews. The major disadvantages of mail surveys are their low response rates, which are often below 10 percent, and the fact that they allow little room for probing. Techniques for increasing direct mail response rates include:

1. Personalizing the questionnaire, such as printing the respondent's name on the questionnaire.

2. Offering a monetary or gift incentive to those who complete and return the questionnaire.

3. Include self-addressed return stamped envelope with the questionnaire.

4. Send a follow-up postcard one week after the questionnaire is mailed to remind people to respond.

5. Use follow-up phone calls to remind people to respond.

DESIGNING QUESTIONNAIRES

The design of a successful questionnaire is an art. Fortunately, there are some established principles and procedures you can apply to design an acceptable questionnaire. For example, each question asked should be directed at obtaining the information needed to qualify your market. All solicited responses should apply toward solving your marketing problems by providing you with the information you need. Questions should be easy to answer and, whenever possible, you should use checklists to solicit answers.

Questions should be phrased in simple and unambiguous words. Avoid using any words, or phrases that could irritate the respondents. Each question asked should stand on its own, and not conflict with other questions. For example, if you asked the question "Do you like our product idea?" and in the next question asked "What is it that you don't like about our product idea?" you could confuse the respondents, who indicated they liked your product idea in the first place. Perhaps a better way to phrase the follow-on question would be to ask, "What improvements would you like to see in our product idea?"

After you have designed your questionnaire, pretest the form. Show it to your friends and ask them if they understand the questions you're asking. How would they respond? If you are using "checklist" responses, find out if you have all the possible response options covered.

When you are satisfied with the format of your questionnaire, cross-check the answers you're looking for against the marketing problems you are trying to solve. Will the answers provide you with the information you need to answer the questions in the market analysis? Will you know more about your target market when you complete the survey?

SAMPLING PROCEDURES

The selection of survey participants is an important part of the survey process. In most surveys, you do not need to include every possible respondent in the survey. A sample of the people in a target market population is usually sufficient to derive market conclusions about the total target market.

The obvious benefit of surveying a sample of the population, as opposed to the entire population, is the cost and timed saved. Sampling can also produce more accurate results. Imagine how long it would take if you attempted to interview every fisherman in Colorado? By the time you finish the interview process, the business environment may have changed. The results you obtained during the early stages of the interview process may no longer be valid.

RANDOM SAMPLING

How do you select a sample population for your survey? There are two basic sampling procedures to use: random, and selective sampling. In random sampling, all members of the target population have an equal chance of being included in the survey. Sampling is done according to statistical rules that leave no room for the researcher's judgment. In random sampling, a complete list of the target market members is obtained. Names are randomly selected from the list until enough names have been selected to meet the desired sample size.

For example, suppose you had a list with a thousand names that represented your target population. The names could be sequentially numbered beginning with one through a thousand on individual cards, and mixed in a barrel. The researcher chooses the sample by randomly selecting cards from the barrel to obtain a desired random sample of, let's say, one hundred names.

SELECTIVE SAMPLING

In selective sampling, respondents are selected on the basis of the researcher's judgment. The target market is divided into subgroups. Each subgroup becomes an independent market and is subjected to all the rules that govern the random sample approach. This approach is used when the researcher knows, or suspects, that certain subgroups in the target population might have an unusual influence on the overall results of the survey.

For example, suppose that the research objective was to determine the average amount of time people spend using personal computers for home use. The people who are retired probably have more time for home use than working people. Thus, to ensure that the sample does not reflect the bias of retired people, the researchers might divide computer users into two groups, working and retired people, and they would independently survey the two groups.

SAMPLE SIZE

How many people do you need to survey to obtain qualified results? The answer to sample size questions are covered in detail in any good statistics book. If you intend to conduct extensive surveys, you should learn more about how statistics are used to select sample sizes. For those of you who have no interest in learning any more than you have to about statistics, this section offers you a "crash course" on the subject.

First, let's establish what it is that we are trying to accomplish when we survey a sample of a target market. We hope that the answers obtained from the sample represent the answers we would have obtained, had we surveyed 100 percent of the target market. This basic principle is the foundation for market research, and it is supported by the statistical laws of probability.

Two elements go into the survey sample size formula to assure that the answers obtained from the sample reflect the answers of the total target market. The random selection process covered in the previous section was the first element.

The second element is the sample size. Suppose

Exhibit 7-2. Rule-of-Thumb Sample Sizes for Different Populations

Size of Population	Sample Size
Less than 100,000	3% to 5%
100,000 to 200,000	2.5%
201,000 to 500,000	2%
501,000 to 1,000,000	1%
Over 1,000,000	.5%

that the target market was composed of a population of one million people. If we chose to sample one person out of the million about our product, would we be able to formulate conclusions about what the remaining 999,999 people thought? The answer is an obvious "no."

Would we have been able to form significant conclusions if we had randomly surveyed 1 percent of the population? The statistical answer is "yes." Statistics tells us there is an inverse relationship between the size of the sample and the size of the target market. The percent surveyed decreases when the target population increases. Again, this concept is all covered in any good book on basic statistics.

As a "rule-of-thumb," we have identified the sample sizes you should use for a survey, based upon different target market populations sizes, in Exhibit 7–2. The sample sizes assume that all respondents are selected randomly.

TABULATING SURVEY RESULTS

Marketing people use a variety of techniques to turn raw marketing data into useful information. First, they tabulate all the data they collected from interviews, surveys, and secondary sources. Support data collected are carefully organized into marketing categories. The first step in the analysis process is to determine if the support data reinforce the primary marketing information.

Three numbers are typically derived from the market analysis process: the mode, the median, and the mean. The mode is the number that occurs most often. The median is the number in the middle, which divides the list in half. Half of the respondents are above the median and half are below the median. The mean is the average, or the sum of all scores, divided by the number of respondents.

SEGMENTING THE MARKET

Once you have decided on the business you are going to start, and have collected enough market information so that you understand the basic structure of your market, you need to segment the market. Rarely is the market a homogeneous block. Instead, it is usually composed of individuals who have diverse needs. The American automobile industry offers a classic example of what happened to an industry that did not segment its market. For years, Detroit automakers were convinced that all Americans wanted big cars. They did not follow the market trends that indicated some buyers were concerned with fuel economy, and others were interested in smaller cars that were as comfortable as large cars. The Japanese segmented our market by making cars that precisely fit the needs of each market group. It took several decades for the U.S. auto industry to recover from their failure to properly segment their markets. There are four variables that enter into the market segmentation formula:

1. The price of the product or service.
2. The quality and characteristics of the product or service.
3. The promotion techniques used for the product or service.
4. The method of distribution of the product or service.

Let's return to the auto industry example for a moment, to see how you would apply the four variables to segment the market. If we assume that the

consumer market could be divided into four market
groups, we can apply the variables as follows:

1. Individuals who want utility and economy
   (price).
2. Individuals who want performance (quality).
3. Individuals who want perceived luxury (promotion).
4. Individuals who want service (distribution).

Now that we know what our customers want, we
need to identify who our potential customers are by
market segments. Where do they live and how do we
reach them? There are three basic market segmentation methods that are commonly used: (1) demographic segmentation, (2) geographic segmentation,
and (3) census tracks.

DEMOGRAPHIC SEGMENTATION

Demographic segmentation involves breaking out the
market in terms of social statistics and charactristics.
Examples of demographic market segmentation
would be breakouts by age, sex, religion, education,
ethnic group, income, family size, and occupation. It
is one of the most popular and easiest methods used
to segment the market. Most demographic data is
available through secondary information sources.

To demonstrate how demographic data could be
used to segment the market for a product or service,
let's assume that you are interested in opening an income tax service. Your first concern is to determine
the profile of an average customer who uses tax
preparation services. What are their demographic
characteristics? Based upon the market research that
you conducted, you have discovered that your average customer fits the following demographic profile:

- Their income exceeds $45,000 per year.
- 60 percent are married working couples.
- 75 percent are college graduates.
- 80 percent are homeowners.

You have now developed a demographic profile
that shows what the average income tax service customer looks like. Now that you have the answer to

this critical question, it leads you to discover the answer to the next question: Where do the predominance of people that fit this demographic profile live? The answer to this question will be important for several reasons. First, it will help determine if there is a viable market of sufficient size to support your business venture. The information can be used to select the best location for your business. You need to conduct a geographical analysis to further segment the market.

GEOGRAPHIC SEGMENTATION

Geographic market segmentation involves segmenting the market by population density and demographic criteria. In the tax service example, you identified a demographic profile of the most likely customer for your service. You want to locate your business in an area where a predominance of these people live. Secondary information sources may provide you with the geographical information that you need to make an intelligent marketing decision.

For example, if you want to locate your business in either city A or B, which one has the greater population of people who fit the market demographic profile? Two possible sources for this information would be the respective Chambers of Commerce, or the advertising departments of the local newspapers. Most newspaper advertising departments maintain extensive geographic and demographic profiles of the markets they serve. In the next section, we will show how you can obtain precise geographic information from census track data.

USING CENSUS TRACKS

Every 10 years, the United States conducts a census of the country's population. As one would expect with the dramatic improvements in computer technology, each census count becomes more probing and sophisticated, in its quest for geographic and demographic information. The most recent census was taken in 1990, and it included the collection of extensive information. The following is only a partial list of the data that were collected.

1. Income, family status, age, and sex by household.
2. The types of fuels the households burn, and average mortgage payments.
3. All levels of education.
4. How household occupants get to work.

The United States is divided up into standard metropolitan statistical areas called SMSAs. Most SMSAs include at least one major metropolitan center and the adjacent communities. There are numerous subdivisions within an SMSA, which are called census tracts. The data collected by the Census Bureau is available to the public at a very reasonable fee.

Census track data can be an important component in segmenting a market. For example, let's assume that you want to locate a business somewhere in Denver, Colorado. Like all metropolitan areas, Denver is a SMSA that is divided into numerous census tracts. You can locate the various census tracts that are within any SMSA by obtaining a census tract map for that area from the Census Bureau. For the purposes of this example, we have assumed that you are interested in opening a business in the southeast section of Denver, if the demographic data supports your market segmentation requirements. You ordered the tract demographics from the Census Bureau and have extracted the following information.

Southeast Denver area

There are 3,356 households in this portion of Denver, of which 2,500 are homeowners and 856 are renters. The homeowners' median income is $51,185, and the mean income is $57,990. The renters' median income is $37,876, and the mean is $43,984.

The median monthly rent payment is $580.

The median asking price for a house is $148,000, and the median value is $124,875.

The total number of individuals who live in this tract is 6,775, of which 3,125 are married, 1,685 are single, and 1,965 are either separated or divorced.

58 percent of the individuals 25 year or older have at least 3 years of college.

Based upon your analysis on the census track data, you decide to open your business in southeast Denver. All of the Census Bureau's data have been incorporated into TIGER, which stands for Topological Integrated Geographic Encoding and Reference System. TIGER is a digital map data base that automates the mapping activities required to support the census. The map data base is computer readable, and can be used by automated mapping applications. The TIGER data base covers census area boundaries, political boundaries, address ranges within ZIP codes, and much more. Hard copies and electronic media copies of all, or parts of the TIGER data base, can be ordered by contacting the Census Bureau, Washington, DC 20233.

ESTABLISHING YOUR MARKET NICHES

Today's marketplace is extremely specialized, and as a result, many big businesses find it hard to offer everything for everyone. This gives the small business the advantage, because it can tailor its operations to serve what are called market niches — areas that are too small to generate the volume needed by big businesses to make a profit. Once you find your niche, target your marketing and sales efforts to reach your target market customers. Initially, keep your focus on a narrow plane.

For example, let's assume that you are planning to open a computer consulting business. Your proposed business plans to set up computers for accountants and provide the necessary training. Your business could logically be expanded to include attorneys and doctors. However, accountants are subjected to their own set of regulations and custom computer needs. To be successful at target marketing, you need to apply the following to your marketing program:

- Become an expert. Target one market group so that you will know it well and can anticipate the needs of the market.

- Look for patterns. Find out who your customers are by talking to them and checking credit card receipts to find out where they come from.

- Know your niche customers. Talk to your customers and take notes of what they say, where they like to go, and what they like to buy.
- Crunch the numbers. Check sales and credit card receipts and note the addresses on checks so that you know where they come from.

SELECTING A LOCATION

A highly successful and respected entrepreneur was once asked what she thought were the three most important success factors in a startup business. She responded with "location, location, and location." There are a number of other factors to consider when selecting a location for your business, which we have summarized as follows:

1. Is the area increasing in population over the national average?
2. Is the climate suitable for the business?
3. Where are your customers concentrated?
4. What are the costs and availability of transportation?
5. What is the availability of materials and supplies?
6. What are the construction and land costs?
7. What is the area's attitude toward your business?
8. What is the labor skill availability?
9. Are police, fire, and utility services adequate?
10. Is there adequate parking, lighting, and public transportation?
11. Are there any tax and cost incentives?
12. Can the population in the area support your business?
13. How close will you be to your competitors?
14. What level of walk-in traffic does the location support?
15. Is the rent or lease expense reasonable for your type of business?

16. Are there any zoning laws that could restrict the operation of your business?

Our list of questions is not all-inclusive, but it provides you with the start of a good checklist that you can use, when you begin your search for a business location. As you review the checklist, decide which factors are most important and weigh them accordingly. Be deliberate in your choice and avoid making a decision in haste.

USING PROFESSIONAL MARKETING SERVICES

Up to this point, we have assumed that you will be conducting your own market research program. However, there are firms that specialize in providing market research for a fee. There are three types of research firms. Syndicated firms sell specialized marketing information. For example, you can buy demographic profiles for just about any geographical location you want from syndicated companies. Custom firms design customized market studies tailored to your exact specifications. Specialty line companies make up the final category. They perform specialty functions such as field interviewing, telephone interviews, and direct mail surveys.

Research fees vary depending upon the type of work you want to contract. Some firms will quote a fixed price for a defined project, whereas others may charge a level of effort hourly rate. If you are interested in learning more about research firms, you will find them listed in major metropolitan area yellow pages. Look for them under the "market research" heading.

PREPARING YOUR FINAL PLAN

At this point, let's assume that you have analyzed all of your primary and secondary market information. You understand your market and feel confident that you have all of the information you need to develop a good marketing plan. Your marketing plan will identify where you want to go and the marketing objectives you want to accomplish. If properly designed, the plan projects what events are likely to occur in the future. It is used as an antidote to implement changes, to minimize any adverse conditions that may affect your business, and to leverage advantageous conditions when they occur.

There are two critical parts to a marketing plan. The sales forecast comes first and shows anticipated sales dollars and units. The second part is the market strategy, that when deployed, achieves the figures shown in the sales forecast. Like all good plans, the marketing plan is dynamic. You are constantly adjusting and tuning it as changes occur in the business environment. A good plan anticipates changing conditions and includes "what if" strategies. If a change occurs, you are not caught by surprise and forced into a reaction mode. You simply implement the subset of your plan that was designed to accommodate the anticipated change.

SOURCES FOR ADDITIONAL INFORMATION

There is nothing difficult or mysterious about undertaking a market research project. Research is nothing more than searching out information in an organized manner and putting the data together in a logical arrangement. The two books listed below are excellent introductions and guides for undertaking research:

Knowing Where to Look: The Ultimate Guide to Research by Louis Horowitz (Writer's Digest Books).

The Research and Report Handbook for Business, Industry, and Government by Ruth Meyer (John Wiley).

The Encyclopedia of American Facts and Dates (Writer's Digest Books) contains thousands of facts, dates, and events throughout America's history that can be useful to you if you need actual market data.

Marketing organizations offer many sources for marketing information. The names and addresses of the major marketing organizations are listed as follows:

American Marketing Association (AMA)
250 S. Wacker Drive, Suite 200
Chicago, IL 60606
(312) 648-0536

American Telemarketing Association (ATA)
444 N. Larchmont Blvd., Suite 200
Los Angeles, CA 90004
(213) 463-2330

Direct Marketing Association (DMA)
11 W. 42nd St.
New York, NY 10036-9096
(212) 768-7277

Promotion Marketing Association of America
(PMAA)
322 Eighth Ave., Suite 1201
New York, NY 10001
(212) 206-1100

Public Relations Society of America (PRSA)
33 Irving Place
New York, NY 10003
(212) 995-2230

8

Pricing Your Products and Services

It is the market, and not your cost, that determines the price of your products and services. Market prices are controlled by the laws of economic supply and demand. As a general economic rule, the demand for a product increases as its price decreases. If the price is too high, your customers will either attempt to reduce their consumption of your product, or seek an acceptable alternative. The supply of a product normally decreases as prices decrease. If the price is too low, producers will reduce their production of the product. In this chapter, we'll show you how to apply various costs and pricing strategies to develop the best possible pricing strategy for your products and services.

DEFINING PRICING CONSIDERATIONS

You will establish your prices based upon several considerations. For example, your pricing goals may be to maximize your total profits, or to maximize total sales. However, price may not be the most important selling factor. How consumers perceive value in differentiated goods and services may be more important than price. Product and service quality, brand name appeal, and convenience, are a few of the purchase considerations that can override the importance of price. In the perfect scenario, you would know precisely where consumer preferences fit in the minds of your customers. For example, if you knew that price ranked first, followed by convenience and quality, you could implement advertising campaigns to take advantage of consumer preferences.

We showed you how to determine consumer preferences in the chapter on marketing. In the process, we touched upon the importance of price preferences. Product and service pricing strategies are vitally important to your business, and must be consistent with the image that you want to establish for your business. We have all seen several examples of image-setting pricing in retail outlets that add words like "discount" to the store name to imply a "low price" image. In the final analysis, pricing is always an important and powerful selling criteria, especially in the following circumstances:

1. One-time lower prices may be used to introduce a new product or service.

2. The use of different prices for the same product can be used to test-market demand and to find the optimum price.

3. Discount pricing can be used to sell off excess product inventory.

4. Price changes can be used to take advantage of competitive situations such as job bidding.

5. Pricing strategies can be used to help minimize down-turns in the economy or to take advantage of economic up-turns.

APPLYING ECONOMIC THEORY TO PRICE

Many new entrepreneurs often ignore economics because they do not understand the principles of economic theory and therefore, do not know how to apply economics to the operations of their businesses. This is unfortunate because economic theory, if properly applied, can have a positive affect on the development of any business. The economic events of the past 25 years have included inflation rates that have soared and declined, high and low unemployment, recession and recovery, all of which have had a dramatic effect on every business.

This section will help you understand the basic economic principles that directly — and indirectly — influence price. In the process, your ability to analyze various pricing alternatives will be significantly enhanced. Although economics will not provide you with all of the pricing answers that you will need, it will show you how economic events influence consumer prices.

THE LAW OF ECONOMIC DEMAND

The income of most consumers is much too low to cover everything they want to buy. As a result, consumers are forced to make decisions every day in terms of what they will and will not buy. They may want a Mercedes, but can only afford to buy a Buick. They will place a preference on what they buy first, before they will buy other goods and services. How do consumers decide which products to buy and which products to forego?

Economists suggest that they will first buy necessity items, such as food and shelter-related items (e.g., housing, utilities, etc.). This behavior implies that consumers will buy the things they get the most satisfaction from for every dollar they spend. They will allocate their limited income to maximize, as best they can, their overall level of satisfaction.

If the price of one of their essential goods or services increases, they must give up some other desired item to balance the limited dollars they have to spend. If their personal income increases from a salary raise, they may elect to use the increased income to acquire new goods and services. In summary, an increase in the price of an item will reduce the likelihood that it will be purchased. Conversely, if the price of the item is lowered, there is a likelihood that more of the items will be sold. This inverse relationship between the price of goods and services, and the amounts consumers will buy, is called the law of economic demand.

The availability of substitute goods helps to explain the logic of the law of demand. Margarine can be substituted for butter, aluminum can replace steel, and nonessential services can be eliminated. To estimate the influence of price on quantity, economists measure prices on the vertical, or y-axis of a graph, and the amount demanded on the x-axis (see Exhibit 8–1). The demand curve slopes downward and to the right to show that the quantity of an item demanded will increase as price declines.

Some goods and services are much more responsive to changes in price. If there are a number of viable alternatives for a given product or service, then a change in price can have a significant affect on demand. For example, if one airline carrier suddenly

Exhibit 8-1. The Consumer Demand Curve

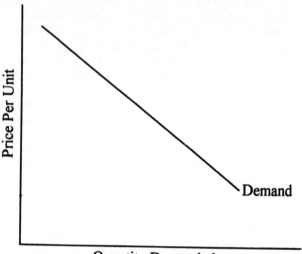

drops its round-trip airfare prices, there is usually a sudden surge of consumer demand for their services, as opposed to the services of the other carriers. That is precisely why the other carriers will almost immediately drop their fares to match the lower rate carrier.

If an airline drops its price for round-trip airfares, then there will be a corresponding increase in consumers' demand for tickets. The quantity demanded of some goods and services may be less responsive to changes in price.

Products with established brand names that enjoy a high degree of consumer loyalty are often less sensitive to changes in prices than "generic" brands. Essential services in the medical field, such as those of the cardiovascular surgeon, are another example. However, despite the degree of responsiveness, the fundamental law of demand holds for all goods and services. A price increase will induce a consumer to turn to a substitute, which will lead to a reduction in the demand for that item. A price reduction will make a commodity relatively cheaper, inducing consumers to purchase more of it as a substitute for other commodities.

THE LAW OF ECONOMIC SUPPLY

How does the market process determine the amount of goods and services businesses will produce? In order to answer this question, we need to understand the factors that influence businesses to supply goods and services. Business owners have to pay a competitive price for the resources they need to operate their business. The resources could be made up of any combination of raw materials, finished products, or labor, depending upon the type of business. The sum of the amounts paid for the resources to run the business will equal the total cost of the product or service offered for sale by the business.

Most entrepreneurs have a strong incentive to run profitable businesses. Profit is the reward that is earned by the entrepreneurs who carry out business activities that are successful. It is what is left over after all costs have been paid. To be profitable, the revenue derived from the sale must exceed the cost of the employed resources. If the sales revenue is less than the costs that were incurred to produce the items sold, then a loss occurs.

The entrepreneur must then decide what products and services to produce to make a profit. Because profitability will be affected by the price consumers are willing to pay and the cost of doing business, entrepreneurs must understand the basic principles of economics. For example, how will you respond to a change in price for your product? If consumers are willing to pay a higher price, then you will probably be motivated to supply more of the product for sale. However, other entrepreneurs, encouraged by the high prices you are getting, may be motivated to enter the market and supply the same product. Over a period of time, this activity will lead to an expansion in output for the product. The direct relationship between the price of a product, and the amount of it that will be supplied, is called the law of economic supply.

REACHING THE
MARKET EQUILIBRIUM POINT

In the world of economic demand and supply, buyers and sellers make decisions independent of each other. However, the market will ultimately influence their choices and actions through a process that economists call market equilibrium. To an economist, the market is not a physical location, but rather an abstract concept that is influenced by buying and selling.

At some point in the market process, buyers and sellers will reach an agreement on a price that buyers are willing to pay, and sellers are willing to accept for a given product. This point is called the market equilibrium point, a state in which conflicting economic forces are in perfect balance. Before a market equilibrium point can be attained, the decisions of the buyers and sellers must be coordinated.

The market price will tend to change in a direction that will bring the price that buyers are willing to pay, into balance with the price sellers will accept. If the quantity supplied is not precisely equal to the quantity demanded by consumers, there will be a tendency for the market price to rise or fall, until a balance is reached.

If we combine the demand and supply curves that we created in the previous exhibits, we can show in Exhibit 8–2 how this relationship works for a hypothetical product (e.g., widgets). At the high price of $12, widget producers will supply 650 units at point "A" on the exhibit whereas consumers will only demand 450 units at that high price (see point "B"). An

Exhibit 8-2. Market Equilibrium

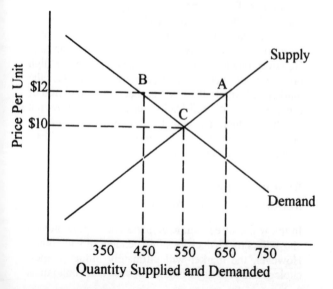

Quantity Supplied and Demanded

excess supply of 200 units will result, since production (supply) exceeds sales (demand).

As a result, the inventories of the widget producers will increase. To reduce undesired inventories, some producers will increase their sales by cutting prices. Other businesses will have to match the lower prices, or risk selling even fewer widgets. The advent of lower prices forces the marginal producers out of the business as the remaining businesses reduce their levels of output.

How low will the widget price go? When the price has declined to $10 in Exhibit 8–2, the quantity supplied by producers and the quantity demanded by consumers will be in balance at 550 units. The market equilibrium price is reached at the point where the supply and demand curves intersect at point "C." At the $10 price, the coordination of buyer and seller desires is achieved. The production plans of producers are in market equilibrium with the purchasing plans of buyers.

What happens if the price of widgets is lowered to $8, as we have shown in Exhibit 8–3? At the new low price, consumers will demand 650 widgets but producers' supply will be only 500 units. Because demand exceeds supply by 150 units (650 − 500 = 150),

Exhibit 8-3. The Affect of a Lower Price on Market Equilibrium

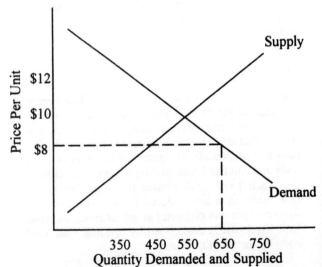

some consumers who are unable to purchase widgets at $8 are willing to pay a higher price. Recognizing this fact, producers will raise their prices and expand their output to meet the increased demand. Market equilibrium is again restored at the $10 price.

As these exhibits illustrate, competition is the great regulator in the small business economy. The presence or entry of independent businesses protects the consumer against the sole-source seller who seeks to charge prices that are substantially above costs. The existence of alternative resource suppliers makes it possible for new entrepreneurs to enter a market that might otherwise be dominated by a single "price gauging" supplier. If you understand how these basic economic forces work to influence the pricing of products and services, you will be in a much better position to establish and control viable prices for your business.

COST ANALYSIS

In a competitive economic environment, not every business can raise prices or increase sales volume to meet their profit objectives. However, they can realize their profit objectives by reducing costs. The implementation of systematic cost controls requires a basic understanding of cost accounting. Successful entrepreneurs understand the nature and behavior of the different types of costs. In addition, they know how to control the two primary cost categories: fixed costs and variable costs.

FIXED COSTS

Fixed costs are costs that do not change when there is a change in the sales or production volumes. Examples of fixed costs include rent, utilities, taxes, and salaries that are not directly related to the activity. Exhibit 8–4 graphically illustrates the behavior of fixed costs and unit fixed costs at different levels of output.

Total fixed costs remain the same, no matter how many units are produced or sold. However, the fixed cost per unit decreases as output levels increase. Unit fixed cost is determined by dividing total fixed costs by the quantity of output.

Exhibit 8-4. Total and Unit Fixed Cost Curves

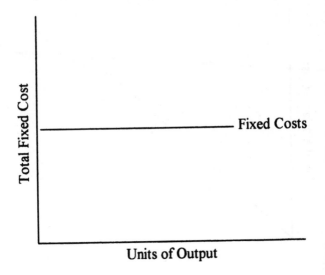

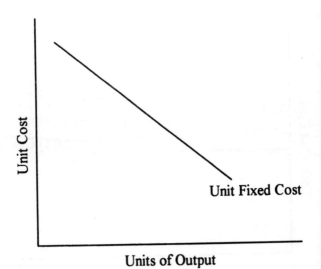

Exhibit 8-5. Variable Cost Curve

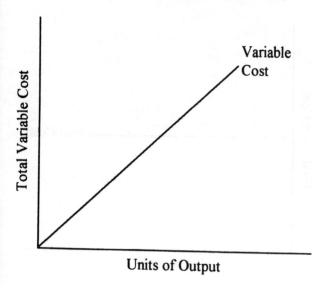

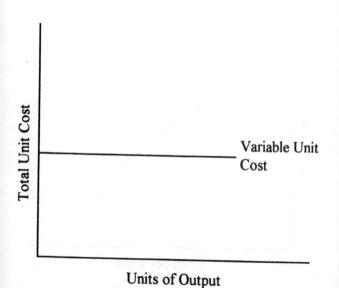

VARIABLE COSTS

Variable costs increase or decrease in response to changes in the number of units sold or produced. Examples of variable costs include the cost of materials, direct labor, factory supplies, and sales commissions. Exhibit 8–5 graphically illustrates the behavior of variable costs and unit variable costs at different levels of output.

Variable cost increases at a constant rate as output rises, whereas variable cost per unit remains the same. Of the four cost relationships illustrated, the unit fixed cost is the only nonlinear relationship. The higher the production or sales volume, the lower the unit fixed cost. This is an important competitive cost issue to contend with if you are competing against a high-volume producer, who can also reduce unit variable costs by buying in volume.

TOTAL COSTS

Total cost is the summation of total fixed and variable costs at various level of output. As one would expect, the total cost curve in Exhibit 8–6 slopes up and to

Exhibit 8-6. Total Cost Curve

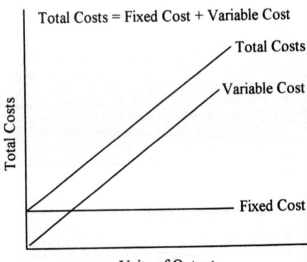

Total Costs = Fixed Cost + Variable Cost

Total Costs

Variable Cost

Fixed Cost

Total Costs

Units of Output

the right to reflect this relationship. Once you have established what your total cost curve is for a given product or service line of business, you can determine total unit cost based upon your projected sales estimates. Unit pricing can be established by adding a "markup" to your cost to achieve a desired profit margin. We will cover several different pricing methods in the next section.

PRICING METHODS

The pricing method that you adopt for your business will depend upon a number of factors that are unique to your particular market, such as the number of competitors. You should first think about what your overall business objectives are before you make any pricing decisions. For example, your pricing objectives may include:

1. Maximizing the profits of your business.
2. Achieving a certain level of return on your investment.
3. Capturing and dominating your market.
4. Meeting or beating the competition.

Calculating your fixed and variable costs will help you determine your price floor, or the lowest price that you can accept without incurring a loss. However, sales quantities can have a direct bearing on whether or not you achieve your pricing objectives. We showed you how to develop a sales unit forecast in Chapter 7 (Marketing). In this section, we will show you how to pull the sales forecast and cost variables together to determine what is the best pricing alternatives for your products and services. Pricing methods vary among the four general business types: retail, wholesale, manufacturing, and service.

RETAIL PRICING METHODS

Retail businesses make profits by providing products and services to customers at a time and place that is convenient to them. Competitive prices are an important factor in the retailer's pricing equation. In many cases, a retailer cannot charge more than competitive retail outlets without losing sales. Higher retail prices are possible if they offer "value added" features that customers are willing to pay for, such as later store hours. If the economy is strong, retail prices can be maintained and even raised. In a slow economy, it may be necessary to lower prices to stay in business. Most retail stores use two basic pricing methods: the markup percent method and competitive markup method. Both methods are illustrated in the examples that follow.

Example 8–1. Markup percent method

The markup percent method is used to achieve a desired target profit, which is expressed as a percentage of gross sales. For example, if we want to make a desired profit of $25,000 on a retail operation with projected net sales of $250,000 and $75,000 in total operating costs, then what price markup must the store achieve?

$$\text{Markup \%} = \frac{(\text{Total operating costs} + \text{desired profit})}{(\text{Net sales})}$$

$$= \frac{(\$75,000 + \$25,000)}{(\$250,000)}$$

$$= 40\%$$

An average price markup of 40 percent is required to achieve the desired $25,000 profit level for the retail store in this example. The markup percentage can be improved by increasing prices or reducing cost. The competitive markup method is used to price your goods similar to those of your competitors. In effect, your markup is controlled by your competitors, and it fluctuates based on what your competitors are charging for their products and services. The competition is, in effect, dictating the profits of your retail business (see Example 8–2).

Example 8–2. Competitive markup method

In this example, let's use the same operating cost and net sales numbers that we used in the previous example. If we know that our competitors are using a 50 percent average markup on everything they sell, what would be the profit expectations from our store:

$$\text{Profit} = (\text{Competitive Markup} \times \text{Net Sales})$$
$$- (\text{Total Operating Costs})$$
$$= (.50 \times \$250,000) - (\$75,000)$$
$$= \$50,000$$

In a competitive markup situation, the base prices of your products and services are controlled by your competition. In this context, you must somehow differentiate your business from competitive businesses if you intend to establish some control over your prices. Areas to concentrate on include:

1. Product and service quality levels.
2. Preferred business location and store hours.
3. Unique advertising, promotion, and discounting programs.

WHOLESALE PRICING METHODS

The function of most wholesale businesses is to provide inventory in the form of products, and in some cases services, to their customers at the precise time when they are needed. Wholesalers are confronted with a different set of pricing methods than retailers in that their prices depend on whether they are distributing unique or standard products. If the product is unique, then the wholesaler is generally under a distribution agreement that covers territorial distribution rights. In this case, the manufacturer usually determines the price that can be charged by wholesalers to retail outlets. In some cases, the manufacturer may simply provide the wholesaler with sales quotas and allow the wholesaler to negotiate prices to meet assigned quotas.

If a wholesaler is distributing standard and highly competitive products, then wholesale prices must be competitive. The retail product differentiation points that we listed in the previous section apply to the wholesale business that wants to establish some control over their prices. The success of a wholesale business may depend upon how well you can satisfy your customers' needs through timely delivery and good service.

If you are considering a wholesale business, you should become familiar with the Robert Morris Associates (RMA) guide to industry financial data, which lists average financial data by industry, such as gross margins and operating expenses as a percent of sales. The RMA guide is available in the reference section of a good public library. The guide can be used to help establish pricing methods for any business, including a wholesale business, which we illustrate in the following two examples.

Example 8–3. Determining the break-even price

Let's assume you want to start a wholesale business that, according to the RMA guide, has an average gross profit of 25 percent of sales. Gross profit is the excess of the sales price over the net delivered cost of the products sold. Assume that average operating expenses are 20 percent of sales. Given this information, you want to determine how you should price your products. You have completed a financial and economic analysis of the business and have developed the following cost estimates:

Fixed Costs (FC) = $75,000
Expected Unit Sales (US) = 400,000
Variable Cost Per Unit (VC) = $4.00

Your initial interest is to determine the average price you must receive for each unit sold to break-even. The break-even formula and calculation follows:

$$\text{Break-even price} = \frac{FC + (US \times VC)}{(US)}$$

$$= \frac{\$75,000 + (400,000 \times \$4)}{400,000}$$

$$= \$4.19$$

In this example, $4.19 was the break-even price, or the average price the wholesaler must charge to cover costs. The break-even price is heavily dependent upon the wholesaler's ability to sell large quantities of products (400,000 units at a relatively low fixed cost of $75,000). In Example 8–4, we want to determine the price that must be charged to make a desired profit margin.

Example 8–4. Determining a price to obtain a desired profit

In this example, we will use the assumptions that we made in the previous example to determine the average price we must charge to make a profit (PF) of $50,000. Our calculation follows:

$$\text{Profit price} = \frac{PF + FC + (US \times VC)}{US}$$

$$= \frac{\$50,000 + \$75,000 + (400,000 \times \$4)}{400,000}$$

$$= \$4.31$$

Exhibit 8-7. Comparing Operating Costs with RMA Standard Costs		
Standard Category	**RMA Standard**	**Standard for Your Business**
Product or Service Price	100%	
Cost of Goods Sold	75%	
Gross Margin	25%	
Operating Expense	15%	
Pre-tax Profits	10%	

If the wholesaler can maintain an average sales price of $4.31 per unit, the wholesaler will make a profit of $50,000 for every 400,000 units sold at this price. As was previously noted, according to the RMA guide, the average industry gross profit for the business in the examples was 25 percent. Average operating expenses are 20 percent of sales. Based upon our calculations in the previous examples, we are interested in comparing our projections against the RMA guide averages. The worksheet in Exhibit 8–7 shows you how to make this relatively easy comparison.

MANUFACTURING PRICING METHODS

Manufacturing businesses are primarily concerned with their internal cost to arrive at an acceptable price. Most manufacturing businesses will establish prices that are somewhere between their industry's price floor (i.e., break-even point) and the price ceiling (i.e., highest price charged in the industry). Both floor and ceiling prices can change, depending upon changes in the general economy, market factors, competition, technological changes, and the availability of resources. If your costs are substantially above the industry's price floor, you may want to reconsider your pricing strategy. Your first pricing step for your product is to establish the price floor. There are three common methods that are used to establish the price floor: (1) the full-cost markup method, (2) the incremental cost method, and (3) the cost conversion method.

Full-cost Markup Method

The full-cost markup method is one of the most common and easiest ways to determine the price floor. In the basic calculation, all product-related costs are added together. Total costs are then multiplied by a desired markup percentage to determine the product's selling price. For example:

Cost per unit

Direct labor	$3.00
Direct materials	$1.50
Total direct costs	$4.50
Overhead cost	$0.75
Total unit costs	$5.25
Markup (assumes 25%)	$1.31
Unit selling price	$6.56

Overhead cost includes the various costs that cannot be directly allocated to unit manufacturing costs, such as rental and utility expenses. Unit overhead costs are determined by dividing total overhead by the number of units produced. The following assumptions and calculations were used to determine overhead cost in this example:

$$\text{Total overhead} = \$7,500$$

$$\text{Units produced} = 1,000$$

$$\text{Overhead per unit} = \frac{(\text{Total overhead})}{(\text{Units produced})}$$

$$= \$.75$$

Incremental Cost Method

The incremental cost method is used when overhead costs are considered immaterial to total manufacturing cost or are included in the direct costs.

Cost per unit

Direct labor	$2.50
Direct materials	$1.95
Total direct costs	$4.45
Markup (Assume 25%)	$1.11
Unit selling price	$5.56

Cost Conversion Method

The cost conversion method is used to establish manufacturing costs for cases in which labor and overhead costs are relatively high compared to material
cost. The cost of materials is covered in the markup
percent. Our formula follows:

Cost per unit

Direct labor	$2.50
Overhead cost	$0.75
Total costs	$3.25
Markup (Assumes 25%)	$0.81
Unit selling price	$4.06

Now that we have established the price floor for
our manufactured product, the next step is to determine the product's price ceiling. Compared to the
price floor, the price ceiling is more difficult to determine. Many of the techniques that we discussed in
the previous chapter on marketing can be employed
to help you determine the potential price ceiling for
your products. For example, you may conduct a pricing survey of your current and potential customers to
determine the highest price level they would be willing to pay for your product.

Price testing is another effective method to measure the upper price demands for your product. You
simply place your product on the market at different
incremental prices above the price floor, and carefully
measure your sales at the different price levels. You
are in effect determining what the economic demand
curve looks like for your product.

SERVICE PRICING METHODS

In a standard service business, pricing is dependent
upon the pricing standards that are already in place.
When standard service pricing exists, a service cannot charge more than the going rate, unless there is a
customer-perceived difference in your business versus competitive services. There are two common
pricing methods that are used by service businesses:
(1) the job cost method and (2) the job multiplier
method. Both pricing methods employ the use of

markup factors to arrive at a final job price. The markup margin can vary depending upon several factors, such as the uniqueness of your services, and quality discriminators that you have established with customers.

Job Cost Method

The job cost method adds all direct job-related costs (i.e., labor, overhead, and materials) to determine total cost (floor price) for the job. In the calculation that follows, we have added a 25 percent profit margin to arrive at a job price.

Total direct labor	$2.50
Total material cost	$1.95
Total overhead costs	$0.75
Total cost	$5.20
Profit margin	$1.30
Job price	$6.50

Overhead includes the various costs that cannot be directly allocated to the job such as the front office expenses (e.g., secretary, rent, utilities, etc.) that are required to accept and coordinate job service requests. Job overhead costs per hour are determined by dividing total overhead by the number of projected job hours to determine how much should be allocated on a per hour job basis.

$$\text{Overhead per hour} = \frac{\text{(Total overhead)}}{\text{(Projected job hours)}}$$

Job Multiplier Method

The job multiplier method is based upon a target level of sales that you must achieve to reach the profit objective of your business. For example, if your target costs are:

Direct labor and materials (DL) = $135,000
Overhead costs (OV)　　　　　 = $45,000
Profit (PR)　　　　　　　　　 = $75,000

Total sales = DL + OV + PR
　　　　　 = 135,000 + $45,000 + $75,000
　　　　　 = $255,000

Based upon total sales of $255,000 and direct costs of $135,000, you can calculate the job multiplier needed to meet your profit objectives.

$$\text{Job multiplier} = \text{Total sales} / \text{direct costs}$$
$$= \$255,000 / \$135,000$$
$$= 1.88$$

The job multiplier tell you how much you need to charge for your direct labor to cover overhead costs and meet your profit objectives. For example, if you are bidding a job that requires 10 hours of direct labor that cost you $20 per hour, the job would be bid at:

$$\text{Total job cost} = (\text{direct hours} \times \text{hourly rate})$$
$$(\text{job multiplier})$$
$$= (10 \text{ hours} \times \$20) (1.88)$$
$$= \$200 (1.88)$$
$$= \$376$$

As you can see from our discussion, there are numerous pricing methods that you can apply to your business. The methods that we showed you in this section covered the four primary types of businesses. However, it should be clear to you that the pricing methodologies covered overlap and can be applied to any business pricing situation. In the next section, we will cover the different pricing strategies that you can use to "fine-tune" the prices for your business.

SELECTING A PRICING STRATEGY

A pricing strategy is a plan of action that you implement to price your offerings, based upon the information you have collected. You understand the economic supply and demand relationships that are unique to your product. You know what your fixed and variable costs are at various levels of output. You understand the various pricing strategies that are currently employed by your competitors. The three basic pricing strategies that you can implement are covered in the balance of this section.

THE INTRODUCTION PRICE STRATEGY

The introduction strategy is used to penetrate into an existing market with a new product. Low price tactics are typically employed to encourage people to try your product because of the significantly lower price. The actual price of the product may be the same as the competitive products, to protect your future efforts to compete on an equal price basis with the competition. Temporary discounts are therefore employed to effectively reduce your price during the market penetration stage. Other price reduction schemes may include two-for-one offers or complimentary gifts. You must be careful that you do not force yourself into a low price image unless that is one of your business objectives. Charging a low price today and then asking for a higher price tomorrow can become a challenging task.

THE LEVELING PRICE STRATEGY

The leveling price strategy is an effective way to discover what consumers are willing to pay for your product. This strategy works well for products and services that are unique or so new that there is very little competition. To initiate the strategy, you price your product at the price ceiling — the highest price you believe consumers will be willing to pay. You then begin to selectively lower the price and carefully measure changes in consumer demand at the different price levels. You are in effect plotting the demand curve for your product, which will ultimately allow you to set a price that best meets your profit objectives.

THE COMPETITIVE PRICE STRATEGY

This strategy is used to price your product or service at the same level as your competitors. Because they have already established their market, you must have something else to offer to encourage consumers to switch over to your product. You might choose to mount an extensive advertising program that features the quality benefits of your product over the competitive products.

SOURCES FOR ADDITIONAL
INFORMATION

Pricing Strategies by Alfred Oxenfeldt (AMACOM, a division of the American Management Association)

Pricing for Profit and Growth by Albert Bergfeld, James Early, and William Knobloch (Prentice-Hall)

Price and Price Policies by Walton Hamilton (Mc-Graw-Hill)

9

Developing an Effective Sales Program

The implementation of an effective sales program to promote sales for your business is a necessity in today's competitive marketplace. Many entrepreneurs consider their sales program and salespeople their most potent competitive tool. In this chapter, we will cover all of the important issues that you must consider if you want to develop an effective sales organization and program for your business.

THE SIX SELLING STEPS

The basic objective of the sales organization in a business is to make profitable sales on behalf of the business. Sales strategies and plans are implemented to help the sales force achieve its sales goal. For example, advertising programs may be implemented to promote specific products or services. There are six important steps that successful salespeople take to close a sale:

1. Prospecting
2. Pre-sales planning
3. Sales presentation
4. Dealing with sales objections
5. Closing the sale
6. Sales follow-up

PROSPECTING

Prospecting is the first step in the selling process. A prospect is a qualified individual who has demonstrated an interest in buying your product or service. Prospects are the lifeblood of any business because they form the foundation of your customer base. Without a solid customer base, your business will fail. There are two primary reasons why your business must constantly look for new customer prospects: (1) to incrementally increase sales and (2) to replace lost customers.

Some entrepreneurs confuse the sales term "sales prospect" with "sales lead." The name of a person or business who might be a prospect, is referred to as a sales lead. Once a lead has been qualified, the lead becomes a prospect. There are six questions that must be answered with a "yes" to qualify a prospect:

1. Does the prospect need your products and services?

2. Does the prospect perceive a need or problem that can be satisfied by your product?

3. Does the prospect have a sincere desire to fulfill this need or solve the problem?

4. Can the prospect afford to pay for your product?

5. Does the prospect have the authority to make a buy decision?

6. Will the potential purchase be large enough to make it profitable?

Most salespeople operate in a sales territory that includes customers, prospects, and leads. Although locating leads and qualifying prospects are important sales activities for any business, the selling of large ticket items is more dependent on prospecting than retail store sales. However, prospecting and qualifying customers is vitally important to any sales program.

How to Find Prospects

Prospecting, like other sales activities, is a skill that can be constantly improved upon by dedicated salespeople. Some entrepreneurs charge themselves with finding X number of prospects per week. In the process, they are constantly evaluating and improving upon their prospecting methodologies. Prospects can come from a number of sources including the following:

- Personal acquaintances, such as friends and relatives.

- Leads from people who are directly or indirectly involved in your business (i.e., suppliers, etc.).

- Leads from newspaper articles.
- Lists and directories, such as the telephone directory or association membership lists.
- Current customers who refer prospects to you.

Sales Leads

Sales leads from personal acquaintances are usually easy to obtain and are often overlooked. Maintain a list of all your personal acquaintances and contact them on a regular basis to solicit referrals. Expert leads come from people who are in a business that may relate to yours. For example, if you own an accounting service business, you may want to contact the bankers in your market area. Bank customers will often ask bank officers for accounting service source recommendations.

The local newspaper can be a source for all types of sales leads. If a new company is moving into your market area, and you are in the office supply business, you may want to make a sales call on their office manager before they move. You can obtain customer prospect directories for just about any target market group imaginable. Direct mail businesses are just one source of specialized customer directories. Many can provide you with directories for customer demographic parameters that you select such as location, income, age, areas of interest, and many other qualifying criteria. Direct mail businesses are listed in the yellow pages.

Current customers are an important source for prospect leads. Satisfied customers generally like to share their successful buying experiences with their friends. Some businesses offer rewards, such as gift certificates and discounts, to clients who refer new customers to the business. The business cost of the gift is usually far less than what it costs to find a new customer through traditional sales channels.

PRE-SALES PLANNING

The sales call is still the basic foundation to most sales programs, and planning a sales call is the foundation of a successful sale. You would never start a long-distance drive to an unfamiliar place without first looking at a road map. Similarly, you should plan what you want to accomplish in a sales call and later measure yourself against your plan.

Good salespeople are convincing and impressive. You can prepare yourself to be convincing and impressive by knowing your products, and more important, how the product can be applied to the needs of your customer. Know your customer before you make the sales call. You can gain a wealth of customer background information from sources such as annual reports, local newspapers, and conversations with people who already know your customer. The elements of pre-sales planning include the following:

- Sales objective. Always have a sales objective in mind before you make the sales call. Your objective should be specific, measurable, and directly beneficial to your customer.

- Customer profile. Obtain as much customer profile information as you can regarding the firm, buyer, and the individuals who can influence the buying decision prior to the sales call. This will allow you to customize your presentation to the needs of the customer.

- Customer benefits. Develop a specific set of benefits that you believe the customer will realize if they buy your product. The customer benefit plan should be the nucleus of the information you will use in your sales presentation.

Overall, good sales planning shows up and pays off in increased sales when you do your homework before you make the sales call. At the end of every sales call, critique your plan so that you can improve upon your next sales call.

MAKING A SALES PRESENTATION

The sales presentation is where all of your preplanning efforts come together. Here are the procedures and steps that you should follow in planning a sales presentation.

1. First, develop your sales call objective.
2. Determine what product you will be presenting to your prospect.

3. Based on your objective and what you know about your prospect, determine what specific product benefits to present.

4. Prepare a business proposition showing alternative purchase options.

5. Establish a suggested order.

Visual aids and demonstrations can be developed to help you create an informative and persuasive sales presentation. If properly delivered, your presentation should influence your prospect to make a purchasing decision. Make sure you rehearse your presentation before the sales call.

HANDLING SALES OBJECTIONS

Sales prospects may raise objections at any time during a sales call. Accept objections as a challenge that, when handled correctly, will benefit both you and your prospect. The more effectively you can meet the customer's needs and solve his or her problems, the more successful you will be in sales. If you develop a fear of objections, you will fumble with your response and probably lose the sales.

Although people may want to buy, they do not want to be forced to buy something they do not want. If they cannot see how your offering will fulfill their needs, they will ask questions and raise objections. If you cannot answer the questions effectively and meet the objections, you will not close the sale. The salesperson who can overcome objections and smoothly move back into the presentation will succeed.

Objections can occur at any time during the sales presentation. However, the prospect may allow you to make your presentation and must be prompted before raising any objections. The experienced salesperson will use a trial close technique to determine the prospect's attitude toward the product. The technique simply involves asking the prospect for the order. For example, you might say: "Mr. Jones, if you like everything you have heard, when may I place the order?" You should be prepared to respond in one of four ways:

1. If there is a positive response to the trial close, then move in to close the sale because there are no apparent objections.

2. If an objection is raised, respond to it, and initiate another trial close to see if you have met the objection.

3. After meeting one objection, be prepared to meet a sequence of objections, which can be a benefit in that it allows the prospect to get everything out on the table.

4. If you have responded to the objections, initiated trial closes, and have not been able to overcome the objections, return to your sales presentation to further discuss your product relative to the objections.

There are several sales strategies salespeople use to master objections. Always take notes after a sales call to help refine the process. What responses worked best for different objections? If you had the opportunity to repeat the sales call, what would you have changed in your presentation or responses?

CLOSING A SALE

Closing a sale is the process of helping prospects make a buy decision. You help people make that decision by asking them to buy. As successful salespeople know, there are no magic phrases and techniques to use in closing a sale. It is simply the end result of your presentation.

Although it may seem obvious, some salespeople forget that prospects already know the salesperson is there to sell them something. They are predisposed to buy something or you would not be there. During the course of your presentation, they may be ready to make a buy decision. Unfortunately, most salespeople are not mind readers and must therefore interpret when a prospect is ready to buy.

When should you attempt to close a sale? The answer is when the buyer is ready, and in the "conviction stage" of the sales presentation. Prospects can enter the conviction stage at any time during the presentation. They may indicate that they are in this stage by asking you buyer signal questions. A buying signal is anything a prospect says or does to indicate that they are ready to buy. The following questions illustrate buying signal questions:

- What is your price and what types of payment terms do you offer?
- Can I get a special price if I pay cash?
- What are my color or model options?
- How soon can you deliver the product?
- How large an order do I need to place to get a discount?

The accurate interpretation of buying signals should prompt you to attempt a trial close. Your trial close starts with a brief summarization of the major features of your product or service. If you receive a positive response from the prospect, you close the sale. The formal close is where you will ask for the order. You must put the prospect in the position of having to make a buy or no-buy decision. At this stage in the sales process, a good sales person stops talking as they wait for their prospect to respond to the closing question.

If the prospect makes a no-buy decision, you can begin to ask appropriate probing questions. For example, if price is the major issue in the prospect's mind, you might ask: "What price are you willing to pay?" If you believe that you have obtained sufficient information from the probing questions you have asked, you can initiate another trial close. Courtesy and common sense should set the limits on the number of closings you attempt in any one setting.

ESTABLISHING SALES FOLLOW-UP

Providing service and follow-up after the sale to a customer is important, no matter what type of company, product, or service you represent. Follow-up and service create goodwill between the salesperson, your company, and the customer. By contacting the customer after the sale to check on customer satisfaction, you develop a positive foundation for repeat business and customer referrals. The following checklist will help you get started:

1. Develop an account penetration program for each of your accounts that will help you make friends within an account and increase sales.

2. Never allow an account to run out of stock. If they are out of stock, you not only lose the sale but your account also loses the sale. Maintain adequate levels of inventory to minimize out of stock situations.

3. Fight for shelf space and position. If you are selling retail products, you should constantly seek to obtain the best retail space in the store for your products.

4. Offer technical assistance to your customers. If you are selling industrial products and services, help your customers learn all they can about your offerings. For example, make your users aware of product accessories that might aid them in performing a function in a safer or more profitable manner.

5. To ensure the enthusiastic promotion of your company's product, assist your distributors. Experiences show that companies that cultivate a professional relationship with their distributors, by providing them with product knowledge and promotional materials, are much more likely to succeed.

6. Demonstrate your willingness to help. If an account has a problem, offer your help to resolve the problem, even if it's not your problem. Your actions, rather than just your words, are what build customer respect.

This checklist should help you develop a customer follow-up program. Sales follow-up is an essential ingredient if you want to maximize your sales. Numerous studies have shown that it cost ten times as much in advertising cost to attract a new customer as it does to attract an existing customer. In many respects, your customer base is one of the most valuable assets your company owns.

IMPLEMENTING PERSONAL SELLING

Personal selling involves the personal communication of information about a product or service to persuade a prospective customer to make a purchase decision.

It is in contrast to mass impersonal selling, which is generated by advertising and sales promotional programs. Personal selling has the advantage of being more flexible than other promotional techniques. For example, you can tailor your sales presentation to fit the needs of individual customers. During the presentation process, you can see the customer's reaction to a particular sales approach, and then make the necessary adjustments to accommodate the needs of the customer.

A second advantage of personal selling is that it can be focused on a specific set of prospective customers to minimize wasted time. By contrast, most forms of advertising involve sending a message to a large block of people who are not interested in your product or service. That is not to say that advertising and promotion should not be an important part of your overall sales program. We will cover the important aspects of advertising and promotion in the next chapter. The primary point that we want to make in this chapter is that personal selling and one-on-one customer prospect contacts are essential ingredients to a successful sales program.

USING DISTRIBUTION NETWORKS

If you decide to use distributors to promote your products or services, what are your distribution options? Can your business perform the service better and more effectively than the distributor? To assist you in the cost comparison process, here is a list of self-distribution costs that you should consider:

- Salaries. Inside employee commissions and salaries are reduced or eliminated.

- Administrative costs. Invoicing, accounting, and other administrative costs are reduced.

- Overhead. Overhead expenses for sales support and supply expenses are reduced.

- Storage. Warehouse and delivery costs are reduced.

Let's assume you have decided to use a distributor, because you believe it would be the most cost effective method for distributing your company's products and services. The following list describes the types of distributors for you to consider.

- Wholesalers. Wholesale firms buy in quantity and generally sell to retailers or other wholesalers. They can carry a variety of lines that are dictated by the companies they represent. Wholesalers provide value by shipping orders, storing merchandise, invoicing, granting credit, and distributing into outlets that otherwise might be not be available to your business.

- Rack jobbers. These firms use retail stores and display racks to sell products. The rack jobber essentially rents space from the retailer. In a typical rack jobber arrangement, you sell your product directly to the jobber.

- Brokers. Brokers usually deal in transactions within a given market. The major reason why companies use brokers is because of their knowledge of the marketplace and the buyers in the market. Hence, they can usually shorten the sales cycle.

- Commission agents. These are independent sales agents who work for you on a commission basis and are paid as independent contractors. You may assign them a sales territory and provide them with office support. As independent contractors, commissioned agents control their own hours.

ESTABLISHING SALES TERRITORIES

A sales territory comprises a group of customers or a geographical area assigned to a salesperson. Most territories have geographical boundaries that contain present and potential customers. Some of the reasons for establishing territories are summarized as follows:

- Coverage. To obtain thorough coverage of a target market and competitive territorial assignments.

- Jurisdiction. To establish a salesperson's responsibilities over an established jurisdictional area.

- Performance. The total sales over an established period of time can be used to evaluate a salesperson's performance.

- Qualifications. To match a salesperson's qualifications with the needs of the customers in a territory.

The salesperson is responsible for generating sales in a territory based on its sales potential. The same manager typically establishes a total sales quota that each salesperson is expected to reach. Once this quota is set, it becomes the responsibility of the salesperson to develop and implement a territorial plan for reaching the quota. While there is no standard planning sequence to follow, the following six factors should be considered.

1. Evaluate your territory.
2. Assign territory sales quotas.
3. Perform account analysis.
4. Establish account objectives.
5. Develop a customer sales plan.
6. Initiate sales calls.

The sales territory planning function is critical to the success of the salesperson. Due to the increasing cost of direct selling and the limited resource of time, salespeople have to focus their attention on productivity. Proper management of a territory is an effective method for a salesperson to maximize territorial sales and profits.

STAFFING A SALES FORCE

Sales force staffing involves the process of matching the right people to the right sales job and territory to achieve the sales objectives of the company. The staffing process initially starts by determining how many salespeople you need to maximize your sales. Staffing size considerations may include factors such as the number of prospects to be covered and the geographical size of the different sales territories. Once the sizing issues are resolved, the employment planning can begin.

- **Job analysis.** Determine the type of sales person to recruit for each sales job. Develop a job description and job specifications.
- **Job description.** The job description is a formal written statement describing the nature, requirements, and responsibilities, such as sales quota requirements of the job.
- **Job specifications.** The job specification converts the job description into people's qualification, such as abilities, experience, and education.
- **Recruiting.** Recruiting begins with the initiation of a search plan by which you prospect for salespeople. Once all of the activities leading up to and including the actual decision to hire an applicant are completed, the recruiting process ends.

TRAINING SALESPEOPLE

Sales training is the effort to provide the opportunity for salespeople to acquire job-related skills that will improve their performance in the selling environment. Good sales training is designed to change or reinforce behavior to make salespeople more efficient in closing sales. The three basic training methods are:

- **Discussion.** The discussion approach involves the use of case studies. At a sales session, small discussion groups may be formed to analyze a case and present their findings or recommendations to a larger group. Case study discussions may be supplemented with lectures and demonstrations.
- **Role playing.** In role playing, the sales trainee tries to sell a product or service to a hypothetical buyer. Often the trainee's presentation is videotaped and replayed for critique by the group and trainer.
- **On-the-job training.** On-the-job training may take several forms. New salespeople may accompany a veteran salesperson on a sales call. After a series of calls have been made, the

trainee is allowed to make a sales call under the watchful eye of the trainer.

Sales training is a continuous process for both experienced and novice salespeople. Training should be initiated whenever new sales techniques and ideas are developed to assure the ongoing productivity of the sales force.

MOTIVATING SALESPEOPLE

Sales motivation involves the arousal of an individual to achieve a set of job-related goals. There are four broad motivation factors that can be deployed to motivate salespeople.

- **Compensation.** Salespeople are compensated by one of three methods; straight salary, straight commission, or a combination of salary and commission. The straight salary plan offers a sense of security to the salesperson, but lacks monetary incentives to increase sales. The straight commission is a complete incentive plan, but lacks the security benefit of a guaranteed salary. The combined salary and commission plan was designed to offer the advantages of both plans by combining security with an incentive motivation.

- **Awards.** In addition to compensation plans, many companies use award systems to motivate their salespeople. The award is something that is given in addition to what is earned by the sales person. An award could include a Christmas bonus based upon the overall performance of the company, and not an individual's performance. Performance awards can fall into several categories and are typically initiated for job performance that is considered exemplary.

- **Recognition.** Non-financial rewards can be very effective in motivating salespeople. Recognition rewards are commonly presented at sales meetings, where the salesperson receives recognition for a contribution they have made to the company. Although there are usually no financial benefits with recognition rewards, they serve to show the sales force

that the company (i.e., management) appreci-
ates individual efforts.

- **Leadership.** Leadership is the process by
  which management attempts to influence the
  activities of its salespeople. For example, a
  sales manager might offer his or her direct assistance to help salespeople in reaching their
  quotas. To be an effective leader, you need to
  know your salespeople, their territories, and
  customers. Play the role of a coach whose aim
  is to aid salespeople in reaching their personal
  goals.

HANDLING COMPETITIVE
SELLING TECHNIQUES

Competition is something all salespeople must contend with on a daily basis. There are three basic rules
that you can apply to handle competition:

1. Do not refer to your competitor unless it is
   absolutely necessary.
2. If required, acknowledge your competitor only
   briefly.
3. Know how to make a favorable comparison
   of your product against your competitor's
   product.

- **Do not refer rule.** You can lessen any competitive surprises the buyer may present by
  properly planning your sales call. Find out
  what competing products your prospect is using and, if possible, their attitude toward the
  product. Based on your findings, you can develop a presentation that will leverage the
  drawbacks of the competitive product without
  specifically referring to the competitor.

- **Briefly acknowledge rule.** Your competitors
  should not be discussed during a sales call unless the prospect brings the subject up. Then
  acknowledge your competition in a brief
  statement and return to your presentation.
  "Yes, I am familiar with their product. In fact,
  the last five of my customers who were using
  their product switched over to ours." You
  have briefly acknowledged the competition

and, in a positive manner, moved the prospect's attention back to your product.

- **Favorable comparison rule.** At times, it is necessary and desirable to make a detailed comparison of your product to a competing product. If the products are very similar, emphasize your company's service, guarantees, and what you personally do for customers. If your product has unique features, then it might be appropriate to make a global statement, such as, "Our product is the only one on the market with this feature." Play down the importance of features that your product may lack when compared to the competitive product.

BUILDING A REPEAT SALES BUSINESS

It can take days, weeks, and even months to convert a prospect into a customer. Many businesses assume that once they close a sale, repeat customer sales will become automatic. This simply will not happen unless you initiate specific steps to foster repeat business. There are six basic steps you can implement to build a repeat customer business.

1. Concentrate on improving your account penetration. Account penetration is critical in uncovering additional customer needs and problems that can be solved through the purchase of your products. In the process, you will be demonstrating to customers that you have their best interest in mind.

2. Contact all of your customers on a frequent and regular basis. There are no set guidelines for the frequency of calls you should make. Typically, you should invest your sales time in direct proportion to the actual or potential sales represented by each account.

3. Handle your customer's complaints promptly. This is an excellent opportunity to prove to your customers that their business is important to you. The speed and efficiency with which you handle even the most trivial com-

plaint will go a long way to ensure the repeat business of your customers.

4. Follow-up. Always do what you say you will do within the promised time frame. Nothing can destroy a customer relationship faster than not following through on what you have promised. They have placed their faith in you by purchasing your products, so you must be faithful to them to ensure their future support.

5. Provide service to your customers as if they were royalty. By providing your customers with money-saving products and problem-solving ideas, you can become an indispensable member of their team. Become their advisor and provide all of the service-related assistance that you can.

6. Show appreciation. Customers contribute to your success, and in return you should show your appreciation. Thank them for their business and always look for ways you can help them.

SELLING ON CREDIT

In many businesses, credit sales are not an option — they are a requisite if you want be competitive. The extension of credit depends on several considerations that, when analyzed separately and as a group, can be used to form the foundation of a credit policy. Whatever credit policy you choose to implement, it should reflect the needs of your business and be competitive at the same time. Let's look at each of the credit factors you should consider.

- *Judgment.* Many potential credit problems can be eliminated by simply exercising good judgment when granting credit. For example, if one of your accounts is seriously past due, it doesn't take any special insight to know that extending them additional credit would probably be a poor business decision. Always remember that a sale is not a sale until you get paid for it. If a customer defaults on their payment, the sale becomes a bad debt expense to your business.

- *Checking.* Always run a credit check before you grant any sizable amount of credit to a customer. There are a number of firms that offer relatively inexpensive credit checking services in most metropolitan areas (see Credit Services in the Yellow Pages). This will help protect you from individuals and companies that are slow payers, or that have a history of not paying their bills.

- *Applications*. Credit applications can be used to obtain the basic information you need to verify an individual's payment history. You can design your own form, or purchase predesigned forms from a good stationery store.

COLLECTION PROCEDURES

Timing is one of the fundamental laws of successful collection procedures. The longer you wait to collect your money, the higher the probability that you will not get paid. Therefore, to increase your collection percentage, always ask for payment immediately after a service has been performed, or a product has been delivered. Other techniques that you can employ to reduce the time it takes to collect money are summarized as follows:

- Send invoices. An invoice should be sent out immediately after a service has been completed or a product has been delivered. The payment terms should be clearly identified on the invoice along with any other credit terms. For example, if full payment is due in 30 days and a late charge will be added after 30 days, print those conditions on the front of the invoice.

- Establish late fees. Late fees have become increasingly popular as a method to encourage timely payments. Late fees can include a billing charge and a percent on the remaining balance after an established number of days (i.e., 1% on balances past 30-day due date).

- Follow-up. If a customer does not pay within the allotted time period, you should initiate immediate follow-up action in the form of a letter or a telephone call. If you are afraid to make the call, then you should be prepared to lose your money. Record in writing any payment commitments a customer makes to you. If the "check is in the mail," allow a reasonable time

for the check to arrive. If it does not arrive, call
the customer back for an explanation.

- Send collection letters. Most collection letters
  are form letters that are designed to motivate
  people to pay on past due accounts. The typical set of collection letters uses more aggressive words as the past due period becomes
  older. Ultimately, the final letter in the series
  may simply advise the customer that the account is being turned over to a collection
  agency. You can obtain samples of different
  types of collection letters by checking out a
  book on the subject at your local library.

- Use collection agencies. Collection agencies
  are in business to collect past due accounts on
  behalf of their clients. A good agency is experienced in the latest collection techniques because this is their primary business. Their services are not cheap. Most agencies charge a
  percentage of the amount they collect, which
  can be as high as 50 percent or more.

TRUTH-IN-LENDING LAWS

The truth-in-lending laws are one part of the Consumer Protection Act. They were designed to protect
consumers, and enable them to shop intelligently for
the best interest rates and terms when they purchase
goods and services on credit. There are two important
features of the law you should be aware of if you offer
credit terms to your customers. You are required to
provide information to customers that clearly shows
them the dollar amount of your finance charges and
the annual percentage rate.

The law applies to most businesses who extend
credit to individuals. In addition, there are provisions
in the act to insure that consumer reporting activities
are conducted in a fair and equitable manner and that
the consumer's right to privacy is protected. For further information, contact:

Director
Office of Public Information
Federal Trade Commission
Washington, DC 20580
(202) 523-3598

HANDLING EXPORT SALES

If you plan to broaden your markets by exporting products, you will probably need the services of a freight forwarder. International freight forwarders are licensed by the Federal Maritime Commission and provide the knowledge to move domestic products to foreign destinations. A good forwarder is trained to advise you of the best ports of shipment at the least possible cost. In addition, they will prepare the necessary shipping documents, obtain the necessary licenses, book space on ocean vessels, arrange for transportation to and from the appropriate docks, and oversee all other shipping details.

The National Customs Brokers and Forwarders Association of America publishes a membership directory that can be purchased from the association. Members are listed both alphabetically and geographically. The directory also includes the addresses and telephone numbers of the Federal Maritime Commission's district offices. For further information, write:

National Customs Brokers and Forwarders
   Association of America
5 World Trade Center
New York, NY 10048
(212) 432-0050

Federal Maritime Commission
1100 L Street, NW
Washington, DC 20573
(202) 523-5911

FORECASTING SALES

Accurate sales forecasting is critical to any business. In many cases, your sales forecast will determine the level of other forecasts. For example, if you are a manufacturer of product A, and you overestimate the amount of product A you can sell, you may have overstocked raw materials needed to produce the product. The net results of a poor sales forecast is that you may not be running your plant at full capacity and you'll have excess inventory. Sales forecasting can be a very complex process and involve the use of hundreds of alternative strategies. In this section, we will cover some of the basic forecasting concepts.

DETERMINING MARKET POTENTIAL

Most markets are not homogeneous and are composed of groups of individuals and organizations that have diverse needs. In Chapter 7 on marketing, we referred to these groups as market segments and showed you how to use various marketing techniques to define and size each segment. Once that is accomplished, you can then apply various sales forecasting techniques to arrive at a sales estimate for your business. For example, if you were in the business of providing catering services, your market segment could include the following:

- Businesses that have seminars, meetings, banquets, and parties.
- Wedding receptions that could be further segmented by religious beliefs and ethnic groups.
- Charitable and political fund-raisers that could be further segmented by types of charitable organizations and political parties.

Once you have defined the segment of your market, you need to estimate the sales for each market segment. Because we covered this subject in detail in Chapter 7, we will discuss only the basic approaches in this section. In the catering business example, you could survey the businesses in your market area to determine the potential interest in using your ser-

Exhibit 9-1. Worksheet for Estimating the Size of Market Segments			
Market Segment	Estimated Size ($$ and People)	Average Unit Price	Source of Information

vices. The city clerk's office can tell you how many marriage licenses were issued over a period of time. At some point in the market segmentation analysis, you should be able to estimate the total size of each market segment by using the worksheet in Exhibit 9–1.

DETERMINING SALES PENETRATION

Once you have estimated the potential sales in each market segment, the next step is to determine the percent of each segment you believe you can capture. Start by analyzing the competition in each segment and include the following factors:

- Features and benefits of competitive products and services.
- Competitive prices and credit policies.
- The type and amount of advertising used by your competitors.
- Competitive selling and services techniques deployed.

After you have analyzed the competition in each segment, you can estimate the sales you believe you can capture by market segment. Your estimate should be realistic and backed by solid rationale. For example, you may want to first compare the services of your business to the services that are offered by your competitors. The worksheet in Exhibit 9–2 can be used to rank your competitors relative to each other.

Exhibit 9-2. Worksheet for Ranking Competitors			
Name of Competitor	**Estimated Annual Sales**	**Estimated Advertising Budget**	**Rank**

When you complete the competitive ranking analysis, you can develop realistic sales estimates. Let's assume that your business ranks in the "upper third" of the competitors in your market area. Assume that we know the following about a given segment of the market:

Number of competitors = 5
Average annual sales per competitor = $300,000
Annual sales of leading competitor = $550,000
Annual sales of bottom competitor = $200,000

Equal Share Assumption

This assumption assumes that your business successfully competes for an equal share of the market. Because you know there are five competitors with average annual sales of $300,000, you also know that total annual sales for the market are $1,500,000 ($300,000 × 5). Your share of the annual market sales would be one sixth of the total or $250,000 ($1,500,000/6).

FORECASTING SALES PERIODS

We showed you how to develop a total sales forecast for a given period of time (e.g., one year). Unfortunately, most businesses incur expenses on a monthly basis and they rely on monthly sales revenues to pay for expenses. To complete the sales forecasting process, we need to allocate the annual sales estimate into monthly sales estimates. The simple approach would be to divide sales by twelve months to obtain an average monthly sales forecast. Some businesses have stable sales patterns and can use this technique. However, the sales of most businesses are influenced by external forces including seasons, holidays, weather, or economic events.

The external forces that may affect the monthly sales of your business will be dependent upon the type and nature of your particular business. For example, seasonal sales could be influenced by the four seasons of the year — summer, fall, winter, and spring. Let's assume that you have conducted a seasonal analysis and have determined that your sales will occur on a percentage basis as follows:

Summer (June–August) = 40 percent of total sales

Fall (September–November) = 20 percent of total sales

Winter (December–February) = 15 percent of total sales

Spring (March–May) = 25 percent of total sales

If we apply the percentage estimates for each season to an annual sales forecast of $500,000, we can forecast our seasonal sales as follows:

Seasonal sales = (Percent of annual sales) × (Annual sales)

Summer sales = 40% ($500,000) = $200,000

Fall sales = 20% ($500,000) = $100,000

Winter sales = 15% ($500,000) = $75,000

Spring sales = 25% ($500,000) = $125,000

Sales could also be influenced by major holidays, such as Christmas and Easter. Let's assume that you have conducted a holiday analysis and have determined that your sales will occur on a percentage basis as follows:

The Christmas season will account for 25 percent of your total sales.

The Easter season will account for 20 percent of your total sales.

The remaining 55 percent of your sales will be spread equally throughout the year.

Sales could be influenced by weather patterns that are common in your market area. For example, if your business is an outside contracting business and, on average, it rains during the months of January through March in your market area, you may adjust your sales forecast as follows:

Only 10 percent of your total sales will be realized during the rainy season (January–March).

The remaining 90 percent of your sales will be spread equally throughout the year.

Sales could be influenced by economic events. For example, many people receive federal income tax refunds in April and May and are therefore in a "buying mood" for the big ticket items that your business sells. Your sales projection follows:

30 percent of your sales will occur as a result of tax refunds (April–May).
The remaining 70 percent of your sales will be spread equally throughout the year.

In conclusion, there are a number of ways sales forecasts can be spread over time. We have covered just a few examples in this section to show you how it is done, and to introduce you to some of the factors you may need to consider when you estimate monthly sales. When you have completed your forecast, use the following checklist to help verify the validity of your forecast.

Sales Forecast Checklist

1. Compare current sales with expected sales. Are they higher, lower, or the same? Can you explain the reasons for the major variances?

2. Compare current sales with prior period sales. What changes have taken place over the past year and why did they occur? If there were no changes, is that significant?

3. Break your sales down into meaningful categories. What products and services are selling well and why? What are the laggards and why?

4. Break your customers down into meaningful categories. Who were your top customers? Did 20 percent make up 80 percent of your sales? Should more attention be paid to cultivating existing customers or new customers?

5. When do most of your sales take place (e.g., time of day, season, etc.)? How can you apply this information to pricing, advertising, staffing, and the other operational requirements of your business?

6. Where are your sales coming from (e.g., store, region, territory, etc.)?

7. What are your sales categories (e.g., direct sales, distributors, mail-order, etc.)?

8. Rank the sales performance of your salespeople. Who were the outstanding performers and what made them successful?

9. What was the average sales amount and how does it compare to the average amount for the same period last year? Can you explain any deviations?

SOURCES FOR ADDITIONAL INFORMATION

All sales organizations and programs must have access to strategic information to function effectively. In this section, we have listed a few sources of sales information to help you get started.

CONSUMER INFORMATION

In 1970, the federal government established the Consumer Information Center to help other government agencies distribute consumer information to America's businesses. A Consumer Information Catalog is published quarterly and lists all of the best federal consumer booklets that are available through the Consumer Information Center. The catalog includes the prices of all booklets listed. To request a copy of the latest Consumer Information Catalog, write:

Consumer Information Center
Pueblo, CO 81009

CONSUMER PRODUCT SAFETY

The federal government's Consumer Product Safety Commission is responsible for enforcing the provisions of the Consumer Product Safety Act. The Commission requires businesses to report defects in products that could create a hazard to the buying public. Businesses are required to disclose corrective action programs, which are reviewed and approved by the Commission. The Commission also conducts research on product hazards. For further information, contact:

Office of Information and Public Affairs
Consumer Product Safety Commission
1111 18th Street, NW
Washington, DC 20207
(301) 492-6580

TRANSPORTATION SCHEDULES

Salespeople who travel frequently and use various forms of transportation must plan their trips in advance. Although most good travel agencies can provide you with transportation information, it is often helpful to rely on your own guide to assist in preplanning a trip. The Official Airline Guide, and Russell's Official National Motor Coach Guide, are available in a public library or good bookstore.

NATIONAL TELEPHONE DIRECTORY

One of the problems that salespeople face is finding the addresses and telephone numbers of people and companies that are not located in their immediate area. Directory assistance will give you telephone numbers but not addresses. The National Directory of Addresses and Telephone Numbers contains a listing of telephone numbers and addresses that are indexed by phone areas, zip codes, and business types. It also includes a section of selected toll-free numbers and is available in a public library.

PASSPORTS

It is essential that you apply early for a passport if you plan to travel abroad. If you are applying for your first passport, you must present in person a completed DSP-11 passport application form at a federal courthouse or post office. If you want to renew an existing passport, you may apply by mail, if your current passport was issued less than 12 years ago and you were at least 16 years old when it was issued. For complete information about how to apply for a passport, contact:

Passport Services
Bureau of Consular Affairs
1425 K Street NW
Washington, DC 20524
(202) 523-1355

WEATHER INFORMATION

Many sales programs require accurate and up-to-date weather information on a continuous basis (e.g., outside promotional programs). There are a number of private weather services available. Consult the "weather services" section of the Yellow Pages or contact the National Weather Association, which maintains a partial listing of private services.

National Weather Association
4400 Stamp Road
Temple Hills, MD 20748
(301) 899-3784

CONVENTIONS

There is a growing trend to meet and exchange sales information at conventions. Many conventions also feature trade shows and display areas. For more information, contact:

International Association of Conventions and Visitors Bureaus
P.O. Box 758
Champaign, IL 61820

TRADE ORGANIZATIONS

Gale's Encyclopedia of Associations lists a number of trade organizations that represent wholesalers and distributors engaged in various specialized activities. The encyclopedia is available in a good public library, or contact:

National Association of Wholesaler-Distributors
1725 K Street, NW
Washington, DC 20006
(202) 872-0085

10

Developing an Advertising Program

Advertising is the main ingredient of a company's promotional effort. It's also a critical support function to a sales program. Developing advertising and promotional programs that complement the activities of your sales force are an essential ingredient to the success of your business. For example, a sales force may be asked to concentrate on selling product A for the months of April and May. Meanwhile, product A is simultaneously promoted through different advertising media to support the sales program. By incorporating the message of your sales program into an advertising program, you provide your customers with the information they need to initiate a buy decision in your favor. In this chapter, we will cover the basic principles of advertising and show how they can be used to increase your sales.

THE PRINCIPLES OF ADVERTISING

The object of advertising is to communicate to your target market what your business offers to satisfy their needs. Advertising, if properly used, can be a cost effective way of promoting products and services because it can reach a vast number of people at a low contact cost per person. Anybody can develop a successful advertising campaign by following the basic steps that we cover in this section.

A common advertising objective is to increase sales as a result of advertising. Behind every objective, there should be at least one or more measurable goals that will tell you if you met your objective. For example, one your goals may be to increase the sales of product A by $100,000 as a direct result of a proposed advertising program. Will your proposed program allow you to measure the achievement of your objective in terms of new sales dollars? Your objective may be more qualitative in nature in that your intent is to create an awareness, or to educate your customer prospects about the features of your product. In any event, it is crucial that you establish objectives that will direct the context within which all of your advertising decisions will be made.

The following examples illustrate approaches that can be used to measure quantitative and qualitative objectives of an advertising program. Let's assume that you have selected a media for an ad that will cost you $500. You want to measure the effectiveness of the ad by determining if it pays for itself and returns a 10 percent profit to your business. The ad is placed with a coupon that offers a 25 percent discount on the advertised product and you have collected the following data:

$$
\begin{aligned}
\text{Cost of the ad} &= \$500 \\
\text{Retail price of the product} & \\
\text{after the 25 percent discount} &= \$10 \\
\text{Net profit per product} & \\
\text{after discount} &= \$1 \\
\text{Number of products sold} & \\
\text{as a result of ad} &= 1{,}000 \\
\text{Profit (loss) of ad campaign} &= (\text{net profit/product sold} \\
&\quad \times \text{\# of products sold}) - \\
&\quad (\text{cost of ad}) \\
&= (\$1 \times 2{,}000) - (\$500) \\
&= (\$2{,}000) - (\$500) \\
&= \$1{,}500
\end{aligned}
$$

The ad in the example returned a profit of $1,500 to the business. Now, let's assume that you placed another ad for $1,500. You want to determine if this ad improves the name recognition of your business. Based upon a random survey that you ran prior to placing the ad, 10 percent of the surveyed population recognized the name of your company. Your advertising goal is to increase your name recognition by 5 percent (i.e., 15 percent total) as a direct result of this ad. After the ad was run, you conducted the same survey that you ran prior to placing the ad. The survey results show that your name recognition increased to 18 percent. You therefore concluded that the ad program was a success.

MEDIA CONSIDERATIONS

Determining which advertising media to use is your next challenge. Which media options will economically reach your desired target market and appropriately convey your advertising message? There are a number of advertising sources available including newspapers, magazines, television, radio, trade journals, direct mail, and outdoor displays. To answer the initial question about which media to use, research each option to determine which medium best reaches your target market.

Each advertising media has distinct advantages and disadvantages. The medium you select must be consistent with the money you have to spend and must reach your target customers. It also must portray the market image of your products and services. For example, television offers viewers an opportunity to see your product during a spot advertisement and it is effectively used for this purpose. On the other hand, advertising a service on television is more difficult because of the intangible nature of services. It may be more appropriate to advertise services in some other, more appropriate media.

CUSTOMER PROFILES

Customer profile is the advertising term for the type of customer that is on average, reached by a given medium. It is another way of saying that a particular medium appeals to this type of customer. All reputable medium expend a significant amount of time and money to determine their respective customer profiles. For example, they can tell you where their customers reside, the average age, income, and marital status of the customer that fits their profile. Medium customer profile is available by request to the media that you are considering.

The Standard Rate and Data Service is one of the advertising industry's standard publications that covers media rates, audience, and customer profiles for the following:

- Consumer magazines
- Agricultural publications
- Business publications
- Daily and weekly newspapers
- Network radio and television
- Spot radio and television

- Transit sources
- Direct mailing lists

The SURDS is useful in matching your target market to the right media option. Copies of SURDS are available in a good public library. Most advertising agencies subscribe the publication, which has gained national recognition for its accuracy in reporting customer profile information.

REACH AND FREQUENCY

Reach is the total number of households that will be exposed to an advertising message by a particular medium over a given period of time. It is usually expressed as a percentage of the total households in a defined geographic area. For example, if the local newspaper delivers papers to 20,000 homes in a city that has a population of 40,000 homes, then the reach of the paper is 50 percent.

Frequency is the number exposure an advertisement receives by a person in a household. For example, if your newspaper advertisement is seen on average three times by people in a household, then the ad frequency is three. If we apply this frequency rate to our previous example, the total frequency would be 60,000 (20,000 subscribers $\times$ 3 frequency rate = 60,000). Reach and frequency factors vary between different advertising media. One of the keys to the success of your advertising program will be to determine when to spend advertising dollars on reach, versus frequency alternatives.

Reach works best when you want to introduce a new product or service to as many people as possible. It assumes that your advertising message is so compelling that people will respond to the ad on their first exposure. Incentives such as coupons and sales discounts are often used in these types of ads to attract attention.

Frequency works best when you want the customer to order your product or service directly from the ad. Frequency ads act as constant reminders to customers to initiate a buy decision. They are effective when time limits are placed on the ad, such as sale end dates.

ADVERTISING OBSOLESCENCE

The length of time you should run an ad program is an important consideration for two basic reasons: cost and message obsolescence. You should always consider the various factors that may influence ad success as a tradeoff against cost. As long as the value of the success factors exceed the cost of advertising, continue running the ad program. Success factors could include sales that are directly attributable to the ad and improved customer awareness for your business.

Everything ages over a period of time and advertising messages are no exception. Even the perfect advertisement program will, over time, lose its intended impact on your customers. If it is left in place long enough, it can cause a negative backlash among customers that are "tired of hearing the same old thing." As a rule of thumb, the optimum frequency number is between three and six times. The conviction is that once a customer has received your message three to six times, they will know about your product or service. If the frequency extends beyond six, you could be wasting your advertising dollars by paying for redundant messages.

MEDIA OPTIONS

Each advertising medium has its advantages and disadvantages for different businesses, products, and services. For example, television offers broad reach and dynamic presentation advantages. However, it is expensive and its demographic selectivity is limited. Newspaper advertising is relatively cheap, but has a short life cycle of about one day. Magazines offer longer life cycles than newspapers, but require long lead times to place an ad, which can be expensive. A summary of the various media options are shown in Exhibit 10–1.

NEWSPAPERS

One of the main advertising advantages of newspapers is that they are widely read and there is a short lead time to place an ad. The selectivity of ad loca-

Exhibit 10-1. Advertising Media Summary

Medium	Market Coverage	Type of Audience
Daily Newspapers	Single community or entire metro area.	Trends toward men, higher age, and income group.
Weekly Newspapers	Single community with some metro.	Residence of smaller communities.
Shoppers	Single community.	Bargain and convenience shoppers.
Telephone Directories	Geographic area.	Active shoppers.
Radio	Defined by station's location.	Selected audience defined by station broadcast.

Television	Defined by station's location.	Selected audience defined by station broadcast.
Transit	Local and metro communities.	Commuters and shoppers.
Outdoor	Entire metro area.	Auto drivers and commuters.
Local Magazines	Entire metro or state area.	Specialty groups.
National Magazines	Entire country with some regional issues.	Specialty groups.
Direct Mail	Controlled coverage.	Customized demographic selection.

tions allow you to focus in on your target market. For example, a sporting goods store can advertise in the paper's sports section, and the financial service business can advertise in the business section.

Because of the large volume of ads that appear in newspapers, it can be difficult to differentiate one ad from all of the others. Another disadvantage is that much of the paper's circulation is wasted. In our sporting goods store example, the only people that are likely to see our ad are the ones that read the sports section of the paper. There are a large number of newspaper readers who never read the sports section. And yet, newspaper advertising rates are based upon total, and not partial, circulation numbers. There are three general types of newspapers to consider:

1. Daily and weekly community papers
2. Metropolitan area papers
3. Daily and weekly national papers.

Shopper Magazines

Shoppers are magazine size tabloids that are usually printed on newsprint, are free, and displayed in stands at popular shopping locations. They are consumer oriented and offer inexpensive ad rates. Most are published either weekly or monthly. They have a very short shelf life so ads must be well written to be effective. Coupon ads tend to do well in shoppers.

Magazines and Journals

Magazines and journals are an effective way to reach your target market through demographics, geographic, product, or service related magazines. For example, there are magazines that cater to personal computer buffs, homeowners, outdoor enthusiasts, and photographers. There are numerous trade magazines and journals that are written for a particular industry or profession. Some magazines target specific demographic or geographic markets. For example, the American Bar Association publishes the ABA Journal nationwide, while California Lawyer is targeted at lawyers who practice in California. Magazines and journals typically enjoy a long shelf life in that they remain in the home or office for several weeks before they are thrown out. As a result, they are typically read by many individuals, which improves the frequency exposure of your ad. Full color display ads enhanced with special effects is another advantage of magazines.

The two biggest disadvantages of magazine advertising is their high cost and the long lead time needed to place an ad. Advertising in national magazines can cost thousands of dollars just for a single ad. Most ad copy must be submitted at least 60 to 90 days before the publication date of the magazine.

RADIO AND TELEVISION

Radio is an inexpensive broadcast medium that allows you to quickly create and change your advertising message. The medium offers a high degree of demographic segmentation and geographic selectivity. Buyers response is almost immediate, which make radio advertising relatively easy to measure. The disadvantage of radio is that it only provides for an audio message. Messages have a short life and have to be frequently repeated to attract the listener's attention.

Television uses both sight and sound to get your message across. Because television reaches large audiences, the cost per exposure is relatively low. However, the total dollar cost of television is high. Rates vary depending on the audience size, which fluctuates significantly throughout the day. Two well-known indexes that are used to measure television audience size are the Nielsen Station Index and the Arbitron Index.

DIRECT MAIL

You can be highly selective in choosing the target market for direct mail to minimize wasted circulation. The results from a direct mail advertising program are relatively easy to measure. A direct mail program can be initiated at any time without concern for superimposed lead times. Unlike newspapers, there are no other advertising distractions, and thus your advertising message will stand out.

However, direct mail is expensive. Over the years, it has developed the unwanted title of "junk mail," which means that most direct mail is thrown out before it ever gets read. Many direct mail experts consider a 3 to 5 percent response to a direct mail campaign a success. The types of direct mail programs to consider are:

- **Personal letters.** A letter is sent to a prospective customer that describes a product or service and presents a case for why the prospect would buy the offering.

- **Brochures.** Brochures are sent directly to a pre-qualified list of customer prospects. A cover letter is sometimes used to introduce the brochure.

- **Catalogs.** Catalogs are sent directly to pre-qualified customers through bulk mail channels.

- **Newsletters.** Newsletters contain helpful information as well as promotional information. They are sent to customer prospects on a recurring basis.

- **Flyers.** Flyers are similar to brochures, although they tend to cover less content and focus on the promotion of a specific product or service.

- **Price lists.** Price lists work well if customers are already aware of your product or service, which tend to fit shopping categories.

- **Samplers.** Product samples are an effective way of introducing new products.

TRADE SHOWS

Business and consumer trade shows have become a $60 billion industry in the United States. Business shows sell to businesses and tend to specialize by industry. They may or may not be open to the public depending upon the show. Consumer shows are made up of businesses who will sell to anybody at the show and are open to the public. One of the main advantages of trade shows is that they attract very targeted markets. The secret to your success at a trade show is to pick the right show that draws your target customers. Although the cost per sales lead at trade shows is low, the cost of booth space, display materials, and show staffing is expensive.

TELEPHONE DIRECTORIES

Telephone directories, or "Yellow Pages" are they are commonly called, cover a defined geographical area and are very popular with active shoppers. They are typically used by shoppers who have a need to purchase a specific product or service in the immediate future. Yellow page advertising is popular with brand name retailers, and retailers who offer specialized products and services. The primary disadvantage to yellow page advertising is the high advertising cost. Once an ad is placed, the copy can not be changed until the next edition comes out, which is usually once a year.

USING ADVERTISING AGENCIES

Should you employ the services of an advertising agency to assist you in developing and implementing your advertising program? The answer in part will depend upon the size of your business, what the agency can do for you, and how much you can afford. Advertising agencies can provide you with a number of services including:

- **Media selection.** Agencies will match your target market requirements against the most appropriate media options to assure the reach and frequency of your advertising program.
- **Ad copy.** Agency writers can create and edit all of the written copy for your ads.
- **Artwork.** Most agencies employ artists who can produce artwork to supplement your advertising program.

- **Strategies.** Agencies can survey your business and develop and test advertising strategies that leverage the benefits of your company, its products, and services.

- **Monitoring.** Agencies can monitor the performance of different advertising programs to help you determine if your advertising goals and objectives are being met.

If you are qualified, or can find people who are qualified to provide these services for you, you may decide that you don't need the services of an advertising agency. However, developing effective advertising programs can take up important business resources that could be better used elsewhere. A good agency knows how to tie all of the features and benefits of your business together into an advertising program that will probably be better than what you can develop on your own. You may discover that you can't afford the services of an established agency. Some of the smaller startup agencies will accept new clients in the interest of building a client portfolio.

If you are thinking about employing an agency, the check-out procedures remain the same regardless of size and reputation of the agency. Talk with the principals of the agency to find out everything you can about their firm. Some of the question you should ask are summarized as follows:

What is the size of the agency and how long has it been in business?

What types of businesses or industries does the agency specialize in?

What programs does the agency recommend to startup businesses?

Who are some of their small business customers?

What are the different levels and types of services that are offered by the agency?

What make this agency successful over the competitive agencies?

Who would be working with you and what are their qualifications?

What are the agency's fees and compensation terms?

Exhibit 10-2. Comparative Checklist for Advertising Agencies			
Checklist Question	Agency A	Agency B	Agency C
Did their references check out?			
Does the agency represent businesses similar to yours?			
What is the creative capability of the agency?			
How do you rate the people that will work on your account?			
How do you rate the agency's proposed advertising plan for your business?			
What is the overall experience of the agency?			
Total Agency Score			

Score the questions for each agency on a scale of 1 to 5 where 1 = poor and 5 = excellent. The agency with the highest total score should be your first choice.

If you plan to do a considerable amount of advertising, ask the agency to prepare a speculative proposal for your business. Speculative advertising proposals should cover the cost of agency services and an estimate of the expected results to your business. The in-depth contents of agency proposals will vary, depending upon their perception of the size of your account. If your account does not meet their minimum size requirements, they may not be willing to prepare a proposal.

Unfortunately, many of the good agencies will only accept new business clients that can qualify for a minimum monthly or annual fee. Getting an agency to accept your account can become the more challenging of the two problems. To solicit their interest in your business, stress the tremendous growth potential of your company and offer them factual analysis whenever possible. Consider offering the agency an "escalating fee schedule" where, over a period of time, you incrementally increase your monthly agency fees. The advantage of this system is that your fees would increase as the agency helps you grow your business. The worksheet in Exhibit 10–2 will help you select the advertising agency that best meets the overall needs of your business.

USING DISCOUNTS EFFECTIVELY

Discounts and coupons are a way of life for many businesses. The widest variety of discounts are directed at consumers. When you offer a special discount off your product, your salespeople can use the discount to help make the sale. The discount can also be used to motivate the customer to buy larger quantities than what they would normally buy. The different types of discounts are covered in Exhibit 10–3.

The customer can mail in a coupon to receive the discount, or receive the discount by presenting the coupon at the point of purchase. If carefully designed and administered, consumer discounts can significantly increase your sales. They also offer the added advantage of providing a quantitative measurement of the effectiveness of an ad. You can count the coupons to determine how many people responded to a specific ad program.

FREE ADVERTISING

Magazines, newspapers, radio and television stations, are constantly looking for new ideas that would be of interest to their readers, listeners, and viewers. Whenever you are about to offer a new product or service, contact the appropriate media officials to see if they would be interested in featuring an article or spot time to cover your new release. If something exciting and newsworthy happens to your business, initiate the same contacts. Editorial coverage can be more effective than your own advertising — and it's free.

To start a free advertising program, develop a contact list of any media that you believe would be interested in receiving information about your business. The list could include local radio and television news stations, metropolitan newspapers, and trade journals. Contact each source and find out who handles unsolicited news requests. A typical submission

Exhibit 10-3. Promoting with Premiums

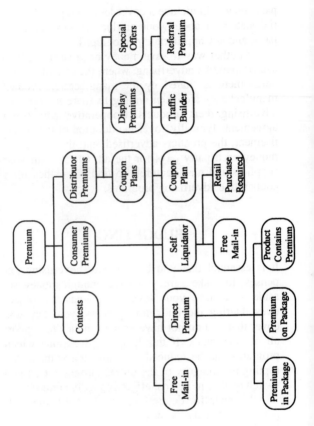

package would include a cover letter, proposed editorial statement about your product, service, or company, and any appropriate photographs.

Another way to save money on advertising is to use cooperative advertising, where the cost of the advertisement is shared by the manufacturer. Product manufacturers are often willing to share the cost for advertising their products. Cooperative advertising agreements typically cover the duration of the advertisement, the products advertised, and the amount of money each party pays for the ad. Check with your suppliers and manufacturers to find out if they offer cooperative advertising programs.

BUDGETING

It is essential that you budget your advertising expenses, to make sure you have enough money set aside to achieve your advertising goals and objectives. During the budgeting process, you may discover that you do not have enough money to support all of your goals. If this happens, determine which programs can be reduced or eliminated without disrupting the integrity of the overall program. Can you switch over to more cost effective media options?

Methods for determining total advertising budgets vary widely between industries and different businesses. Most businesses use one of three approaches to determine how much they should spend on advertising: (1) Percent of sales approach, (2) Top-down approach, and (3) Competitive approach. The three approaches are not mutually exclusive from each other. In many cases, it may be practical to apply all three approaches to develop your advertising budget.

PERCENT OF SALES APPROACH

Of the three approaches covered, the percent of sales approach is the easiest to understand. You forecast sales over a period of time (i.e., monthly or annually) and then allocate a fixed percentage of total sales to advertising. The challenge in the approach is to determine what percent to use for advertising that makes sense. Find out what advertising percent other businesses like yours are using for their advertising budgets. Review the advertisements that are being placed in the local newspaper and estimate the cost of competitor ads. Once you know how much your competitors are spending, you can establish a percentage rate that either takes you above, or below what your competition is spending. The disadvantage of the percent of sales budget approach is that it has nothing to do with balancing advertising expenses against your advertising goals. The percent of sales can be calculated as follows:

$$
\begin{aligned}
\text{Time period covered} &= 1 \text{ year}\\
\text{Annual sales forecast} &= \$500{,}000\\
\text{Advertising percent allocation} &= 5\%\\
\text{Annual advertising budget} &= (\text{Annual sales forecast} \times \text{Advertising percent allocation})\\
&= (\$500{,}000 \times 5\%)\\
&= \$25{,}000
\end{aligned}
$$

TOP-DOWN APPROACH

The top-down approach is used to determine the advertising budget you need to achieve the goals and objectives of your program. Costs are broken down by what is needed to fund the successful completion of each advertising goal. It includes a media breakdown by time period and event. Here is how the top-down approach works. Assume that one of your advertising goals is to sell 1,000 units of product A over the next two weeks. You intend to accomplish this goal by advertising the product in the local newspaper and on a local radio station. The worksheet in Exhibit 10–4 can be used to monitor the success of your ad program.

Exhibit 10-4. Advertising Effectiveness Worksheet for the Top-Down Approach				
Media Source	**Cost**	**Frequency**	**Anticipate Sales**	**Actual Sales**
Radio				
Newspaper				

COMPETITIVE APPROACH

Successful salespeople know their competitor's products, sales tactics, and advertising programs just as well as they know their own. One way they obtain this information is by constantly evaluating the ads of competitors. In the process, they learn about the competitors product features and benefits, where the competitive ads are being placed, and what the competition is spending on advertising. If you know what the per-column-inch rates are for a display ad in the local paper, you can quickly estimate a competitor's advertising cost. The following example illustrates how you can quantify the estimated monthly advertising cost of a competitor:

$$
\begin{aligned}
\text{Column inches advertised}& \\
\text{in local paper per month} &= 50 \text{ inches} \\
\text{Cost per column inch} &= \$25 \\
\text{Total estimated advertising costs} &= (\text{Total column} \\
&\quad \text{inches} \times \text{Cost per} \\
&\quad \text{column inch}) \\
&= (50 \times \$25) \\
&= \$1{,}250
\end{aligned}
$$

THE FINAL BUDGET

Once all of your advertising goals and objectives have been established, and you have determined what you need to spend to achieve your objectives, you need to complete the final budget. A typical advertising budget is prepared monthly and expenses are accumulated on a year-to-date basis in a format similar to what we have shown in Exhibit 10–5.

During the course of any one month, you will be comparing the results of each ad program that you run using the various techniques that we have discussed. At the same time, you should be monitoring your total advertising expenses. Are you within budget and can you explain any actual to budget variances that may occur?

LEGAL ASPECTS OF ADVERTISING

Both the Federal Trade Commission and state enforcement agencies can order you to stop running an advertisement if they consider it to be false or mis-

Exhibit 10-5. Advertising Budget Worksheet				
Budget Account	**Month**		**Year to Date**	
	Budget	**Actual**	**Budget**	**Actual**
Media				
Newspapers				
Radio and TV				
Promotions				
Trade Shows				
Displays				
Overhead Expenses				
Salaries				
Supplies				
Travel				
Total				

leading. These agencies can also order you to run a retraction stating that your ad was deceptive. Deceptive advertising can severely damage the reputation of your business, and could also result in law suits from you customers and competitors. The two checklists that follow cover the basic do's and don'ts of proper advertising:

DO CHECKLIST

1. Do be accurate and truthful about your products and services.

2. Do get permission to use endorsements before you place an endorsement ad.

3. Do get a release if your ad features a picture of someone or uses a person's name.

4. Do have sufficient quantities on hand to cover the demand generated by an ad or state that quantities are limited in the ad.

DON'T CHECKLIST

1. Don't place misleading or deceptive ads. The government merely has to show that your ad had deceptive qualities.

2. Don't make false statements. You can be held liable, even if you were unaware of the fact that the statement was false.

3. Don't state that your product or service is free when there are attached conditions, unless the conditions are clearly stated in the ad.

4. Don't claim that your price is a savings unless you previously offered the same product or service at a higher price.

5. Don't use bait and switch tactics. It is against state and federal laws to advertise a product and then tell customers it is not available, which is an indication that you never intended to sell the item.

SOURCES FOR ADDITIONAL INFORMATION

The practice of good public relations to supplement your advertising program is as essential to the local bakery as it is to General Motors. Public relations is defined as "the act of dealing with people successfully, with an emphasis on activities that are beneficial to the public and the good will of the business." For further information, write:

Public Relation Society of America
845 Third Avenue
New York, NY 10022
(212) 751-1940

BOOKS

Risk Free Advertising by Victor Wademan (John Wiley)

How to Write a Good Advertisement by Victor Schwab (Wilshire Book Co.)

How to Get Big Results from a Small Advertising Budget by Cynthia Smith (Hawthorne Books)

How to be Your Own Advertising Agency by Herbert Holtje (AMACOM, a division of the American Management Association)

How to Advertise and Promote Your Business by Connie McClung Siegel (John Wiley)

PART THREE

ACCOUNTING FOR THE BUSINESS

11

Handling Insurance and Risk Management

Insurance should be an important part of your overall business strategy because it not only provides protection for your business, but for yourself as well. For a relatively small amount of money, you can protect your assets against the potential of a far greater loss. Without the protection of insurance, a major loss could cause you to lose your business, and depending upon your type of business organization (i.e., proprietorship versus corporation), you could also be personally liable.

Risk management is an insurance term that means managing the potential risks that could adversely affect your business. There are many different ways other than buying insurance to manage and minimize business risks. For example, you may decide to install a sprinkler system in your warehouse to reduce the risk of fire damage to your product inventory. The fact that you may have an insurance policy that also covers product damage due to fire, is an added risk management decision you may have made to further protect your inventory.

FOUR TYPES OF INSURANCE YOU NEED

The four basic types of insurance are property, liability, life, and health. Property insurance protects against business property losses. Liability insurance protects the business against accidents that may occur on the premises of your business, or as a result of someone who works for you. Life and health insurance provides compensation to employees for losses sustained as a result of illness or death.

PROPERTY INSURANCE

Property insurance protects the physical assets or property of your business against loss. This includes real property, buildings, equipment, office machines, supplies, and inventories. The different types of property insurance are summarized as follows:

- **Business loss insurance.** This type of property insurance covers you against the loss of profits or commission that occur if some identified event in the policy happens. For example, if a high percentage of business is dependent upon sales in Florida, you could apply for a sales protection policy that would reimburse you for lost sales in Florida that were attributable to a hurricane.

- **Comprehensive property insurance.** This popular form of property insurance covers damages to all company property, except property that is specifically excluded from the policy. You therefore have the assurance of knowing that all company assets are covered with the exceptions specified. You are therefore less likely to duplicate property coverage by caring a single comprehensive policy, as opposed to several individual comprehensive policies.

- **Comprehensive insurance.** Comprehensive insurance can be used to supplement a comprehensive property insurance policy when additional coverage is needed. The specific business assets that are covered by comprehensive policies are identified in the policy. The vandalism part of these policies can be expensive, depending upon where your business is located (i.e., high crime areas). Special protection for unique events like earthquakes can be added to comprehensive policies for an additional fee.

- **Crime insurance.** Burglaries and other acts of crime on or off your business premises, by anybody, including your own employees, can be covered by crime insurance. These policies can be very specific or broad in nature. For example, you can have a policy that covers just the cash in the office safe, company securities, the theft of an employee's personal items when they are working, or a variety of other more complex options. These policies are relatively expensive, since it is often difficult to prove most thefts, and the insurance company must therefore pay for the lose based on the word of the person suffering the loss. Cost preventive tactics include the use of employee lockers, and the removable and off-site deposit of cash at the end of each business day.

- **Fire insurance.** Fire policies cover loses due to fire, lightning, and losses to goods temporarily removed from the site of the fire — such as perishable items that were removed from a burning warehouse and damaged in the process. Additional fire protection, such as theft that may occur as a result of the fire, are usually excluded from standard fire insurance policies. They can be added to the main policy for an additional fee. Make sure you know what is, and what is not, covered by fire insurance policies.

- **Marine insurance.** Marine insurance is used by specialized businesses such as importers who may own imported commodities while they are being transported by ship from their port of origin. The insurance covers damages to imported goods while they are being transported on open water.

- **Power insurance.** Power insurance covers certain types of machinery and equipment, such as boilers and power generating equipment that are susceptible to explosions.

- **Transportation insurance.** Goods are covered while they are being transported from one location to another by land routes. Many carriers carry transportation insurance as a part of their service. Check with the carrier first, so that you don't duplicate coverage.

- **Vehicle damage insurance.** This insurance is usually included as an option under the vehicle liability insurance policy. The policy covers damages that occur to company owned vehicles as a result of an accident with another vehicle, or an "act of God," such as hail damage. One way to help reduce or control your cost for this type of insurance is to restrict the number of people who are authorized to drive company-owned vehicles. Conduct driver record checks on employees before you allow them to drive company vehicles.

LIABILITY INSURANCE

All businesses are subject to laws governing negligence, which includes customers, employees, or anyone else who is a part of your business. If you fail to do something and are found to be negligent, you are liable for damages. You can also obtain liability insurance to protect you against the negligence of others, or from natural events. The different types of liability insurance are summarized as follows:

- **Business interruption insurance.** Interruption insurance covers your business if it is forced to shut down as a result of events that are identified in the policy (e.g., fire, natural disaster, etc.). These policies pay the business a defined sum of money to compensate for the events that have interrupted the operation of the business.

- **Comprehensive liability insurance.** Comprehensive policies can be purchased to cover liabilities that may extend beyond the coverage of your basic liability policies. Sometimes called umbrella policies, they may cover unforeseen multimillion-dollar liability related lawsuits to protect your business against an extreme loss. Although these types of policies offer high end coverage, they are not as expensive as you might think. The low probability of multimillion dollar liability awards against small business is relatively low, which keeps the cost of these policies down.

- **Key employee insurance.** You can purchase insurance that will compensate the business for the loss of life or disability of "key" employees who are identified in the policy. The policies are designed to help reduce the risks that are associated with the loss of an important employee.

- **Product liability insurance.** This type of insurance is important if your business sells a product that could cause injury or damage to the consumer, or user of the product. For example, if you own a restaurant, then the consumers of your food could be susceptible to food poisoning. A toy manufacturer might be concerned about an injury a toy might cause to a child. Services can also be covered under a product liability policy. Judgments against medical doctors for wrong diagnostic decisions are common. However, consultants in all types of services can be held liable for the services they render.

- **Vehicle liability insurance.** Vehicle liability covers the injuries to people that occur as a result of the negligence of a driver in a company-owned vehicle. Your business is also liable for accidents involving employee owned vehicles, if the vehicle is being used for company business (i.e., en route to a company designated function).

- **Workers' compensation insurance.** This insurance is usually required by law in most states and protects the employer against the liability of an employee accident. The basic policy covers medical expenses, rehabilitation costs, and loss of wages to employees injured on the job. In cases of severe injuries where an employee is permanently injured, compensation can be awarded to them in a settlement amount or in payments over a defined period of time. As an employer, you are required to provide employees with a safe place to work, hire safety conscious people, provide safe tools for the job, and advise employees of safety precautions. If you fail to abide by the workers' compensation laws, you can be held liable for damages that extend beyond the standard coverage of the policy.

LIFE AND HEALTH INSURANCE

Life and health insurance provides compensation to the employees for sustained losses as a result of illness or death. Employees are reimbursed for medical expenses and in the event of an employee's death, the beneficiaries receive life insurance benefits.

- **Basic health insurance.** Basic insurance policies include an employee paid annual deductible fee before the basic policy goes into effect. Most health insurance policies are designed to cover routine medical care, such are physician office visits and most routine hospital care procedures (e.g., X-rays, lab tests, etc.).

- **Basic life insurance.** Life insurance provides financial protection to the employee's family or named beneficiaries in the event of the employee's death. The face value of a typical policy is usually some multiple of the employee's gross annual salary or a fixed amount.

- **Major medical insurance.** Major medical generally covers hospitalization and all the associated medical costs that are incurred during an employee's stay in a hospital.

- **Dental insurance.** Reimbursement for routine to complex dental care is covered in dental insurance policies. Routine care includes preventive dental procedures (e.g., cleaning) and normal fillings. Some policies cover more expensive dental care procedures such as orthodontal work and dental surgery.

- **Preventive health insurance.** Some companies will maintain a separate health insurance policy that covers routine physical exams, eye exams, prescription vision products, drug treatment programs, and hearing instruments.

HOW TO ESTABLISH A RISK MANAGEMENT PROGRAM

The insurance program for your business will depend upon the type of business you start, what you can afford, and the amount of risk you are willing to accept. There are three basic steps involved in developing a risk management program:

1. Identify business risks.
2. Assess business risks.
3. Implement a risk avoidance program.

IDENTIFYING RISKS

The first step in the risk management plan is to identify every conceivable risk that can affect your business. This could include losses due to fires, earthquakes, damage caused by one of your products, or some injury that occurs on company property. You must decide which of the risks you have listed are likely, or unlikely to occur, and what the occurrence of the risk would cost. Most risks fall into three categories: property, liability, and life.

Property Risks

Property risks generally cover loss or damage to the property of the business. This includes real estate property, personal property, office supplies, and equipment. Property insurance protects against the loss of business and personal property. Personal property includes employee owned items that are stolen from company property. Property risk categories to consider include:

- **Fire risks.** Fires that result from internal causes (e.g., electrical failure), lightning, or external causes (e.g., arson), are covered by most standard fire insurance policies. Fire risks that may not be covered include smoke damage to products, and the rent for temporary office space. You pay extra for additional fire protection.

- **Natural disaster risks.** Perils such as hail, floods, windstorms, and earthquakes are covered under all risk property insurance. Flood damage and earthquakes are often priced as separate options.

- **Crime risks.** Standard crime insurance covers theft, vandalism, and burglary that occur on business property. Add-on risk coverage options may be needed to cover crime affecting employees on business trips, or the theft of company property in an employee's homes.

- **Motor vehicle risks.** Liability, comprehensive, and collision insurance covers risks to company-owned vehicles including cars, trucks, and service vehicles, such as lift-trucks.

Liability Risks

Liability risks are subject to various state and federal laws that cover negligence. Negligence refers to the failure of a business to exercise a degree of care that results in damages that are incurred by a person, persons, or another business. A negligence example would be a business's failure to remove spilled water from the entrance, which caused a person to slip. If the fall results in physical damage to the person, the business could be financially liable. Liability risk categories to consider include:

- **Standard liability.** Standard business liability policies are similar to the liability part of a homeowner's policy. They cover payments for personal injuries that occur on company property, related medical expenses, and legal costs. Optional coverage is usually required for perils that occur off company property (e.g., company-owned vehicle accident).

- **Product and service liability risks.** If you produce products or provide a service that could cause an injury to a consumer, then product liability insurance covers these occurrences. Product risk examples include food and children's toys. Service examples might include a liability suit brought against a company for providing erroneous financial advice.

Life and Health Risks

Life and health insurance provides compensation to employees, owners, or in some cases the business itself, for losses that are sustained as a result of the illness or death of someone associated with the business. We are all familiar with life and health employee benefits that are common in many business. In some situations, it may make sense to initiate a life insurance policy where the company itself is the beneficiary. For example, there may be a "key employee" who works for the company. If that person should die, his or her death would result in a serious disruption to the activities of the business. Hence, the life insurance benefits would be used by the company to help reduce the impact of the loss.

ASSESSING BUSINESS RISKS

At this point in the discussion, we will assume that you have developed a comprehensive list of risks that are of concern to you and your business. You must now decide if the risks that you have listed are likely or unlikely to occur, and the significance that the occurrence would have on your business. For example, let's assume that you own a construction business. You maintain a main office that is responsible for dispatching your employees to customer locations where the construction work is performed. Account billing is computerized and performed out of the main office. If a fire destroyed your main office and all of its contents, the risks to your business would be $20,000 in office furnishings and equipment.

You are not concerned about the potential loss of the office furnishings and equipment since it can be easily replaced and you can afford the $20,000 potential loss. You are concerned about the loss of your accounting records since your business carries on average $100,000 in accounts receivable. If the records were destroyed, you would have no way to follow-up on customer payments. However, if you backed up you accounting records daily, and stored the disk file in a safe off-site location, you could significantly reduce the risk of fire damage to your business. On a risk scale of 1 to 5 (1 = low and 5 = high), you have rated the fire risk as a 2 after you implemented the file backup procedure.

You are concerned about the liability that could affect your business as a result of negligence. What would happen if one of your customers slips on the floor in your main office? As you consider the liability issues, you realize that your customers seldom visit your main office. Most of your customer contact occurs between yourself and your employees at the customer's site. However, because of the nature of the services that you provide (e.g., construction), any

Exhibit 11-1. Insurance Risk Worksheet				
Type of Insurance	Risk Covered	Cost Per Year	Probability of Occurrence	Risk Ranking*
Liability				
Property				
*Rank insurance risk on a scale of 1 to 5, where 1=low and 5=high.				

one of your employees could be responsible for a negligent act while on a customer's premises. You are also concerned about any liability issue that could occur as a result of an injury to an employee in the main office. On a risk scale of 1 to 5, you have rated liability risk as a 5.

Let's assume that most of the people who work for your contracting business are young married people just starting families. Even though you are in the construction business, the loss of life due to a job related accident is very low for your type of construction business. However, you know that your employees are concerned about what would happen to their families if they were to die. Finding and retaining good employees is important to your business, and you believe that by offering a life insurance benefit, your business would have a better chance of retaining good employees. On a risk scale of 1 to 5 you have rated life insurance as a 3. All of your risk estimates can be summarized in a worksheet similar to the one we have prepared in Exhibit 11–1.

IMPLEMENTING A RISK AVOIDANCE PROGRAM

At this point, you should have a list that identifies the various risks to your business, which can be prioritized on a high-to-low scale (i.e., 1 = low and 5 = high in our examples). Part of the analysis that you may have used to prioritize different risks was to con-

sider different programs you could implement to reduce risk levels. We provided you with an example of
storing accounting records off-site to reduce the risk
of fire.

In theory, all risks can be covered by unlimited
insurance policies. In reality, no business can afford
to pay for every insurance policy they would need
to eliminate all risks. Risk avoidance programs are
important for a number of reasons. The occurrence of
an adverse event that could have been avoided dis-
rupts the productivity of any business. The event
costs money that the business may not be able to afford.

There are many risk avoidance techniques that
can be implemented at little or no cost to a business.
The fact that you may have a risk avoidance program
in place could substantially reduce the insurance premiums for that risk. It is for this reason that we encourage you to develop a risk avoidance program
before you shop for insurance alternatives. The following list of questions can be used to help you develop a program for your business:

Risk Avoidance Questions

1. Can you hire someone else to perform high-
   risk business tasks for the business?

2. Can you save insurance premiums by bond-
   ing certain employees?

3. Can you store backup copies of critical business documents and files at an off-site location?

4. Can you economically install fire prevention
   devices?

5. Can you offer your employees safety manuals that are supplemented with periodic
   safety meetings?

6. Can you encourage or require employees to
   wear safety equipment whenever appropriate?

7. Can you conduct periodic on-site and off-site
   inspections to assure that your business is in
   compliance with the risk avoidance procedures your have implemented?

After weighing all of your prevention alternatives, implement the programs that make sense. Solicit the advice of your employees and associates. They will often come up with viable ideas that you did not consider. In some cases, you may decide to supplement parts of your risk prevention program with an insurance program.

DEVELOPING AN INSURANCE PROGRAM

At this point, you should have developed a shopping list of insurance needs. The focus of this section will be to take you through the steps that must be completed to develop an insurance program. The steps that we cover will provide you with the foundation to evaluate various insurance products that cover different risks.

SEEKING PROFESSIONAL ADVICE

The insurance industry is a complex and highly competitive business that is constantly changing. Most small business people do not have the training or knowledge to master all of the various aspects of the subject. Nor can they justify hiring full-time insurance experts to assist them in developing a cost effective insurance program that adequately covers the critical risks of their business. There are three basic sources to choose from when seeking professional advice: company insurance agents, general insurance agents, and insurance consultants.

Company Insurance Agents

As the name implies, a company agent represents the insurance offerings of a single insurance company. All states require insurance agents to pass different levels of state tests and proficiency exams before they can represent and sell insurance to anybody. For this reason, most insurance agents are professionally qualified to sell the insurance that they represent. In addition to the state licensing requirement, most of the large insurance companies conduct extensive training programs for their agents. However, the emphasis is on selling policies, which can influence the objectivity of an agent during consultation discussions.

General Insurance Agents

General insurance agents represent more than one insurance company and are therefore not bound by the insurance products of any one company. They are usually in a better position to recommend an insurance product from a company that best meets your needs, since they have more than one company to draw from. Like all insurance agents, their primary focus is to sell policies.

Insurance Consultants

Insurance consultants are listed in the yellow pages and offer independent insurance advice and consultation on a fee for service basis. Most insurance consultants charge an hourly fee for their service and many will quote a fixed fee for certain assignments. Fees vary widely throughout the country and depend upon the level of the consultant's expertise. They do not, and should not, work for an insurance company to protect their objectivity. The advantage of working with an insurance consultant is that you have some assurance of obtaining an objective opinion on the various aspects of your insurance needs.

Cross-check the advice that different agents offer you to see if you are getting consistent answers to your insurance questions. If you discover an inconsistent answer, probe for additional information until you are satisfied that you have the right answer.

ANALYZING INSURANCE COSTS

The bottom line of containing risk with any insurance program is costs. Cost for the same coverage can vary widely between different insurance companies. For example, one insurance company may have experienced high fire liability for your type of business, while another has experienced low liability rates. Hence, the fire insurance rate, or any other rates for that matter, can vary significantly between companies. Talk to as many different insurance agents as possible to get advice on the different aspects of your insurance program and to obtain competitive cost estimates. Insurance cost-saving issues that you should consider are summarized as follows:

1. Compare different deductible options to find the one you can afford.
2. Look for policy discounts by consolidating your insurance under one company.
3. Check all policies to make sure you are not paying for duplicated coverage.
4. Perform a competitive review of all of your policies at least once a year.

CREATING AN INSURANCE PLAN

Plan your insurance program to make sure it covers your insurance needs today, and can be modified to accommodate any changes to your business tomorrow. A good plan should provide you with the best coverage possible for what you can afford to pay, and offer you a level of risk protection that meets you expectations. The insurance plan worksheet in Exhibit 11–2 contains the basic information that you, or anyone else in your company would need to access, should it become necessary to initiate an insurance claim.

In the event of your absence, other people in your business should know how to access the insurance plan in the event of an emergency. This would include the location of the back-up plan that should be stored at an off-site location. Keep accurate copies of your insurance policies in the plan document.

Exhibit 11-2. Basic Insurance Plan Informations Worksheet

Type of Insurance	Company	Who to Contact	Risk Covered	Annual Premium
Liability				
Property				
Power				
Theft				

Records of all claims, losses, and recoveries should also be kept in the insurance plan document.

SELECTING AN INSURANCE COMPANY

The selection of an insurance company is dependent upon a number of factors. If possible, select a single company that can cover all of your needs. The advantages are twofold. First, you'll only have one company to deal with for all of your insurance matters. Second, many companies offer premium discounts for multiple policies. The disadvantage is that you may not be able to minimize your total insurance costs by dealing with a single company. One company may offer you the lowest cost on standard liability insurance, but cannot offer you a competitive fire insurance policy.

COMPARING COSTS

Comparing the cost between different policies may not be a simple task unless you are comparing two identical policies. However, there are differences in most policies that you need to be aware of before you can make a valid cost comparison. For example, one company may charge you a higher premium, but pays a dividend at the end of the insurance period that could bring their premium below the cost of their closest competitor. The worksheet in Exhibit 11–3

Exhibit 11-3. Insurance Policy Cost Comparison Worksheet			
Company	**Coverage**	**Deductible Amounts**	**Cost Per $1,000 of Coverage**

has been designed to help you compare the costs of different policies.

Our exhibit demonstrates that cost comparisons between companies can be further complicated by the amount of the deductible. If you are willing to accept a high deductible, then Company A would be a logical choice, whereas Company B would be the best choice for the low deductible policy.

DETERMINING FINANCIAL STABILITY

The A.M. Best Company is one of the insurance industry's most authoritative rating services. They publish Best's Insurance Reports which include insurance company ratings that cover the company's reliability in dealing with policyholders, their net worth, and other important financial factors. The reports are available in a good public library, or you can ask your agent to show you the company's rating report. The three highest rating classes are A+, A, and B+. If you are considering a company that ranks below these ratings, you may want to conduct some additional research.

SOURCES FOR ADDITIONAL INFORMATION

Business Insurance by Edwin White (Prentice-Hall)

Risk Management and Insurance by Arthur Williams and Richard Heins (McGraw-Hill)

Risk and Insurance by Mark Greene (Southwest Publishing)

12

Accounting for Your Business

Maintaining a timely and accurate accounting system is fundamental to the success of any business. Not only will accounting reports help you make the right decisions, but they will be required by third party investors such as banks. In addition, accurate accounting records will help you keep your taxes to a minimum by providing the basis for taking all legal deductions. This chapter will show you how to collect the accounting information that you need to manage your business.

UNDERSTANDING FINANCIAL STATEMENTS

Financial statements are prepared at the end of each accounting period, which is usually monthly. There are two basic statements that every business should prepare — an income statement and a balance sheet. The income statement reflects the operations of the business over a period of time (i.e., one month). The balance sheet reflects the financial position of the company at a reported point in time (i.e., last day of the month). You can prepare these reports yourself, or have them prepared for you by an accountant. First, we want to explain both reports in more detail and show you how to use the information in the reports to run your business.

THE INCOME STATEMENT

The income statement is sometimes called a profit and loss statement because it compares the total income of a business against total expenses over a defined period of time to determine the profits or losses of the business. Most astute businesses owners will prepare an income statement at the end of each month to determine monthly profits.

Exhibit 12-1. Income Statement for the ABC Company		
Account Description	**Month**	**Year to Date**
Sales		
Product Sales	$9,500	$16,800
Service Sales	21,000	47,975
Total Gross Sales	$30,500	$64,775
Less: Returns and Allowances	$500	$10,000
Net Sales	$30,000	$54,775
Cost of Goods Sold		
Product Inventory	$9,200	$17,110
Direct Service Labor	2,000	3,000
Service Related Materials	400	940
Cost of Goods Sold	$11,600	$21,050
Gross Profits	$18,400	$33,725
Total Operating Expenses		
Salaries	$10,200	$23,400
Rent and Utilities	700	3,000
Taxes and Insurance	2,500	3,480
Total Operating Expenses	$13,400	$29,880
Net Profit	**$5,000**	**$3,845**

Total gross sales for the small business in Exhibit 12–1 are the sum of all product and service-related sales. Any sales discount or allowances for returned sales items are deducted from gross sales to determine net sales. The next major column on the income statement is the cost of sales. Cost of sales reflect all of the direct costs that are associated with the actual products and services that were sold.

The calculation for the cost of sales of products is slightly different than for service costs. The product inventory in Exhibit 12–1 was valued at $9,200, which was determined by what the business actually paid for the inventory. The cost of services that were rendered during the month included two cost categories: (1) direct labor and (2) materials. Direct labor was the cost of the labor used to perform the services. The cost of all materials used to perform the services is recorded on the next line. Total product and service costs are summarized in the total cost of goods sold line (e.g., $11,600) and are subtracted from net sales to determine gross profit.

The next column on the report covers operating expenses, which include selling and administrative expenses. Selling expenses include sales commissions, salaries, and advertising. Administrative expenses cover management salaries, office related expenses, rent, and equipment. Total operating expenses are then deducted from the gross profit line to determine pretax profit. Federal, state, and local taxes are deducted from pretax profit to arrive at the "bottom line" in the income statement or the net profits. If the resultant number is negative, then the number reflects the net losses that have occurred.

THE BALANCE SHEET

The balance sheet records the financial condition of a company at a designated point in time, which is usually the last day of the month. There are three main sections on the report; (1) assets, (2) liabilities, and (3) equity. Total assets are always equal to the sum of total liabilities and equity to balance the report and hence the name balance sheet (see Exhibit 12–2).

Here is how to interpret the balance sheet report. The asset column of the report is dived into two asset categories. Current assets are all assets that can be converted into cash within a relatively short period of time (i.e., 30 to 60 days) and includes cash and accounts receivable. Plant and equipment are the assets that the business intends to keep longer than a year and includes items such as real property and equipment.

The depreciation line item below the plant and

Exhibit 12-2. Balance Sheet for the ABC Company

Account Description	December 31
Assets	
Current assets	$66,000
Plant and Equipment	22,000
LESS: Depreciation	(10,000)
Total assets	**$78,000**
Liabilities	
Current liabilities	$25,000
Long term liabilities	30,000
Total liabilities	**$55,000**
Equity	
Owner's equity	$23,000
Total liabilities and equity	**$78,000**

equipment line is deducted from fixed assets. As certain fixed assets get older, they depreciate in value, which is why depreciation is deducted from fixed assets. We will cover the concept of depreciation in more detail later in the chapter. The sum of the two asset categories are added together to determine the total value of asset for the company. The next major column on the balance sheet covers the liability section of the report. Liabilities are the debts and obligations that are owed by the business. Current liabilities are due and payable within the next 12 months. Long-term liabilities are due over a period exceeding 12 months, such as long-term notes payable to the bank. Short and long-term liabilities are added together to determine total liabilities.

The equity line on the balance sheet is sometimes called net worth, since it is the claim that the business owner has on the assets of the business after all business liabilities have been liquidated. In a proprietorship or partnership, the equity belongs to the proprietor or partners. In a corporate organization, the equity belongs to the stockholders.

PURPOSE OF FINANCIAL STATEMENTS

Both the income statement and balance sheet are extremely important management tools. Since they represent the condition of a business at a point in time, the astute entrepreneur can take whatever may be the appropriate management action necessary, based upon the reported financial condition of the company. For example, if sales and profits are up, then it may be appropriate to continue "business as usual." On the other hand, if sales and profits are down, the reports can be used to identify where the problems are, so that corrective action can be taken.

KEEPING ACCOUNTING RECORDS

Accounting records are used to produce financial statements that we just discussed and other essential accounting reports. The record system that you set up for your business must be simple to maintain and use. In fact, every record you keep should have some relevance to your business, such as supporting a tax deduction or providing you with meaningful information. Avoid keeping records that contribute nothing to the overall success of your business just for the sake of keeping records. Worthless records are costly to maintain and make it more difficult to find the record you need.

Because of tax implications, your recordkeeping system should be consistent and accurate. For example, if you intend to deduct automobile mileage for business trips from your tax return, the mileage and destinations should be consistently recorded in a standard travel log. Avoid the shoe box approach, where everything gets recorded on whatever piece of paper happens to be lying around at the time. Although ac-

Exhibit 12-3. Maintaining Sales Records by Types of Products Sold			
Date of Sale	Amount	Units Sold	Product Sold
4/16/199X	$4,900	50	Product A
4/18/199X	$6,300	34	Product B
4/22/199X	$7,900	54	Product C

counting records can be used to create a variety of meaningful accounting reports, we will cover only the three essential sets of records and supporting reports that you must maintain to create an income statement and a balance sheet — sales records, accounts receivable records, and cash disbursements.

SALES RECORDS

Sales records should be subdivided into categories that are meaningful to your business. For example, the income statement in Exhibit 12–1 split sales into two different categories; (1) product and (2) service sales. Therefore, in order to achieve this level of sales reporting detail, product and service sales records should also be maintained in separate categories. Let's assume you are interested in reporting sales at a more detailed level (i.e., types of products sold). The recordkeeping method that we used in Exhibit 12–3 to maintain sales records would provide you with important historical information about how different products have sold in the past.

   If your business sells three types of products (A, B, and C), then daily sales records could be sorted by sales type and date, at any time, to determine the historical sales trends for your business. The sales report in Exhibit 12–4 could be generated from the sales record log, to provide sales information by product or service line.

ACCOUNTS RECEIVABLE RECORDS

Accounts receivable are the moneys owed to the business for sales that were made on credit. It is vitally important to maintain accurate accounts receivable records to assure the timely collection of monies

Exhibit 12-4. Historical Sales Report for the ABC Company				
Sales Month	Product A	Product B	Product C	Total Sales
April	$14,900	$50,010	$23,890	$88,800
May	$6,300	$34,600	$44,500	$85,400
June	$7,900	$54,100	$35,000	$97,000

Exhibit 12-5. Sales and Accounts Receivable Records for the ABC Company

Date of Sale	Amount	Product Type	Sales Type	Billing Information
4/15/19—	$14,900	A	Cash	
4/17/19—	$6,300	B	Credit	John Doe, 123 Main St.
4/21/19—	$7,900	C	Visa Card	

due the company. The payment of your credit accounts are dependent upon the accuracy of these records. If we add additional information to the sales recordkeeping system that we developed in the previous section, we could maintain our sales and accounts receivable records on the same system (see Exhibit 12–5).

By adding the "Sales Type" and "Billing Address" columns to the sales record keeping system, we can record all of the information needed to maintain accounts receivable records. For example, under the sales type column, we would record "AR" for accounts receivable if the sale was a credit sale. We would then add the customer's billing address for all credit related sales. The letters "PD" could be used to designate a "paid in cash" sales transaction.

Accounts receivable are aged at the end of each month in what accountants call an aged accounts receivable report. The report lists unpaid accounts and shows the past due status of customer accounts. A typical aged accounts receivable report is shown in Exhibit 12–6.

The report shows accounts by name that are unpaid for 30, 60, 90, and over-90 days. Let's assume that you have extended credit terms to your customers which allows them to pay for the products they receive in 30 days. By this definition, any account that is in the 60, 90, or over-90 day column on the report is past due. The accounts receivable report is used to contact accounts to solicit past due payments.

CASH DISBURSEMENTS RECORDS

Cash disbursements are the monies paid to fund the operation of the business. Most businesses pay for their expenses by checks, which are retained in the cash disbursements records system for tax audit purposes. Petty cash may be used to pay for items such as small incidental office supplies that do not justify writing a check. Exhibit 12–7 illustrates one method of recording monthly cash disbursements.

At the end of the month, cash disbursement records are sub-totaled and recorded in the income statement under the appropriate expense categories

Exhibit 12-6. Accounts Receivable Report for the ABC Company				
Account Name	Current	30-60 Days	61-90 Days	Over 90 Days
Ryco Corp.	$14,900			
John Doe	$6,300			
S.Jones		$4,600		
Jane Smith			$3,390	
Atlas Steel				$6,780
Total Due	$21,200	$4,600	$3,390	$6,780

Exhibit 12-7. Cash Disbursements Records for the ABC Company			
Date of Expense	Type of Expense	Amount	Explanation
4/15/19-	Direct labor	$5,600	Service related labor
4/17/19-	Taxes	$4,700	State excise taxes
4/21/19-	Inventory	$4,600	30 units of Product A

on the income statement. The following list of questions offers some ideas for reducing the expenses within your company:

Cost Cutting Questions

1. If you had to reduce each expense by 10 percent, what would you lose in real value.

2. If you had to reduce total expenses by 10 percent, what expenses would you cut in order of priority? What would be the subsequent consequences of each cut made?

3. What expenses have you added since you started the business? Why were they added and do you still need to include these expenses in the current operation of your business?

4. Have you recently reviewed all of the purchases that have been made to determine if you are paying competitive prices? Have any of your suppliers increased their prices over the last six months and can you use a less expensive alternate supplier?

5. Do you consistently take discount options when they are offered?

OTHER RECORDS

There are a number of other important accounting records that you will want to keep for your business. Some recordkeeping systems are unique to an industry, while others are unique to your specific type of business. The following list will provide you with some examples of additional records that you may want to maintain.

- **Equipment records.** All the equipment that is used in your business should be included in its own record keeping system. Records should show the date of purchase, the purchase price, the name of the seller, and any applicable warranty information. Equipment records are used to calculate the depreciation on the balance sheet and can be referred to in the event of a fire or theft.

- **Payroll records.** Payroll records must be maintained to accurately record labor expenses on the income statement and to provide proof to a tax auditor that you have paid the appropriate payroll taxes. These records are also used to produce W-2 forms for your employees at the end of the year showing total tax withholding information.

- **Tax records.** The IRS requires that you maintain certain tax records over different periods of time, depending upon the type of record. Contact you local office of the Internal Revenue Service and ask them to send you a copy of their latest Tax Record Retention Schedule. The schedule will show you what tax records you must keep and for how long.

ACCOUNT MANAGEMENT TECHNIQUES

Accounting systems provide information to business owners that can be used to manage their business. In this section, we will cover some of the important account management areas to consider. We'll also show you how to develop an effective account management program for your business.

CREDIT MANAGEMENT

In many businesses, you may need to extend credit to your customers to remain competitive. As we explained in the previous sections, credit sales are recorded in the accounts receivable account and reported monthly in an aged accounts receivable report.

Accounts receivable should be closely monitored to make sure that there is a reasonable relationship between total credit sales and total sales. This statement begs the question of what is a "reasonable relationship?" Unfortunately, there is no standard answer since the relationship varies widely between businesses and industry. However, the following example will help you develop a standard for your business.

Susan owned a small but very successful appliance shop in a growing metropolitan area. Her liberal credit terms were one of the main reasons for the success of her business. She allowed her customers to take up to "90 interest-free days" to pay for purchased appliances. At the end of each month, Susan would calculate the relationship between total receivables and total sales as follows:

$$\text{Receivable-to-sales ratio} = \frac{\text{Total accounts receivable}}{\text{Total credit sales}}$$

$$= \frac{\$700,000}{\$250,000}$$

$$= 2.8$$

The ratio of 2.8 indicated to Susan that on average, it took her 2.8 months to receive, or collect, a credit sales dollar from her customers. The ratio was consistent with the store's 90 day or 3 month credit policy, even though the appliance store industry average was only 1 month. The example illustrates an exception to what most businesses would consider to be a reasonable receivable-to-sales ratio, which would be in the range of 1.0 to 1.5 months.

CREDIT MANAGEMENT CHECKLIST

1. Establish or tighten credit policies to discourage slow-paying customers.
2. Establish a collection follow-up system where you consistently send out collection letters and make appropriate telephone collection calls.

3. Refuse credit to customers who do not meet their past due debt obligations to your business.

4. Charge interest and billing fees on past due accounts.

5. Initiate aggressive collection activities (e.g., small claims court, collection agency) on all accounts that are over 60 to 90 days past due, unless the customer has made payment terms that meet with your approval.

ACCOUNTS PAYABLE MANAGEMENT

Accounts payable cover the purchases that are financed by a supplier through extended credit terms. Terms can vary from very strict, such as cash on delivery terms, to lenient net 90 days terms, which means that the total payment is due in 90 days. The proper management of accounts payable is important to any business that relies on good relations with its suppliers. For this reason, accountants created an aged accounts payable report that is very similar in format to the aged accounts receivable report (see Exhibit 12–8).

The basic purpose of the report is to let you know when payments are due to your suppliers, and to "flag" any payments that are past due. Good supplier relations depend upon the timely payment of their invoices. If your business has always been a prompt payer, and times get tough, your suppliers are more likely to return the favor by extending liberal credit terms to help you through an adverse situation.

INVENTORY MANAGEMENT

In certain types of businesses (i.e., retail and manufacturing), inventory can account for more than 50 percent of current assets. If the maintenance of inventory levels will be a significant part of your business, you need to closely manage inventory levels. You should know at all times if your inventory levels are consistent with the current sales levels, because it costs money to carry excess inventory. Excess inventory is an expensive proposition for a number of reasons.

Exhibit 12-8. Aged Accounts Payable Report for the ABC Company				
Vendor Name	Current Due	30-60 Days	61-90 Days	Over 90 Days
Ryco Corp.	$14,900			
Johnson Inc.	$6,300			
Jones Stores		$4,600		
Smith Co.			$3,390	
Atlas Steel				$6,780
Total Due	**$21,200**	**$4,600**	**$3,390**	**$6,780**

- Storage. It costs money to store and insure surplus inventory levels.

- Finance. Purchased inventory items tie up working capital that can not be used for the operation of the business.

- Theft. Higher inventory levels are more susceptible to theft and pilferage.

- Records. Additional administrative costs are required to maintain excessive inventory records.

- Taxes. In many states, inventory levels are taxed separately. Excess inventory levels can result in additional tax obligations.

One of the primary causes of failures in inventory intensive businesses results from maintaining inventory levels that are either excessive or inadequate. Inventory ratios can be used to indicate whether levels are in line with industry standards. For example, the inventory to cost of sales ratio can be used to compare inventory value to the cost of sales.

For example, let's assume that the ABC Company closed out the accounting month of January, and recorded an inventory value on their balance sheet of $260,000. Their cost of sales for the month was $223,000. The inventory value to cost of sales (IVCS) ratio can be calculated as follows:

$$\text{IVCS Ratio} = \frac{(\text{Inventory value})}{(\text{Cost of sales})}$$

$$= \frac{(\$260,000)}{(\$223,000)}$$

$$= 117\%$$

In our example, we maintained 17 percent more inventory that what was required to support sales. One could argue that the surplus inventory was justified to make sure that no out-of-stock conditions occurred. If the ratio had been allowed to drop below 100 percent, then there would not have been enough inventory on hand to meet sales demands. As a result, the ABC Company would not have been able to meet its sales objectives.

PROFITABILITY MANAGEMENT

As an entrepreneur, one of your goals might be to maximize your wealth. Profitability is one of the most important measures you can use to determine your financial growth. There are several ways profitability can be measured to determine how well your business is performing in the aggregate.

Gross Profit Ratio

This ratio is the relationship between gross profit and sales. Gross profit is sales, less the cost of sales, which includes direct labor and materials.

Gross profit = Total sales − Direct cost of sales

The gross profit ratio is an efficiency indicator for your business and can be calculated as follows:

$$\text{Gross profit ratio} = \frac{\text{(Gross profit)}}{\text{(Sales)}}$$

If the cost of sales are equal to sales, then the ratio will be zero, which would mean that the business would, at best, be breaking even. A positive ratio is an indicator of efficiency and profitability. The ratio is used to monitor the cost of sales from one period to the next. A fall in the ratio would indicate rising costs.

Net Income Ratio

This ratio is the relationship between net income, which is sales less all direct and indirect costs.

Net income = (Sales) − (Direct cost of sales + Indirect cost of sales)

The net income ratio is an overall effectiveness indicator for your business and can be calculated as follows:

$$\text{Net income ratio} = \frac{\text{(Net income)}}{\text{(Sales)}}$$

The number should be positive, which would indicate that the business is making a profit. If net income is a negative number, then the business would be in a loss position.

INTERNAL CONTROLS MANAGEMENT

Internal controls are the organization's plan to safeguard its assets, check on the accuracy of its accounting data, promote operational efficiency, and encourage adherence to managerial policies. It is the means by which the owner can protect and control the successful operation of the business. The essential components of internal controls are:

- Authority. Hiring competent and trustworthy personnel with clear lines of authority is essential to maintain internal controls.

- Responsibilities. The adequate segregation of responsibilities helps to prevent the possibility of collusion between two or more employees.

- Procedures. The implementation of proper procedures help to prevent the violation of internal control standards.

- Records. Proper recordkeeping can discourage internal control violations.

- Assets. Tight controls over assets that have a "street value" can discourage theft.

- Audits. Consistent independent checks and audits on controls is an essential component to the overall control process.

Internal controls work by dividing responsibilities for handling key phases of business transactions. Cross-checking the results will provide early detection of errors, losses from embezzlement, fraud, or carelessness. The deployment of internal control procedures discourages improper actions.

CHOOSING AN ACCOUNTING SYSTEM

In selecting an accounting system that is right for your business, you must examine various options available to you. These options are set forth here, along with their advantages and disadvantages. Keep in mind that the accounting system you select will influence how your accounting records will be maintained.

CASH AND ACCRUAL OPTIONS

Cash accounting systems are simpler to understand and maintain than accrual systems. Many small businesses use cash as the basis for keeping their accounting books. For example, if you are operating a fast food business, and most of your sales result in cash transactions, then you have no need to maintain account receivable records. In a single store operation, there is probably no need to maintain extensive inventories. Your total sales (i.e., cash receipts) are recorded by a cash register at the end of each business day. At the end of the month, you simply deduct the cash that you paid out for expenses (i.e., labor and materials) from total cash receipts to determine your profits.

Cash accounting systems work well for businesses that operate in an environment where there is a close one-on-one relationship between the period in which sales and expenses occurred. For example, at the end of a reporting month, total expenses for the month would closely reflect the actual cost of goods sold during the month. This point is important to assure the accurate calculation of monthly profits and losses.

Let's assume that we are at the end of the month and you want to determine if your fast food restaurant made a profit or loss. The monthly accounting transactions for the restaurant are summarized as follows:

Assume

$$\text{Cash sales} = \$10,000$$
$$\text{Total operating expenses} = \$4,000$$
$$\text{Total payroll expenses} = \$3,000$$

Then

$$\text{Total profit} = (\text{Cash Sales}) - (\text{Total operating expenses} + \text{Total payroll expenses})$$
$$= \$3,000$$

Assume that you close out the accounting books for the month satisfied with the fact that your business made a $3,000 profit. Next month, you receive a $4,000 invoice from one of your suppliers for a food delivery they forgot to bill you for last month. If you had recorded the invoice in last month's income statement, your restaurant would have incurred the following loss:

$$\text{Cash sales} = \$10,000$$
$$\text{Total operating expenses} = \$8,000$$
$$\text{Total payroll expenses} = \$3,000$$

$$
\begin{aligned}
\text{Total profit (loss)} &= (\text{Cash sales}) - (\text{Total operating} \\
&\quad \text{expenses} + \text{Total payroll} \\
&\quad \text{expenses}) \\
&= (\$10,000) - (\$12,000 + \$3,000) \\
&= (\$5,000)
\end{aligned}
$$

As the example illustrates, the major disadvantage of the cash accounting system is timing. If cash sales and expenses are not recorded in the right time period, the income statement for the business will not accurately reflect profits or losses. This problem is eliminated if you elect to use the accrual option.

Under the accrual system, each item is entered into the accounting records as sales or expenses are incurred, without regard for when the sales payment or expense payments are due. In our previous example, we would have recorded the delivery and expense of the food shipment the moment it arrived at the restaurant. At the end of the month, inventory levels would have been adjusted to show the exact costs of the inventory that was used during the month to obtain an accurate accounting of profits or loses.

More accurate recordkeeping systems cost money, which is the disadvantage of the accrual system. However, carefully weigh the intangible "value" of paying more to obtain more accurate or timely accounting records. Talk to your associates who are knowledgeable in accounting principles before you make a decision on the type of accounting system you will select for your business.

SINGLE AND DOUBLE ENTRY OPTIONS

A single entry accounting system is one in which only cash and personal account records are maintained. It is easier to maintain than a double entry system but it is not self-balancing, since debits do not equal credits. For this reason, single entry systems must be carefully maintained. They are acceptable for small business where accounting transactions are infrequent.

Double entry accounting systems are more common and popular than their single entry counterpart. As the name suggests, a debit and credit in the same amount is made for each transaction in an accounting journal. A journal is a chronological accounting record of every accounting transaction. At the end of the month, the debits in the journal will equal the credits — if they were accurately recorded (i.e., the books balance).

ASSET DEPRECIATION OPTIONS

We talked briefly about depreciation when we discussed the concept of the balance sheet. Depreciation is considered an expense to the business just like any other expense. Depreciation expense gets charged against certain fixed assets that depreciate in value over time such as equipment, computers, furniture, and other similar items. The loss of value could be attributable to obsolescence, and the general use of the asset. There are two basic accounting methods that are used to calculate depreciation — straight line and declining balance. Straight line depreciation is based on the expected life of the asset. The following example illustrates how the straight line method is used to determine depreciation expense:

Straight Line Depreciation Method

Let's assume you purchased a $5,000 personal computer that has an expected "asset life" of 5 years. This means that at the end of the fifth year, the computer will be obsolete or worn out, based upon your best judgment. In other words, at the end of the fifth year, the asset will be worth nothing. The annual depreciation expense of the personal computer can be easily calculated.

$$\text{Annual depreciation expense} = \text{Total asset cost/asset life}$$

$$= \frac{\$5,000}{5}$$

$$= \$1,000\,/\,\text{Year}$$

Declining Balance Depreciation Method

The declining balance depreciation method can be used if it is to your advantage to obtain a quicker write-off of an asset. Under this method, assets are depreciated by a percent of their remaining balance each year. The depreciation expense of the personal computer that was used in the previous example can be easily calculated for each year of the asset's useful life of 5 years. The declining balance percentage is based upon twice the equivalent straight line percentage. The following calculation illustrates how the declining balance method is used to determine depreciation expense:

$$\text{Declining balance percentage} = 2(\text{straight line percentage})$$

$$= 2 \times \frac{1,000}{5,000}$$

$$= 2 \times .20$$

$$= .40$$

Annual depreciation expense = (declining balance percentage) (asset value balance

Year 1 = .40 × \$5,000	=	\$2,000
Year 2 = .40 × \$3,000	=	\$1,200
Year 3 = .40 × \$1,800	=	\$ 720
Year 4 = .40 × \$1,080	=	\$ 432
Year 5 = .40 × \$ 648	=	\$ 259
Total		\$4,611

The total straight line depreciation of the personal computer after five years was exactly \$5,000. Under the declining balance method, it was only \$4,611, since it is mathematically impossible to obtain the exact value of the asset under this method. This is one of the disadvantages of using the declining balance method. You cannot take the full write-off if you use the declining balance method. However, the method allows you to take more of the depreciation write-off in the early years of the asset's life. This may be a desirable feature for assets that have a high rate of early obsolescence, or when early tax deductions are beneficial to your business.

USING ACCOUNTING SERVICES

All of the accounting functions that we have discussed can be performed by you, or you can hire an accountant to perform the services for you. There are three different types of accounting professionals to consider: (1) bookkeeper, (2) accountant, or (3) certified public accountant. The choice you make regarding the type of accounting professional you need will depend upon your own level of accounting knowledge, and the accounting complexities of your business. In any event, a good accounting professional will contribute to your business in the following ways:

1. Help you setup an appropriate accounting system for your business.
2. Help organize and supervise the maintenance of all accounting records.
3. Provide timely, accurate, and useful accounting reports.
4. Implement appropriate financial controls to help prevent theft and the loss of money.
5. Prepare timely tax reports to assure that you take advantage of all legal and applicable tax deductions.
6. Provide accounting advice on how to run your business.

BOOKKEEPERS

Bookkeepers are proficient at maintaining the accounting books for the businesses that they represent. They are proficient at recording sales and expenses as they occur and are generally qualified to prepare your end-of-month accounting reports such as the income statement, balance sheet, accounts receivable, and accounts payable reports. Most bookkeepers do not have a college degree in accounting, and hence are limited in their ability to offer you in-depth advice and consultation on the reports that they prepare for your business.

ACCOUNTANTS

The primary difference between a bookkeeper and an accountant is a college degree. A typical accountant has a bachelor of arts degree in accounting from a college or university. In addition, he or she may have an advanced accounting degree such as a masters of business administration (MBA) degree in accounting. Most accountants are fully qualified to prepare financial statements and accounting reports that are needed to run a business. Because of their academic background, they are generally qualified to interpret and offer you accounting advice that may be pertinent to your business.

CERTIFIED PUBLIC ACCOUNTANTS

Certified public accountants (CPAs) have a degree in accounting and have taken an extensive set of state exams to acquire the title of CPA, which is recognized as one of the highest levels of achievement within the accounting profession. CPAs must conform to very strict state and federal regulations relative to the accounting accuracy of any reports that they prepare on behalf of a business they represent (i.e., Financial statements). For example, if your income statement is prepared and certified by a CPA, it implies a much higher level of "report integrity," than if the same report were prepared by a bookkeeper or accountant. This is an important consideration if you are relying on the information in your financial reports to support loan or investor agreements. For this reason, the cost of CPA accounting services is higher than the comparable cost of an accountant's services.

The list of questions that follows will help you when you interview accounting candidates. You can use the same questions in employee interviews for accounting positions within your company.

ACCOUNTANT INTERVIEW QUESTIONS

1. Does the candidate have business experience that matches the needs of your business?
2. Does the candidate belong to a professional association?
3. What are the candidate's views regarding his or her scope of responsibilities to a business?
4. What specific small business experience does the candidate have to offer?

5. What are the candidate's views regarding the most to least important accounting functions?

6. What types of accounting advice and consultation can the candidate offer you that will help you run a more efficient business?

7. What references can you call to verify the candidate's qualifications.

TAX PLANNING

Going into business will expose you to a different set of tax laws that may be new to you. Some of the laws were enacted to encourage individuals to start their own businesses. Others were passed for various reasons that could help or hinder you, depending on how you organize your business.

SALES AND USE TAXES

Almost every business that sells products, and in some cases services, will have to pay a sales or use tax. In some cases, wholesalers are excluded from the taxes. Check with your state's office of the controller to find out if your business will be liable for either sales or use taxes. Sales taxes are imposed for the privilege of doing business in a state. Since the tax is imposed on all retailers, it is really a tax on the buyer and not the seller. The use tax is an excise tax imposed by various states on the storage and use of tangible materials to conduct business in the state. The tax is used to complement the sales tax, so that all tangible items either sold or utilized are taxed.

UNEMPLOYMENT TAXES

The federal and state unemployment tax systems enable workers who have lost their jobs to apply for unemployment compensation. Federal unemployment tax is computed on the first $7,000 in wages paid to each employee and is paid by the employer. Each state has its own unemployment tax requirements. Check with your state's employment tax agency to find out the specific requirements for your business.

EXPENSE DEDUCTIONS

The various tax agencies define business expenses as the normal and current cost of running a business. To be tax deductible, a business expense must be both ordinary and necessary to the operation of the business. An ordinary expense is one that is common and accepted in your field of business. A necessary expense is one that is helpful and appropriate for your business.

Ordinary and necessary business expenses are legally deductible in most small businesses. For example, let's assume that you are conducting fly fishing classes as a part of your outdoor business. Fly fishing tackle are "commonly accepted" tools of the fly fishing educational trade, and hence would be tax deductible. In addition, you also conduct rafting trips. The rafts would be considered a "necessary business expense," and are tax deductible even though this equipment might be considered "pleasure equipment" by the IRS under a non-business situation..

All business expenses must be kept separate from personal expenses. In fact, if business and personal expenses are combined, a tax auditor can disallow the entire business tax deduction. For this reason, always maintain a separate set of accounting books and checking accounts for your business.

COMPUTERIZING ACCOUNTING SYSTEMS

There are many excellent computerized accounting programs available that have been designed to run on inexpensive personal computers. They range in cost from less than a hundred dollars for simple application, to several hundred dollars for the more complex applications. Many of the applications include spreadsheets, database features, and special report generation capabilities that can prove to be very beneficial to use as your business grows and expands. Almost all basic accounting systems will, at a minimum, perform the recordkeeping and reporting functions that we have covered in this chapter.

Selecting the computer system that is right for your business can be fun, and frustrating at the same time. The selection process starts with the basic component — the personal computer hardware. The minimum hardware and operating software configurations that are required to run most accounting applications are summarized as follows:

- **Memory:** 4 megabytes or more of memory are required to support most basic accounting applications.

- **Fixed disk:** 80 megabytes or more of memory is required to support most basic accounting applications.

- **DOS operating system:** Version 6.0 or a later version is required to support most basic accounting applications (e.g., IBM or Microsoft).

- **Windows operating system:** Microsoft version 3.0 or a later version of their Windows operating system is required to support most basic accounting applications.

- **IBM OS/2 operating system:** Version 2.0 or a later version is required to support most basic accounting applications.

Assuming that you have access to a personal computer that meets our minimum configuration standards, visit the computer stores in your area that carry complete lines of application software. Ask the store representative to show you the application accounting software that they carry. Review the advertised features on the shipping cartons, and write down the name of the application and features that appear to meet your requirements. The shipping carton will also list the minimum computer configuration requirements that are needed to run each application.

Make sure the application will run on your personal computer. Write the software manufacturers and ask them to send you a detailed brochure on the applications that are of interest to you. Find out if they have a demonstration disk that you can try before you buy, or a 30-day money back guarantee if you are not satisfied.

Ask your business and accounting associate to recommend brand name accounting applications. If you encounter difficulty in locating specific products, write to software mail order companies and ask them to send you their latest catalog. Egghead Software is a good mail order company to contact at the following address:

Egghead Software
22011 S.E. 51st Street
Issaquah, WA 98027-7299
1 (800) 344-4323

If you decide to automate your accounting systems, you should select the most advanced application that you feel conformable with today, but make sure it also includes features that will support the growth of your business. If you select a very basic accounting system, and later discover that you need more advanced features that are not offered in the basic system, the conversion to another more advanced system can be a costly experience.

Automated accounting systems are not for everybody. There are a number of manual bookkeeping systems that are available for just about every industry and business. To find out what may be available for your business, contact the trade associations that serve your industry. They are listed in the *Gale's Encyclopedia of Associations,* which is available in a good public library. Manual bookkeeping systems are also available through stationery and office supply stores.

SOURCES FOR ADDITIONAL INFORMATION

A number of tax services, national accounting firms, and independent accountants will maintain your accounting record, prepare essential accounting reports, and all appropriate tax returns. They are listed in the yellow pages of your telephone directory under accountants. Write the Small Business Administration, Washington, DC 20416 and request a copy of the Small Business Tax Workshop Guide.

The Institute of Management Accountants can provide you with a list of members who reside in your area. As is the case with many professional organizations, the association stresses the professional services of its members. For further information, contact:

Institute of Management Accountants
10 Paragon Drive
Montvale, NJ 07645
(201) 573-9000

COLLECTION AGENCIES

Accounts receivable that are difficult or impossible to collect can become a serious problem for any business. Collection agencies can help you collect on difficult accounts. They are listed in the yellow pages or you can contact the American Collectors Association and obtain a directory of their members.

American Collectors Association
P.O. Box 35106
Minneapolis, MN 55435
(612) 926-6547

13

Selecting the Best Legal Structure for Your Business

One of the most important decisions you will make when you set up your business will be choosing its legal form of ownership. With changing tax laws and increased concerns over business liability, you need to investigate the various advantages and disadvantages of different ownership forms. Each form has a different level of complexities to consider. Some may require the advice of a specialist, such as an accountant or attorney. In this chapter, we'll cover several organizational options, liability considerations, and employee issues. We'll also cover issues to consider when selecting a name and location for your company. The choices for a business format are sole proprietorship, partnership, and corporation.

EVALUATING ORGANIZATIONAL ISSUES

There are several questions you should ask yourself to determine the legal organizational form that's best for you. Your answers to the questions that we have included in this section will help you to determine the organizational structure that best fits your needs. We have included a brief explanation behind each of the following questions:

- Are you going into business by yourself? If you plan to be the sole owner of your new company, then you may want to consider a sole proprietorship structure.

- Do you possess all the requisite skills and the funds to manage the business until it makes money? If your answer is "no" to this question, consider the partnership or corporate organizational alternatives.

- If you do not plan to go into business alone, how many partners or associates will you need and how active will they be? Consider the two basic partnership structures that are discussed in this chapter.

- Do you need partners or stockholders to help finance the business? If the answer is "yes," carefully evaluate the partnership and corporation structures.

- How much personal liability are you prepared to accept, and are you willing to risk losing your personal assets if the business goes bankrupt? If you are concerned about your personal liability, consider the corporate structure alternatives.

- What degree of control do you wish to retain over your business? The proprietorship and limited partnership structures offer you the greatest amount of control.

- How much government regulation are you willing to accept? Proprietorships enjoy the least amount of controls and regulations.

- Who will run the business if you are incapacitated for any period of time?

Your answers to these questions will help you choose a legal business form that's best for you. Whatever you initially decide, your decision is not permanent. You can always change the form of your company to accommodate changing needs as your business grows.

LEGAL FORMS TO CONSIDER

Laws that govern business forms are under the jurisdiction of the city, state, or federal government, depending upon the form you choose. Each form has different applications affecting personal liability, management, and taxation. There are five legal forms that a business can take:

- **Sole Proprietorship.** A business owned and controlled by an individual.

- **General Partnership.** Two or more individuals who have agreed to pool their capital, work together and share in the management and profits of conducting a business.

- **Limited Partnership.** Two or more individuals who have agreed to pool their capital, share in the profits, and allow a general partner or partners to manage the business.

- **Corporation.** A legal entity that exists separate from the people who create it. The corporation is owned by its shareholders and run by a board of directors elected by the shareholders.

- **Limited Liability Corporation.** A limited liability corporation is a business structure that combines the benefits of a partnership for tax purposes, with the benefits of a corporation for liability purposes.

There are advantages and disadvantages to each legal structure. Examine all of the organizational characteristics presented here to determine the one that best meets your needs.

SOLE PROPRIETORSHIP

The sole proprietorship is the simplest business form to set up, and is the oldest and most common form of business in the United States. It is usually financed by the person who owns the business. Forming a sole proprietorship is simply a matter of contacting the local city, or county clerk's office to obtain a business license. A small registration fee is usually required. If your business is engaged in interstate commerce, you may need a federal permit or license. For example, federal licenses are required for meat processing, interstate transportation, and investment advisory service businesses.

Of all the business forms, the sole proprietorship gives you the strongest control over managing the business. There are no partners to consult with on decisions, or board of directors to satisfy. You may have employees with varying degrees of accountability, but the ultimate decision making responsibility rests with you. If you are the sole owner of the business, all of the profits from the business belong to you.

There are some disadvantages to the sole proprietorship. Banks and other financial sources are reluctant to loan money to sole proprietors. The sole proprietor may have a limited net worth, and therefore may not have sufficient collateral to qualify for a loan. If something happens to the sole proprietor such as a long-term disability, there is the added concern from the investors about who would run the business.

The sole proprietorship and the business are one and the same legal entity, which have liability and tax implications. Unlimited personal liability is the most serious proprietorship drawback. If the business incurs debts that cannot be paid, creditors can claim the business assets and the personal assets of the owner. In light of the high rate of failure among new businesses, liability considerations are important. If you have substantial personal holdings, you may want to consider another form of business that limits your personal liability.

The sole proprietor's business income is treated as personal income. You complete Form 1040 (Individual Income Tax Return), Schedule C (Profit or Loss from Business or Profession), and Form 1040ES (Declaration of Estimated Tax for Individuals). The IRS supplies you with four tax declaration vouchers that you submit in January, April, June, and September, with quarterly estimates of tax payment.

Advantages of a Sole Proprietorship

- It is easy to set up a sole proprietorship.
- Sole proprietorships are less expensive to set up than the other forms of businesses.
- The proprietor owns the profits and is the chief executive officer of the business.
- Sole proprietorship businesses can be terminated as quickly as they can be set up.

Disadvantages of a Sole Proprietorship

The personal assets of the proprietor can be accessed by the creditors of the business.

- It is more difficult to obtain financing for a sole proprietorship than it is for the other forms of business organizations.
- As the sole proprietor, you are literally on your own. You have no partners, or corporate associates, to consult with on business decisions.

GENERAL PARTNERSHIP

A general partnership is a business owned by two or more individuals. Like sole proprietorships, general partnerships are easy to form and are relatively free from government regulations. Most states do not require general partnerships to file formal partnership agreements. General partnerships are formed for a number of reasons.

- Partners may pool their capital to start or buy a business, which may have been beyond the financial reach of the individual partners.

- Partners may pool their labor to share the workload and the management of the business.

- A partnership adds strength to the business by combining individual skills that are strategic to the growth of the business.

Although not required by law, partnerships should not be formed with handshakes or verbal agreements. A partnership agreement should be drawn up with the help of an attorney. Partnership agreements become legal instruments that spell out the role of each partner in the business. Be sure the following are included in a partnership agreement:

1. The name, purpose, domicile, and duration of the partnership are documented.

2. The role and authority of each partner is clearly defined.

3. The financial contributions and obligations of each partner are defined.

4. Business expense guidelines are documented showing how expenses will be processed and approved.

5. How much of the business each partner owns is documented.

6. The accounting books and financial records that will be maintained to run the business are identified and approved by the partnership.

7. How profits and losses will be allocated between the partners are documented.

8. The salaries and performance criteria of all partners are established.

9. Succession and buy out options are clearly identified.

10. Arbitration and the settlements of disputes procedures are defined.

11. Absence and disability policies for the partners are defined.

General partnerships are formed in a manner similar to the sole proprietorship. If you wish to operate under an assumed name, some states require that you file a "Certificate of Conducting Business as Partners" with the county or state. Like sole proprietorships, each partner is personally liable for all business debts. If a partner incurs a debt on behalf of the partnership, all the partners are responsible. Therefore, it is important to select individuals that you trust. The death of a partner, unless covered in the partnership agreement, can automatically terminate the partnership.

The partnership itself is not a taxable entity. It does file a consolidated income tax return (Form 1065) that, by itself, is not subject to income taxes. Income for the business is taxed as personal income to each partner. The partners' share is reported on their individual tax return.

Advantages of a Partnership

• The partners provide additional capital to start up the business.

• Although partnerships are more difficult to form, they are still relatively easy to set up.

• The partners can pool their knowledge to assist in the running of the partnership.

Disadvantages of a Partnership

• Organizational problems can develop, if one or more of the partners becomes dissatisfied with the terms of the partnership.

• Each individual partner is personally liable for the total liabilities of the partnership.

• Partnerships can be difficult to dissolve.

LIMITED PARTNERSHIP

Most states allow for the formation of what is known as limited partnerships. A limited partnership is a business owned by two or more individuals, where some of the partners have limited liability. There must be at least one general partner who is personally responsible for all the partnership's liability. Because of the more complex formation and regulatory requirements, limited partnerships are more like corporations than general partnerships.

The most common reason limited partnerships are formed is to raise capital. Partner contributions may include cash, property, or the performance of a service. Limited partnerships can raise capital by selling additional limited partnership interests in the business. A typical limited partnership includes a general partner, who manages the day-to-day operations of the business, and a group of limited partners. Limited partners do not exercise control over the general operations of the business. They invest capital into the partnership in return for a share in the profits (or losses) and are personally liable only up to the extent of their investment.

Unlike a general partnership, a limited partnership agreement must be drawn up and filed with the state. For this reason, they are more complex to set up than general partnership agreements. If you use a fictitious name for the partnership, you are required to file a "doing business as" (D.B.A.) form with the county clerk or state. The tax filing requirements for limited partnerships are the same as for the general partnership.

Advantages of a Limited Partnership

- The partners provide additional capital to start up the business.
- Limited partnerships are more difficult to form than general partnerships and must comply with state regulations.
- The partners can pool their knowledge to advise the general partners.

Disadvantages of a Limited Partnership

- Organizational problems can develop if one or more of the partners becomes dissatisfied with the terms of the partnership.

- Each individual partner is personally liable for the total liabilities of the partnership.
- Partnerships can be difficult to dissolve.

CORPORATIONS

A corporation is a legal entity that exists separate from the people who create it. The corporation is owned by its shareholders and run by a board of directors elected by the shareholders. Corporations are created by filing "Articles of Incorporation" with the state in which they are created, and have a life of their own. Once formed, the corporation can buy and sell property, file lawsuits, enter into contracts, merge, and buy other companies. Corporations pay taxes and are liable for all corporate debts.

State laws permit the formation of corporations under strict registration and taxation guidelines, which vary in complexity. You should hire an attorney if you are thinking about incorporating. To set up a corporation, three or more individuals (depending on the state) submit an application called a Certificate of Incorporation, or an Articles of Incorporation, to the state office that grants corporate charters. This application identifies the names and addresses of the corporate shareholders, the scope of the company's business, and the amount of stock authorized. The application process includes a filing fee. In addition, there is an annual state tax that is based on the corporation's net income, which varies from state to state. Additional fees are charged if you want a permit to issue stock or other securities.

If you want to save money on attorney fees, you can form your own corporation. There are a number of "how to incorporate" books on the market. However, in most instances, you'll need professional help in setting up a corporation to avoid problems during the start-up process.

The cost of incorporating is one of its disadvantages. Not only are costs incurred during the formation stage, but the corporation pays annual taxes on corporate income, as well as a host of other employment taxes. Once formed, the officers or directors of the corporation must adopt by-laws that govern the operation of the corporation. Shareholder meetings must be held and minutes recorded. In certain cases, the corporate officers must sign incorporation agreements.

The primary benefit of the corporation is that the personal liabilities of the stockholders are limited to the amount of their personal investment in the company. Another advantage is the credibility corporations maintain with banks and other lenders. Lending institutions are more willing to advance loans to corporations because of their broader investor base.

Corporations are allowed to raise capital by issuing stock, which represents ownership in the business. Stock may be issued in exchange for cash, property, or services rendered on behalf of the corporation. The primary advantage of financing with stock is that the corporation is not required to repay the stock loan. Instead, the shareholders acquire ownership interest in the corporation, and share in its future profits or losses.

The tax reporting requirements are more complex for a corporation than they are for any other form of business organization. As an employee of a corporation, you draw a salary and report your annual income on IRS form 1040. As a separate entity, the corporation completes Form 1120 (U.S. Corporation Income Tax Return). You therefore have two tax returns to contend with if you work for a corporation.

Advantages of a Corporation

- Corporate liabilities are limited to the amount of an individual's personal investment in the company.

- A large amount of capital can potentially be raised through the sale of corporate stock.

- It is easier to obtain financing from lending institutions than it is for the other forms of business organizations.

Disadvantages of a Corporation

- There is a significant amount of paperwork that must be filed with the state and federal governments to maintain a corporation.

- The corporation, and the individuals that work for a corporation, are subject to government taxes.

- Corporations are governed by a significant amount of state and federal government regulations.

LIMITED LIABILITY CORPORATIONS

A limited liability corporation (LLC), which is sometimes referred to as an "S corporation," is a business structure that combines the benefits of a partnership for tax purposes, with the benefits of a corporation for liability purposes. The difference between a LLC corporation and a standard corporation is in the formation requirements and tax treatment. The LLC corporation is a "hybrid" corporation that enables the business owners to enjoy the limited liability of a standard corporation, and not be taxed as two separate entities. This can be an ideal structure for a new business.

In many ways, LLC corporations are like partnerships. They pay no federal taxes on net income. Instead, the corporation's profits or losses flow back to the shareholders, who are taxed at the shareholders' individual rate. However, some states tax the income of LLC corporations. To form a limited liability corporation, you must comply with the following requirements:

- The LLC must be a domestic corporation with shareholders holding residency in the United States.

- Only one class of common stock can be issued.

- The number of shareholders is limited to 35.

Once you elect to be treated as a limited liability corporation, shareholders report their shares of the corporation's taxable income or loss on their personal tax returns. Although the LLC corporation has some significant advantages over the general corporation, the limited liability corporation tax laws are complicated. Limited liability corporations are a relatively new business structure. Not all states recognize them as legal business structures. Seek out tax advice from your accountant before you form a limited liability corporation.

Advantages of the Limited Liability Corporation

- Corporate liabilities are limited to the amount of an individual's personal investment in the company.
- Capital can be raised through the limited sale of corporate stock.
- It is easier to obtain financing from lending institutions than it is for the other forms of business organizations.

Disadvantages of the Limited Liability Corporation

- There is a significant amount of paperwork that must be filed with the state and federal governments to maintain a corporation.
- Corporations are governed by a significant amount of state and federal government regulations

SELECTING A COMPANY NAME

The name of your business is important because it can be used to convey an image of what the business offers in the way of products and services. When a business goes by a name other than the owner's name, the business is operating under a fictitious name, which is also known as "doing business as" or "d.b.a." in the abbreviated form. Most states require all businesses operating under a fictitious name to file a fictitious name statement with the county clerk. In most states, you must publish a fictitious name statement in an acceptable newspaper in the county where the business is located, for a period up to four weeks. Fictitious name requirements by type of business organizations are summarized as follows:

- **Sole Proprietorship.** The business name is considered fictitious if it does not contain the surname of the owner. John Doe Enterprises would be considered a fictitious name.
- **Partnership.** The business name is considered fictitious if it does not contain the sur-

name of all the general partners and suggest the existence of additional partners. For example, John Doe and Associates would need to file a fictitious name statement because the word "associates" suggests the existence of additional owners.

- **Corporation.** A corporation is not required to file a fictitious name statement, unless it does business in an area under a different name than the one used in its article of incorporation.

The purpose of the statement is to inform the public of the name of the real owner of the business. Filing a fictitious name statement will prevent any other business in the county from using the same business name. Once you decide on the name of your business, you need to find out if another business is operating under the same name. At a minimum, you will need to request a name check with the secretary of state, or the county where you will be doing business.

One of the greatest pleasures in starting your own business is selecting the company name and logo. There are several points to consider when selecting a company name. The name of your company is one of its most frequently encountered advertisements and should say something about what your company does. This is one argument against using your own name for the company. For example, the name Smith and Associates doesn't tell anyone what the company does.

There are other reasons for not using your own name. What if you sell your company and then it later gets sued? It could be embarrassing to have your friends ask "are you connected with the company that was indicted for polluting?" You can, of course, explain that you were, but not during the time of the pollution episode. Why put your name in the control of other people? If you are setting up a professional business such as a legal, brokerage, consulting, or similar service business, and your name is well known (i.e., prestigious), then it may make sense to use it in the company name for its marketing advantage.

Company names consisting of initials tell prospective customers nothing about your company, its products, or services. In most cases, they aren't appropriate names for new businesses. Names like IBM and 3M took decades before name recognition set in, which you don't have.

Enterprise names like Smith Enterprises don't do much for a company's credibility. The word enterprise suggests that you are trying out several different lines of businesses with the hope that one will work. This may indeed be the case, but why broadcast it to your customers and prospective investors? Avoid using names like Smith & Associates, which carries the same connotation as the enterprise name. What are associates and who are they?

Again, a company name should convey to your customers an impression of what your company does. If you're setting up a high-tech operation, the use of technical buzzwords may be appropriate (i.e., The Byte Store for a computer store). Unfortunately, selecting a good name may be tough, because many of the clever ideas have already been discovered. Come up with several good names and conduct a name search at your local library to make sure your name is not already in use. The research librarian can provide you with a directory of state and national business names that are already in use.

Once you have selected your name, request a name check from the secretary of the state or the county where you will be doing business.

LICENSING YOUR COMPANY

Most cities and counties in the country require businesses to obtain a local business license, which is issued by the city, county, or in some areas, both agencies. The failure to obtain a business license can result in fines and penalties. You can also be penalized if you apply for a license after you have been in business. As a rule, if you sell or buy a business, the business license is not transferable. You must obtain a new license.

All states require business licenses for specific occupations such as doctors, lawyers, and CPAs. As states expanded their control over consumer protection interests, they have expanded their requirements for licensing over other businesses as well. Contact your state's attorney general's office to find out what the licensing requirements are in your state.

SOURCES FOR ADDITIONAL INFORMATION

LEGAL ADVICE

Although we do not advocate that you become your own lawyer, you can save on legal fees if you become informed about a legal subject, before you seek legal advice. Knowing something about what may be involved, and what the lawyer may have to do, will also allow you to obtain better legal advice. In the process, you may discover that what you want to do is not practical, so there is no sense in consulting an attorney. An excellent reference on the subject is a book entitled, *Do You Need a Lawyer* by Philip Hermann (Prentice-Hall, 1980).

INCORPORATING YOURSELF

It is possible to incorporate your business by yourself by applying the information that is provided in one of the following books:

Incorporation Made Easy, Alvin Baranow (Wolcotts, Inc. 1984).

How to Profit After You Incorporate Yourself, Judith McQuown (Warner Books, 1985).

FEDERAL TRADE COMMISSION

The objective of the Federal Trade Commission is to maintain competition throughout the American economic system. In brief, the Commission's legal responsibilities include; enforcement of the Consumer Credit Protection Act and enforcement of the Federal Trade Commission Act. For further information, write:

Federal Trade Commission
Office of Consumer Affairs
Washington, DC 20580
(202) 523-3830

PARLIAMENTARY PROCEDURES

If you are required to chair a meeting where you are
responsible for coordinating procedural problems or
even dissension, you need access to the information
that is contained in two books that cover parliamentary procedures:

Robert's Book of Order, Henry Robert (Scott Fores-
man, 1993).
Sturgis Standard Code of Parliamentary Procedure,
Alice Sturgis (McGraw-Hill, 1966).

STOCK EXCHANGES

For details about stock exchange listing requirements,
write to the one of the following exchanges:

American Stock Exchange
86 Trinity Place
New York, NY 10006-1818
(212) 938-6000

Boston Stock Exchange
1 Boston Place
Boston, MA 02108-4499
(617) 523-5625

Cincinnati Stock Exchange
49 East 4th Street
Cincinnati, OH 45202-3892
(513) 621-1410

Intermountain Stock Exchange
3735 Main Street
Salt Lake City, UT 84111-2705
(801) 363-2531

Midwest Stock Exchange
120 South LaSalle Street
Chicago, IL 60603-3402
(312) 368-2222

New York Stock Exchange
11 Wall Street
New York, NY 10005-1916
(212) 623-3000

Pacific Stock Exchange
301 Pine Street
San Francisco, CA 94104-3301
(415) 393-4000

Spokane Stock Exchange
225 Peyton Building
Spokane, WA 99201
(509) 624-4632

14

Leasing Equipment for Maximum Efficiency

To run an efficient business, you must have the necessary equipment. If your equipment is limited, your business may have difficulty competing with well-equipped competitors. On the other hand, too many assets can drain your investment potential. In this chapter, we will show you how to analyze the cost of new equipment, potential revenue contributions to consider, and how to acquire equipment under different lease options.

ANALYZING EQUIPMENT COSTS

The decision to acquire or replace existing equipment is based on two essential considerations—costs and productivity. There are several cost elements that should be reviewed first before you can consider the productivity issues. In some cases, replacing of older equipment with newer equipment can be justified on cost analysis alone. Let's first look at the cost issues.

DEPRECIATION EXPENSE

Depreciation expense is the amount by which an asset decreases in value over the designated life of the asset (covered in Chapter 12). Depreciation is an important cost element because you can deduct depreciation expense from your tax return. Once the book value of old equipment reaches zero (i.e., fully depreciated), you can no longer deduct the depreciation expense from your taxes.

We can demonstrate the importance of depreciation on the "true cost" of new equipment in an example. Let's assume that the ABC Company wants to acquire a machine that costs $50,000. The machine can be fully depreciated over 5 years using the straight line depreciation method. On average, the company pays 25 percent in annual taxes on annual gross profits of $10,000. How much will the company pay in taxes before, and after, it acquires the new machine over the next five years?

Before Equipment Acquisition

$$
\begin{aligned}
\text{5 Year tax obligation} &= (\text{Annual gross profits} \times 5 \text{ years} \\
&\qquad \times 25\% \text{ tax bracket}) \\
&= (\$10,000 \times 5 \times .25) \\
&= (\$50,000 \times .25) \\
&= \$12,500
\end{aligned}
$$

After Equipment Acquisition

$$
\frac{\text{Annual depreciation}}{\text{expense for machine}} = \frac{\$50,000}{5 \text{ years}}
$$

$$
= \$10,000 \text{ per year}
$$

$$
\begin{aligned}
\text{5 Year tax obligation} &= (\text{Annual gross profits} - \\
&\qquad \text{depreciation expense} \times 5 \\
&\qquad \text{years} \times 25\% \text{ tax bracket}) \\
&= (\$10,000 - \$10,000 \times 5 \times .25) \\
&= (\$0)(.25) \\
&= \$0
\end{aligned}
$$

As the example illustrates, the $10,000 annual depreciation expense on the new machine was sufficient to offset profits and hence, eliminated the company's tax obligation. To complete the analysis, we need to determine the actual cost of the new equipment after taxes. We know the purchase price was $50,000, and that the depreciation expense tax deduction would, in effect, save the company $12,500 in taxes. Therefore, the real cost of the equipment would be $37,500 ($50,000-$12,500).

OPERATING COSTS

Operating costs include all of the expenses that are associated with the operations and running of equipment. Operating costs could include labor, materials, utilities, and maintenance. These costs may be higher for older equipment. It usually costs more to maintain older equipment, which may also use more energy than the new "energy efficient" equipment. Operating costs need to be considered in your analysis for new equipment. If we continue with our

Exhibit 14-1. The 5-year Effect of Operating Costs on Old and New Equipment			
Cost Category	**Old Equipment**	**New Equipment**	**Savings (Loss)**
Labor	$19,000	$6,000	$13,000
Materials	$24,000	$26,000	($2,000)
Utilities	$12,000	$8,000	$4,000
Maintenance	$15,000	$10,000	$5,000

previous example, we can illustrate the effect operating costs have on acquiring equipment in Exhibit 14-1.

As the exhibit illustrates, the company can save $20,000 in operating costs over the 5 year asset life of the new equipment. To complete the analysis, we need to determine the revised actual cost of the new equipment. We know that the $50,000 purchase price was reduced to $37,500 due to tax savings. The revised purchase price can be further reduced by $20,000 to $17,500 ($37,500 − $20,000 = $17,500) to reflect the savings in operating costs.

OPPORTUNITY COSTS

The costs that are associated with alternative investment opportunities for the business are called opportunity costs. For example, we know the proposed acquisition of the machine in our examples will cost the company $50,000. Let us assume that the company has a surplus of $50,000 in its checking account that can be used to purchase the machine. As an alternative, the company could choose not to buy the equipment and invest the $50,000 in a certificate of deposit (CD) or other investment alternative. Hence, CDs represent an opportunity cost option to the company. If we assume that based upon current CD rates, a $50,000 investment today would return $10,000 in interest over the next five years, then we need to once again revise the "true" purchase price of the equipment. The affect of opportunity cost on new equipment can be calculated as follows:

$$\text{Revised equipment cost} = (\text{Current revised cost} + \text{opportunity cost})$$

$$= (\$17,500 + \$10,000)$$
$$= \$27,500$$

In this example, we assumed that the company did not need to borrow money to purchase the new machine, since they had $50,000 in their checking account. Let's change the assumption, and assume that the company will need to borrow the money to buy the machine. If the interest over the 5-year life of the loan is $5,000, then the cost of the loan should be added to the cost of the machine ($27,500 + $5,000 = $32,500).

REVENUE CONTRIBUTION CONSIDERATIONS

In certain situations, there is a direct relationship between sales revenue and the production output of equipment, which is often the case in manufacturing companies. For example, if a piece of equipment is used to produce end products, then the equipment contributes to the sales revenues of the business. This issue becomes important in the "old versus new" equipment analysis, if the new equipment adds more sales revenue to the business than the old equipment.

There are several ways in which this can happen. If the new equipment is capable of producing more units of output than the old equipment, and the business can sell the additional units, then the revenue advantage of the new equipment needs to be taken into account, before you can complete your analysis. The new equipment may be capable of producing additional by-products that will also contribute to the revenues of the business. If you assume that the new equipment will produce an additional $35,000 in products per year and that the net profit from the additional production will be $5,000 per year, you can again adjust the acquisition cost of the new equipment by using the following calculation:

Revised equipment cost = (Current revised cost)
$\quad$ −(Annual net profit
$\quad$ × 5 years)

$\quad$ = ($27,500)−($5,000 × 5)
$\quad$ = $27,500−$25,000
$\quad$ = $2,500

$\quad$ In the final analysis, you were able to reduce the $50,000 equipment purchase price to $2,500 over a five-year time period. In the pure economic sense, you have concluded that the new equipment would cost $2,500 more than the old equipment over the next five years. From a strict business view point, you could conclude that your business would be better off financially by keeping the old equipment. Let's consider some of the other issues that may or may not fit in the economic part of the analysis.

$\quad$ The safety and reliability of the old equipment must be considered. If safety is an issue, what is the potential risk to your employees and subsequent cost exposure to your business? Reliability becomes an important issue if equipment down-time can seriously disrupt the operation of your business. If rapid technological changes are occurring in the industry, perhaps a new unannounced model can be uncovered through a discussion with a manufacturer's representative that will make your previous analysis more attractive. In the process, you may be able to negotiate the $50,000 purchase price down to a more attractive price.

LEASING EQUIPMENT

Leasing equipment offers an alternative to buying equipment, and does not require the large cash outlay of a purchase. Many small businesses lease everything they can, including office furniture, computers, and motor vehicles. However, the advantages and disadvantages of leasing should be carefully considered before you lease. The financial consideration should be carefully analyzed to assure that you can make a cost effective decision.

$\quad$ A lease is an agreement to rent an asset over some defined period of time. The company that leases equipment is known as the lessee. The lessee makes periodic lease payments to the company that owns the asset, known as the lessor. Your payments generally cover the lessor's payments on the equipment, plus an additional fee for their service. Lease periods typically cover the IRS allowed depreciable life of the asset.

There are many different types of leases to consider. Each lease option offers advantages and disadvantages that must be carefully weighed, before you can make the right decision for your business. The different types of leases are summarized in the balance of this section.

- **Financial lease.** The most common lease is called a financial lease. The term of the lease generally covers the depreciable life of the asset. The lessee is responsible for making payment to the end of the lease term, and maintains the asset during the lease term. At the end of the term, the ownership reverts back to the lessor. Most financial leases cannot be canceled.

- **Conditional sales lease:** Several different types of leases are covered under conditional sales leases. The basic concept of the lease, is that the Lessee is considered the owner of the asset during the lease period for tax purposes. At the end of the lease period, the lessee has the option to acquire the asset by exercising a "buyout option", that is specified in the lease terms. Some conditional sales leases include "put" and "call" purchase limits in the lease terms. The "put" represents the minimum price, and the "call" represents the maximum price a lessee can pay for the asset at the end of the lease term. In effect it sets the high and low negotiating limits for a purchase price.

- **Leverage lease:** The lessor initiates a partial down payment on assets acquired under a leverage lease and finances the remaining balance. The tax benefits of the lease belong to the lessor. As a result, they can lease the asset at a lower monthly cost than would be the case with other lease types.

- **Net lease:** As the name implies, the lessee is responsible for most, or all costs, that are associated with the leased asset. In addition to lease payments, they are also responsible for other payments such as taxes, insurance, and maintenance.

- **Gross lease:** In a gross lease, the lessor is responsible for most, or all costs, that are associated with the leased asset, including the payments for taxes, insurance, and maintenance.

- **Operating lease:** This type of lease includes conditional lease cancellation provisions in the terms of the lease. The maintenance of the asset is usually the responsibility of the lessor.

- **Payout lease:** In a payout lease, the lessor is paid what the asset costs over the term of the lease. The lessor recovers their costs by the end of the lease term, and makes a profit by selling the used asset.

- **Non-payout lease:** Under the terms of this lease, the lessor is paid less than what the asset costs over the term of the lease. This type of lease is popular with assets that have high established resale value in the used market. The lessor recovers their costs at the end of the lease term when they sell the asset.

- **True lease:** A true lease is where the lessor owns the asset throughout the term of the lease. The lessee does not accumulate any equity from lease payments in the asset. If the lessee wants to purchase the asset at the end of the term, the purchase price is negotiated, independent of the terms and conditions of the lease contract.

- **Sales lease:** In a sales lease, the owner of the asset sells it to another party (i.e., lessor) and then leases the asset back under specified lease terms. This allows the lessee to take advantage of the lease tax laws, and use the money from the sale of the asset for other purposes.

ADVANTAGES AND DISADVANTAGES OF LEASING

Leasing can offer certain advantages to your business, depending upon your situation. For example, does your business need the tax advantage of ownership to help reduce its current tax liability (i.e., conditional sales lease)? If you do not need the tax advantage, and are more interested in minimizing your lease payments, a true lease may satisfy your needs. If you believe that the asset will have some value after the term of the lease, then it may be to your advantage to negotiate purchase terms in the lease contract.

Advantages of Leasing

1. It allows for the use of an asset without requiring a large outlay of cash.
2. Leases require minimum to no down payments to initiate.
3. Lease payments can be spread out over a long period of time to reduce the payment amounts.
4. Flexible payment structures can be incorporated into the lease contract.
5. Lease payments can be deducted as a part of your operating expense to reduce your tax obligation.
6. Leases can protect your business against equipment obsolescence, since you return the equipment to the lessor at the end of the lease term.
7. Many leasing firms specialize in the assets they lease, and can therefore offer excellent technical advice.

Disadvantages of Leasing

1. Since you do not own the asset as the lessee, you must either purchase the asset, if you still need it when the lease period expires or enter into a new lease agreement.
2. Leasing can cost you more than what it would have cost you if you had purchased the asset. Analyze all cost options first before you lease.
3. It is very difficult to terminate a lease contract. This can become a problem if your business encounters cash flow problems.

CONDUCTING A PURCHASE VERSUS LEASE ANALYSIS

It is important to compare the costs of a lease to the equivalent purchase option, so that you can make an informed financial decision. The comparative analysis must consider a number of important factors, including lease payments, purchase prices, maintenance, and tax considerations. Exhibits 14-2 and 14-3 compare lease versus purchase cost options for equipment based upon the following assumptions:

Equipment cost: $25,000.

Estimated economic life: 8 years.

Lease terms: $415 per month, and the lessee must maintain the equipment.

Purchase loan terms: 8 year $20,000 loan at 10% interest. The monthly interest and principle payments are $385.

Annual depreciation: $4,000.

Taxes: Assume 25 percent tax bracket for the company.

Salvage value: $4,000 at the end of the eighth year.

You could determine from our two exhibits that you would be ahead financially if you purchased rather than leased the equipment. If you had purchased the equipment, your total net cash flow would have been $25,781 at the end of the eighth year, even though you had accumulated interest expenses over the eight years. Total expenses were offset by tax deductions you realized on interest and depreciation expenses.

If you had leased the equipment, your total net cash flow would have been $30,000 at the end of the eighth year. However, our lease assumption was based on a 25 percent federal income tax bracket. If your company was in the 35 percent tax bracket, you could deduct a total of $21,000 from $40,000 over the eight years of lease payments to achieve a net cash flow of $19,000 ($40,000 − $19,000).

LEASING SERVICES

Most leasing services are provided by commercial banks, insurance, and finance companies. Many of these institutions have subsidiary companies that spe-

Exhibit 14-2. Cash Flow from Purchasing Equipment

Year	Payment	Interest	Loan Balance	Depreciation	Tax Savings	Net Cash Flow
1	$4,620	$2,500	$22,880	$4,000	$1,625	$2,995
2	$4,620	$2,288	$20,548	$4,000	$1,572	$3,048
3	$4,620	$2,055	$17,983	$4,000	$1,514	$3,106
4	$4,620	$1,798	$15,161	$4,000	$1,450	$3,170
5	$4,620	$1,516	$12,057	$4,000	$1,379	$3,241
6	$4,620	$1,206	$8,643	$4,000	$1,301	$3,319
7	$4,620	$864	$4,887	$4,000	$1,216	$3,404
8	$4,620	$489	$756	$4,000	$1,122	$3,498
					Total	$25,781

Exhibit 14-3. Cash Flow from Leasing Equipment

Year	Payment	Tax Savings	Net Cash Flow
1	$5,000	$1,250	$3,750
2	$5,000	$1,250	$3,750
3	$5,000	$1,250	$3,750
4	$5,000	$1,250	$3,750
5	$5,000	$1,250	$3,750
6	$5,000	$1,250	$3,750
7	$5,000	$1,250	$3,750
8	$5,000	$1,250	$3,750
		Total	**$30,000**

cialize in leasing. The popularity of leasing has propagated the formation of companies that specialize only in leasing. Some companies will lease just about anything you need, while others specialize in specific types of assets (i.e., cars, airplanes, etc.). Leasing companies are listed in the yellow pages under "leasing and rentals." Many of them advertise in the financial sections of major newspapers and in trade journals. Some manufacturers offer leasing plans to their customers.

In your search for a leasing company, you may come across the names of lease brokers. Lease brokers work with prospective lessees to determine their needs, and then solicit bids from the appropriate leasing companies. Most leasing brokers are paid by the leasing company.

CHOOSING A LEASING COMPANY

The leasing industry is very competitive. If you shop around, you should be able to find several competitive companies to consider. In your initial search, check lease rates and the reputation of the companies. Rates can vary significantly between companies, and an established reputation is important since you will probably be leasing from the company for a number of years. When you compare rates, make sure you are comparing comparable lease terms, such as the length of the lease, the brand, and the model of the equipment.

The reputation and reliability of the leasing company can be checked by talking to other people who have leased equipment from this company. Ask the company's representative for references. Check with the Better Business Bureau in your area to see if any complaints have been filed against the company.

All leasing companies will require that you sign a lease contract to validate the lease agreement. Lease contracts are legal documents that cover lease obligations. It is important that you understand all of the terms in the contract. Make sure the contract covers the points that are important to your business, such as the following:

- The duration of the lease obligation, which is usually expressed in months, or an end date.
- The financial terms and obligations of the lessee to the lessor.
- The terms for the disposition of the asset at the end of the leasing term, which may include the lessee's purchase option.
- Insurance requirements and coverage obligations of the lessee and lessor.
- The maintenance obligations of the lessee and the lessor.
- Renewal options and cancellation penalties.
- Who is entitled to the tax benefits.

Lease contracts differ depending on leasing company and the type of assets that you lease. Some will include special terms and conditions for the use of equipment, such as how it must be stored.

SOURCES FOR ADDITIONAL INFORMATION

According to the American Association of Equipment Lessors, leasing is the method most frequently used to finance assets in the United States. Over 80 percent of American businesses use leases to finance a part of their assets to take advantage of certain tax laws. The Association publishes a guide entitled *Equipment Leasing Is Good Business*. For a copy of the guide or additional information, contact:

American Association of Equipment Lessors
5635 Douglas Avenue
Milwaukee, WI 53218
(703) 527-8655

MANAGING PEOPLE AND YOUR BUSINESS

PART FOUR

MANAGING PEOPLE AND YOUR BUSINESS

15

Managing People

Hiring the right employees can have a major impact on the success of your business. If you hire the right person for the job — who is motivated and eager to contribute to your success — you are in good shape. On the other hand, if you make a mistake and hire the wrong person for the job, your business will suffer from a loss of productivity. as well as additional problems as you attempt to replace the poor performer. In this chapter we will cover all of the basic issues, checks, and balances you need to consider to make sure you hire the right person for the job.

DETERMINING PERSONNEL REQUIREMENTS

The first step in determining your personnel requirements is to plan ahead. Employees are expensive resources, and if you are forced to hire someone quickly without the benefit of a plan, you may end up hiring the wrong person for the job, which can be a costly proposition. Not only will your company suffer from the lack of employee productivity, but you could also incur additional expenses and aggravation in terminating the person.

PERSONNEL PLANNING

The following list will help you develop an employment plan that meets the needs of your organization:

1. Determine objectives of the organization first, before you analyze the types of people you will need to meet your objectives.

2. What are your sales requirements and will you need qualified people to help you meet your requirements?

3. Will your company be introducing new products or services that require the support of qualified people? What kinds of technical qualifications do you need?

4. Where is your company going in the next 2 to 3 years and do you have access to the people that will help you get there? If not, what kinds of people do you need to meet your long-term business goals?

5. What types of employees do you need to fulfill the current jobs and do you already have these people?

6. Do you have any key employees who, if they quit, could disrupt the operations of your business? How can you minimize the impact of this possibility?

ESTABLISHING JOB SPECIFICATIONS

After you have determined that your business needs additional people if it is to reach its goals and objectives, you next must determine the specifications for each job that you need to fill. The job specification is a detailed description of the job, and covers all of the desired qualifications the "ideal" candidate should have. A job specification should include the following basic elements:

- The job title

- Who the person will report to

- A list of the tasks and responsibilities of the position

- Prior experience and educational requirements needed for this position

- Any special requirements, problems, or other factors that would exclude a person from this position

- How this position will contribute to the success of your business

- The salary range and compensation package for this position

After you have analyzed the job, write a job description. The job description is an outline of how the job fits into the company. Start by writing down the job title and who the person will report to. Next, develop a job statement and summarize the job's goals, responsibilities, and duties. Finally, define how the job relates to other positions in the company. The Bureau of Labor Statistics publishes a good reference source for developing job specifications every other year. The handbook describes in detail over 200 occupations, and includes salary information about the jobs it features. For more information, contact your local library or:

Superintendent of Documents
Government Printing Office
Washington, DC 20402

RECRUITING TECHNIQUES

Good recruiting techniques demand that you know exactly what you are looking for in a candidate. Make sure that any of your employees who may answer the phone in your absence have enough basic information to answer an applicant's questions. The information in this section will help you find viable candidates.

PERSONNEL SOURCES

Finding the best people to fit your job specifications and requirements can be a challenging and time consuming task. In this section, we will talk about alternative sources for personnel. The advantages and disadvantages of each source covered will also be discussed.

Current Personnel

Staffing a new position with one of your existing employees offers a number of advantages. You can fill the position immediately, if you already have somebody who is qualified for the job and is familiar with the operations of your company. If properly handled, the promotion of an existing employee into the new position can act as a motivator to your other employees (i.e., you will promote from within the company). One of the obvious disadvantages is that you will have to find someone to fill the old position. In addition, some of your staff may be concerned over why they were not chosen for the job.

Outside Personnel

Perhaps no one in your current organization has the specific qualifications that you are looking for. It is often appropriate to find a person for the new position who may be working for another company or is looking for a job. When you search for someone on the outside, you have the opportunity to find a person who has the exact qualifications that you need and is currently performing the type of job that you want to fill. This can increase the chances of success the new person will have in the job. However, it may be a time consuming and costly process to find the person with the exact qualifications that you need. Even if you find the right person, but he or she is already working for another company, how do you convince them to quit their current job? You must be careful not to oversell your position and end up with a new disgruntled employee.

New Graduates

Students who are about to graduate from a trade school, high school, college, or university can be excellent prospects for new positions. Many of these people may have received training in the specific area that you are looking for and be eager to demonstrate what they have learned. One of the best ways to gain access to new graduates is to contact the placement offices of local schools, colleges, or universities. Send them a company flyer that announces your open position and ask the school to post your flyer in an appropriate location.

Temporary Employment Agencies

Employment agencies can be a source for qualified employees. Many agencies allow you to hire their temporary for a fee or at no charge after you have employed one of their people for a specified period of time. This option offers you the advantage of hiring a worker on a temporary basis to determine if he or she can perform the job to your satisfaction. At the end of the trial period, you can either hire the person as one of your own employees or return him or her to the temporary agency. The disadvantage of this arrangement is that you pay the agency an hourly fee that not only covers the employee's salary expectations but the agency's service fee as well.

Contract Employees

Contract employees are the "new breed" of self-employed employees who offer their services, on a contract basis, to any company that will hire them. The advantage of hiring contract employees is that they are usually highly motivated individuals since they are eager to build their business reputations. The hourly rates for these workers can be highly competitive because many of them operate out of their homes to minimize overhead costs. The disadvantages of hiring contract employees are that they may not be a qualified "contract employee" in accordance with IRS regulations. This could result in a tax penalty to your business, since withholding taxes is required for legitimate contract employees. Contact your local IRS office for a detailed list of the independent contractor guidelines.

Independent Contractors

Independent contractors offer their services to businesses at a negotiated or established rate. They generally provide their own tools and materials to perform the work they have been trained to do. Independent contractors are under a legal obligation to complete contracted jobs, and therefore manage their own work schedules. They are typically paid by the job, or at an hourly rate for a specific job.

JOB RECRUITERS

There are many factors and alternatives to consider when you develop the recruiting techniques you will use to find the right person for your company. Some techniques are expensive to implement while others require a significant amount of time to implement.

A good recruiting firm or employment agency specializes in finding people that specifically match your job specifications and needs. You tell the recruiter exactly what you need and the recruiter conducts a job search and advertises for candidates on your behalf. The recruiter will arrange for you to interview pre-qualified candidates. In most cases, you pay the recruiter a "finders fee" if you hire one of their candidates. Some recruiting firms charge service fees to supplement their search costs. In any event, job recruiter fees are usually expensive, and can amount to as much as 30 percent or more of a person's first year's salary.

REFERRALS

Many jobs are filled by implementing informal referral systems. It is relatively easy to do and is cost effective. You simply contact your business associates and friends to advise them that you are looking for someone to hire for a particular position. If they know of someone, or learn of someone who might fit your job requirements, they refer the person to you for an interview. This system offers you the advantage of gaining access to candidates who have been referred by someone you know. However, the "friend-of-a-friend" may not have all of the qualifications that you need.

ADVERTISING

Advertising for personnel can be an expensive proposition, depending upon the types of advertising media you use. The classified sections of newspapers are one of the least expensive sources to use and are the most popular. Regional and national papers like *The Wall Street Journal* offer broader geographic coverage, but at a substantial increase in advertising rates. Display advertisements can be placed apart from the classified sections to allow your ad to stand out from all of the other advertisements that appear in the classified section. You pay a premium for display advertising space.

Many of the trade journal magazines offer both display and classified ad options. The disadvantage of using magazines for this purpose is the cost of space and the lead time required. It can take up to two months for an ad to run in a magazine. Many of the professional associations publish trade magazines and newsletters that feature "open positions" sections. The cost for listing an open position in this section is often free, or inexpensive relative to other forms of advertising.

SELECTING THE RIGHT PEOPLE

The selection process covers the screening and inter-viewing of applicants that ultimately leads to a job offer. This overall process can be the most time con-suming activity of the entire recruiting effort. It is also the most important, because it involves personal contact with candidates, and checking references, and ultimately leads to an offer.

SCREENING APPLICANTS

Applicant screening involves reviewing information such as resumes, that candidates submit in response to your recruiting and advertising program. In many cases, the number of applications that you receive can be extensive, and can require a significant amount of time to process. It may be cost effective to have one of your employees match the applications against your job specifications first to eliminate applicants who are not qualified for the position. As a result of the screening process, you should end up with a manageable number of candidates that you can inter-view.

You may have asked candidates to submit job references for you to check. If you have only a few viable candidates to consider, it may be worth your time to conduct reference checks before you set up an interview appointment. Many employers will wait until after the interview before they begin checking references. They want to make sure the candidate is interested in the job — and that they are interested in the candidate — before they spend time qualifying ref-erences.

Before you interview a candidate, have him or her fill out an employment application. It should ask for specific information such as educational back-ground and work experience. You can buy generic application forms at an office supply store, or you can develop your own to meet your specific needs. Make sure the application form you use conforms to federal Equal Employment Opportunity (EEOC) guidelines. It is against the law for an employment application form to ask about arrests, race, sex, religion, marital status, pregnancy, child care, or sexual preference.

TESTING APPLICANTS

Be careful when testing applicants. Tests that demonstrate a key ability required for the job — such as typing — are perfectly legitimate. Personality or intelligence tests may violate EEOC regulations. For instance, if a certain group of minorities are rejected at a greater rate than other groups based on the test, or if the test has no demonstrated predictability as to probable success on the job, you could be in violation of EEOC regulations.

CONDUCTING INTERVIEWS

Interviewing can be an uncomfortable experience for some people because they may be unsure of their ability to ask the candidate pertinent questions. An improperly conducted interview can literally "turn-off" a highly qualified candidate, who will subsequently reject whatever job offer you make.

To assure that an interview goes well, plan the interview ahead of time. Keep in mind that it is the goal of the interviewer to find the right candidate, and eliminate those who are not qualified for the position. If time permits, send a job application to the candidate and ask that he or she complete the application and return it to you before the interview date. The job application will allow you to review specific areas of the candidate's background that may not have been covered in the resume.

Review all of the information that you have on the applicant and carefully cross-check their background against the specifications for the job. Prepare a list of what you believe are the candidate's strengths and weaknesses. Develop a set of interview questions that will allow you to better determine how well qualified the candidate is for the job.

When you first meet with the candidate, set a relaxed tone for the interview. Select a place where you can conduct the interview without being interrupted. You may choose to start the interview by asking a social question like "What did you think of the ball game last night?" Ask the easy questions first and move into the more difficult questions as the conversation progresses. If appropriate, introduce the candidate to a colleague in your organization whom you have asked to conduct an independent interview. This will allow you to "cross-check" your opinions with someone else after the interview is over.

Encourage the candidate to ask you questions about the job and your company. A candidate who is seriously interested in your company and the job will have conducted their own research to learn something about the company. Give extra marks for well prepared and thought-out questions.

During the interview, observe the person, their dress, mannerisms, and words. Let the person talk freely, so that they can reveal additional information. For example, if a person complains about bosses they had in the past, it may be an indication that he or she has problems taking direction from others. When preparing your interview questions, be sure to keep the EEOC guidelines in mind.

CHECKING REFERENCES

Following the interview process, conduct reference checks on any candidate you are considering hiring. Reference checks allow you to validate what the candidate has told you about their past performance. In this step, examine their education, training, and experience. If academic transcripts are important, ask that they be sent to you.

Work references can be an important source for determining a person's work qualifications and their ability to get along with others. Many employers are reluctant to give out any negative information regarding their previous employees. Keep this in mind when you ask questions and make sure your questions conform to the equal employment opportunity guidelines.

MAKING THE JOB OFFER

Once you have settled on the top candidate, it is time to negotiate an offer. You should have more than one candidate in mind in the event that your first choice declines the offer. Any offer that you make should be done either in person, or over the telephone. It is often best to offer 10 to 15 percent less than what you are really prepared to offer. This will allow you some room to negotiate during the conversation.

If the candidate counters with an unreasonably high salary figure, you can counter with your "high end" salary offer and explain to the candidate that you cannot meet their salary request for whatever reasons (e.g., more than the going rate). You may want to reiterate the benefits of your company and the job. However, be careful that you do not "sell" a candidate on the job, only to discover after they are hired that they will continue to be dissatisfied with the lower salary offer.

HANDLING RECORDKEEPING AND LEGAL ISSUES

Always let unsuccessful candidates or applicants know that they did not get the job. If possible, contact the candidates that you have met on a face-to-face basis and thank them for their time and effort. If they ask you why they were not selected, you may simply tell them, that although they were qualified for the job, you found someone with more qualifications.

After interviewing an applicant, create a file containing the resume, application, and your interview notes. If you hire the applicant, that file will become the person's employee file. Federal law requires that a job application be kept at least three years after a person is hired. If you do not hire the applicant, keep the file for at least one year after the no-employment decision has been made. In today's legal climate, applicants sometimes sue an employer who has not hired them. You should be familiar with the following federal laws:

- **Equal employment laws.** The laws state that you may not discriminate against an applicant on the basis of the applicant's race, religion, sex, national origin, or age.

- **Equal pay act.** The law prohibits employers from paying lower wages to employees because of the sex of the employee.

- **Right-to-know laws.** Any employee has the right to review, copy, or rebut the contents of their personnel file. Employees must also be informed about the presence of any hazardous materials that are present in the workplace. For more information, contact:

Equal Employment Opportunity Commission
Office of Program Operations
2401 E. Street, NW
Washington, DC 20507
(202) 634-6922

DEALING WITH EMPLOYEE PROBLEMS

Employees who have problems can cause trouble in the workplace. In some cases, assignments will be poorly performed and seldom completed on time. There may be a lack of cooperation with the other employees, a tangible lack in pride, spirit, and general dissatisfaction with the job. Dishonesty, absenteeism, and the sabotage of company property can follow.

HANDLING ALCOHOLISM

Alcoholism is a widespread problem among employees that is seldom acknowledged by many businesses. One of the most effective means of dealing with the problem is to refer the addicted employee to the nearest Alcoholics Anonymous group or an alcoholism treatment center. For further information, contact:

National Council on Alcoholism
12 West 21 Street
New York, NY 10010
(212) 206-6770

Alcoholics Anonymous World Services
PO Box 459
Grand Central Station
New York, NY 10163
(212) 686-1100

HANDLING ABSENTEEISM

Absenteeism is a serious problem for any company. It is difficult to resolve because all an employee needs to say is, "I'm not feeling well" and you have little recourse to prove them wrong. Some companies discourage absenteeism by paying their employees a cash bonus at the end of the year for any unused sick leave. However, persistent and randomly occurring absenteeism should be brought to the attention of the employee. All warnings should be documented in writing. If the problem persists, you may have to ask the employee to leave the company.

HANDLING THEFT

Employee theft is one of the most emotionally devastating problems that can occur in a business. It can cast a shadow of doubt over everybody working for the company until the person who is actually responsible for the theft is caught. You should be alert to the following:

1. Office supplies and equipment are missing.
2. Inventory is disappearing from storage areas.
3. Cash is missing from the cash registers.
4. Accounting books do not balance.
5. Purchases are made for products and services that are never delivered.
6. The petty cash drawer is always short of cash.
7. Employees do not charge their friends for goods received.

To help limit your losses from employee theft, check the background of all prospective employees. Get to know your employees to the extent that you can detect signs of financial or personal problems. If they trust you, they may ask you for help before they take their problems out on your business. Initiate tight controls over check signing authorization in the business. Have company payments mailed to a post office box, rather than directly to the company. Double check all daily cash deposits. Spot check all accounting records and let all of your people know that you will do this on a random basis.

HANDLING DRUG PROBLEMS

If you encounter employees who have drug problems, you need to seek professional assistance for them. If they refuse counseling and treatment, you will have to ask them to leave the company. For information, contact the following:

Narcotics Anonymous
PO Box 9999
Van Nuys, CA 91409
(818) 780-3951

U.S. Department of Justice
Drug Enforcement Administration
1405 Street, NW
Washington, DC 20537
(202) 633-1000

U.S. Department of Health and Human Services
Information Center
Washington, DC 20201
(202) 245-6296

TERMINATING EMPLOYEES

The termination of an employee for cause is a tough issue to confront, but it must be done if an employee is not meeting your expectations for the job. In most cases, you have invested a considerable amount of time and money hiring and training the individual in question. For this reason, an employee's performance problems must be shared — by you as well as the employee. Employee warnings and consultations should be carefully documented prior to initiating any formal dismissal process. If the termination of an employee is required, the following guidelines will help you get through the process:

1. Meet with the employee and explain the reasons for the termination.
2. Pay all wages and compensation that are due to the employee at the point of termination.
3. If you believe the termination interview will result in a confrontation, have a second person join you during the interview process.

4. Prepare a document that outlines the reasons for the employee's termination. Ask the employee to sign the document. If he or she refuses to sign the document, note this on the document.

5. After completing the termination session, document in writing the important points that were covered during the session.

IMPLEMENTING WAGE AND BENEFIT PROGRAMS

The wage and benefit programs that you offer to your employees are extremely important. If the levels of your program are below what the competition is offering, you will not be able to hire and retain the best employees. On the other hand, if your program is too liberal, you may have trouble remaining competitive.

ADMINISTERING WAGES

You should consider the competitive aspects when you develop a salary level for a job. If your salaries are not competitive, your employees will lack motivation, which can lead to high turnover rates. If you pay too much in salaries, you'll have to raise your price, which could limit your competitiveness.

Businesses frequently need comparative wage and salary figures to use as yardsticks when they develop wage scales or hire new employees. It is difficult to obtain this information from other companies, since many consider their wage information proprietary. Some businesses may be willing to trade wage and salary information with you on a confidential basis.

To determine what a competitive salary should be in your area, conduct a salary and benefits survey. Call personnel managers in other companies, employment recruiters, industry associations, labor organizations, and management consultants. Find out salary levels for the position you're filling, as well as any benefits offered like bonuses, health insurance, retirement plans, or life insurance plans.

There are some external sources that can offer

wage and salary information. Trade associations frequently publish such information for the use of their members, or nonmembers on a fee basis. Some state labor departments compile and publish this data for distribution to businesses. The Bureau of Labor Statistics publishes a number of helpful monthly reports in this area, including Current Wage Developments and Employment and Earnings. For more information, contact:

Superintendent of Documents
Washington, DC 20402

ADMINISTERING FRINGE BENEFITS

Fringe benefits include pensions, paid holidays, or health insurance programs that are extended to employees by the employer as an added reason for working for the company. Fringe benefits are generally regarded by employees as an extension to their wages. There are two basic issues that you should take into consideration when you develop your fringe benefit program:

1. Once benefits have been offered over a period of time, employees accept them as their due, and no longer consider them as extras.
2. Fringe benefits cost money, are subject to increasing costs, and affect profits.

Before you can develop a competitive fringe benefit program for your company, find out what other companies in your area are offering in your area. Unlike wages, most personnel managers and business owners will share their fringe benefit information with you.

SELECTING RETIREMENT PLANS

The major retirement plans are covered in this section. We'll show you how they work and discuss the advantages and disadvantages of each. The costs and complexities for the various plans vary, depending on how you implement them, and which one you select.

Salary Employer Plans (SEP)

SEP retirement plans are popular with companies that have 10 or fewer employees. You simply open an Individual Retirement Account (IRA) for each employee and yourself. SEP plans are administered through mutual funds, banks, and insurance companies. Many of these companies offer multiple investment options.

You set the contribution amounts, which can equal as much as 15% of a person's income, up to a maximum of $30,000 per employee. The percentage must be the same for all employees, but you can change it yearly. Employees cannot contribute to the SEP directly, but they do pay a yearly custodial fee to the company administering the plan. They also decide where the funds in their account are be invested.

If the simplicity of a SEP appeals to you, but you don't want to make all the contributions yourself, look into a salary reduction SEP. It's basically a collection of employee IRA accounts where the contributions are made by the employees and not you, unless you elect to participate. Fifty percent or more of eligible employees must participate in the plan, and you must have no more than 25 employees to qualify for a SEP under IRS rules.

Money Purchase Plans

If your company's profits are stable from year to year, a money purchase plan is a good retirement option. You set aside a fixed percentage of payroll every year for the employees' retirement, regardless of your profit or loss position. The annual contribution can be as much as 25% of salary, up to $30,000 per employee. The disadvantage to the plan is that you must contribute in good and lean years. The retirement outlays become part of your overhead costs. If you can't make the payment, you have to seek a waiver from the IRS, or risk paying a 10% penalty.

Target Benefit Plans

A target benefit plan allows you to decide the amount each employee receives in retirement benefits. Certain employees, including yourself, can have a larger sum set aside for them each year. Target plans are popular with companies employing older people. The annual contribution limit is 25% of a person's salary with a $30,000 annual limit per employee.

401k Plans

Employees contribute to their own 401k retirement plan. These are by far the most complex of the contribution plans and are suitable for companies with 20 or more employees. If you're competing against big companies for new employees, a 401k plan may be a necessity, since 40 percent of large businesses have them. Employees can contribute up to 20 percent of their salaries to the plan. Your company can match all, some, or none of the employees' contributions as long as the total does not exceed 25% of a person's salary or $30,000 per employee. Even a company match as small as 10 percent is usually enough to encourage employees to participate.

Profit Sharing Plans

If your profits fluctuate from year to year, you might benefit from a profit sharing plan. You choose how much of your company's profits to invest on your employees' behalf each year. You can specify the investment account for the money, or leave that decision up to the employee. You can reward people by giving them a larger percentage as long as you treat all employees equally. If your company has a bad year, you can reduce or eliminate the plan.

Profit sharing can be used to motivate employees and associates. For example, you might promise that if your employees meet a certain sales goal, you'll add an amount equal to some percentage of their pay to their profit sharing plan. In effect, you are conveying a message that says "if the company makes money, then we all make money."

The Profit Sharing Research Foundation issues a number of profit sharing publications that may be of interest to you. Some of the titles include: *Profit Sharing as a Motivator, Increasing Profits Through Profit Sharing,* and *Does Profit Sharing Pay?* For more information, contact:

Profit Sharing Research Foundation
20 North Wacker Drive
Chicago, IL 60606
(312) 868-8787

USING CREDIT UNIONS

Credit unions offer an inexpensive way of offering financial service benefits to your employees. Credit unions are typically owned and operated by their members, who make their savings available for low-cost loans to other members. Many employees have found that credit unions help their companies by contributing to the financial well-being of their employees. For further information, contact:

Credit Union National Association
P.O. Box 431
Madison, WI 53701
(608) 231-4000

CONTROLLING HEALTH INSURANCE COSTS

Health insurance is one of the fastest-growing small business expenses. Premiums for many small businesses have risen 70% in the past four years. The size of a small business' workforce compounds the problem. Some insurance companies don't like dealing with small companies, because small businesses represent a greater risk. For example, one catastrophic expense for saving the life of an employee's premature baby can wipe out the insurance company's profit on a small business for years.

For these reasons, many small companies do not qualify for lower group rates and pay considerably more per employee for coverage, than their larger corporate counterparts. Here are some options to consider to help reduce your medical insurance costs:

- **COBRA.** COBRA was an act passed by Congress that allows former employees of a company with at least 20 employees to keep their company health plan for at least 18 to 36 months after leaving the company. Under the COBRA plan, a former employee retains the exact policy they had while working for another company. The individual must pay the premium to receive coverage. It may be cheaper for you to pay for the employee's COBRA coverage than to add them to your own policy.

- **Organizations.** Find out if health insurance is available from any organizations to which you belong. Many religious, fraternal, and professional organizations provide health insurance for their members at competitive rates.

- **Multiple Employer Welfare Arrangements (MEWA).** Check with the local chamber of commerce. Many chambers offer MEWA health insurance coverage to small businesses and the self-employed. Since several employers are bunched together under the same plan, this coverage allows employers with few employees to benefit from the cost savings of a plan with many members. Some local business organizations also provide MEWA coverage.

- **Blue Cross and Blue Shield.** These companies are mandated to insure all people without regard to most of the criteria commercial insurers normally use. Blue Cross often charges more because they can't refuse to cover those with pre-existing problems or employees who live in high-risk areas. A one-person business can expect to pay even higher rates, but if you can afford it, Blue Cross is readily available. Many associations now offer medical insurance policies for their members. If your business is eligible for membership in an asso-ciation, find out which ones offer health insurance coverage.

- **National Health Care.** Some states such as Hawaii, Vermont, Oregon, and Florida are implementing their own universal health plans, in advance of proposed national health care plans. For example, Minnesota started a comprehensive program of state-subsidized health care several years ago. New York passed legislation that will force commercial insurers to accept all applicants. New Jersey has passed a subsidized insurance plan. If your business is located in one of these states, you may be able obtain affordable coverage.

Shop for group coverage, which tends to be less expensive than individual coverage programs. If you can not find an acceptable group-coverage program, then your only recourse may be to purchase individual health insurance. This is not difficult, but individual policies are usually the most expensive type of health insurance. Call every available insurance agent to find the best price and coverage. The insurance market is extremely competitive, so it pays to shop around for any insurance policy.

IMPLEMENTING EMPLOYEE TRAINING

There may be a number of areas in which you want your employees trained, such as specific job skills, company policies, or productivity techniques. The following outline describes several techniques you can use to introduce training in your company:

- **Apprenticeship training.** The concept of apprenticeship training usually goes hand in hand with the type of jobs that demand training in specialized skills that can only be acquired through a long period of practice and experience. For example, one hour of classroom theory is typically supplemented with ten hours of supervised hands-on training.

- **On-the-job training.** This type of training is used where there is no class theory. The employee begins the job after some brief instructions and learns through the guidance of other employees and management.

- **Simulated work conditions.** On-the-job training may not be an effective approach if the type of work that is demanded from the new employee takes time to learn and can substantially disrupt the work flow of others. To overcome this problem, the work situation is created in a simulated environment, where the employee learns without disrupting the work of others.

- **Classroom instruction.** The theory behind classroom instruction is that many times complicated information cannot be effectively assimilated on the job because there are too many distractions. Employees are therefore placed in a classroom where disruptions can be controlled. Hence, they are allowed to concentrate on the information that is presented to them.

KEEPING EMPLOYEE MORALE HIGH

One of the best ways to boost employee morale is to increase employees' self-esteem. When employees have high self-esteem, they're much more productive. If you choose to ignore the self-esteem issues, which is common practice in large corporations, you will be undercutting one of the biggest potential advantages small businesses have over their larger counterparts. Poor employee self-esteem can cripple productivity, cause absenteeism, high turnover, and poor work attitudes.

How do you create a company climate that radiates high self-esteem? The first step is to create an environment where you always have motivated employees who want to come to work. Set up guidelines for employees that establish the parameters necessary for the success of the business — such as always being on time. Draw up a list of guidelines and ask employees to sign the list indicating they understand the rules and will abide by them in order to remain a part of your company. If employees break the rules, they have no one to blame but themselves.

ESTABLISHING A SUGGESTION PROGRAM

All successful business owners are constantly looking for business improvement ideas. Employees are one of the best sources you have for good ideas. They are often the people closest to the operations of the business, who know what the problems are and how to solve them. Tapping into employee suggestions also increases their self-esteem. To get the most from your employee suggestion program, conduct regular meetings to discuss employee ideas. Offer rewards to employees who come up with ideas that help the company become more efficient.

ESTABLISHING REWARD PROGRAMS

A good way to improve your staff's performance is to create incentives for superior work. You might establish a bonus system that rewards people for more, or better work. One way is to set a company-wide goal to increase sales. Offer rewards to employees if the

goal is met to your satisfaction. If you can't afford
raises or bonuses, try to increase productivity by taking advantage of the fact that many employees grow
bored or dissatisfied with the same job. Offer them
the opportunity to switch into new areas where they
can learn fresh skills. As employees become more enthusiastic about their jobs, their productivity will increase. Above all, remain flexible, and always look
for new ideas to increase employee productivity.

SOURCES FOR ADDITIONAL INFORMATION

EMPLOYMENT AGENCIES

Private employment agencies are listed in the yellow
pages under the heading of "employment agencies."
State employment agencies will also help you find
people who are looking for work — and there is no
fee. The Federal Trade Commission publishes a guide
entitled *Job Hunting: Should You Pay?* The guide includes advice on selecting employment services and
the different types of services that are available. For
further information, contact:

Federal Trade Commission
Washington, DC 20580

INTERVIEWING

If you feel that you need more information about interviewing techniques, perhaps one of the books listed
below will help:

The Evaluation Interview by Richard A. Fear (Mc-
Graw-Hill).

Employer's Guide to Hiring and Firing by Paul Preston (Prentice-Hall).

*One to One: Interviewing, Selecting, Appraising, and
Counseling Employees* by James J. Goodale (Prentice-Hall)

Occupational Health and Safety

The Occupational Safely and Health Act of 1970 covers just about every employee in the United States. The law is intended to reduce the incident of personal injuries, illness, and death of American workers. For further information, contact:

The Occupational Safety and Health Administration
Department of Labor
Washington, DC 20210
(202) 523-8017

National Safety Council
444 North Michigan Avenue
Chicago, IL 60611
(312) 527-4800

Personnel Administration

The Society for Human Resource Management is the largest national organization dedicated to the development of human resources. Through conferences, educational programs, and publications, the association provides information on personnel policies, practices, and management. For further information, contact:

Society for Human Resource Management
606 North Washington Street
Alexandria, VA 22314
(703) 548-3440

Labor Publications

The United States Department of Labor is the largest publisher of materials pertaining to all aspects of labor. The breadth of their coverage is contained in the Department's annual directory entitled Publications of the Department of Labor. A copy should be available in your local library or contact:

Office of Information and Public Affairs
U.S. Department of Labor
200 Constitution Avenue, NW
Washington, DC 20210
(202) 523-7316

DISABLED EMPLOYEES

Employers interested in hiring disabled employees should contact Mainstream, a national non-profit organization that provides employers with information, training, and technical assistance on diverse disability issues. Write for a copy of their catalog at the following address:

Mainstream Inc.
1200 15th Street, NW
Washington, DC 20005
(202) 833-1136

SOCIAL SECURITY

Many people are unaware of the fact that the Social Security program is more than an old age assistance program. The program also covers unemployment compensation, child welfare services, public health, and vocational rehabilitation programs. For further information about the Social Security program, contact the local or national Social Security office at the following address:

Social Security Administration
Office of Public Service
6401 Security Blvd.
Baltimore, MD 21235
(410) 965-7700

16

Protecting Your Business with Copyrights, Trademarks, and Patents

Many entrepreneurs have unique ideas that they have discovered and are anxious to develop. In this chapter, we will discuss ways you can protect your ideas as you proceed through the development cycle. In some cases, you may be successful at obtaining the exclusive rights to your invention, trade name, or written material that can be applied to the startup of your business. As your business grows, these protection features can add significant value to your business.

COPYRIGHTS

A copyright is a form of protection that is granted by the U.S. Copyright Office to the originator or author of written work. A copyright prevents others from doing the following:

1. Reproduce copies of written work or electronic recordings (e.g., records, videos, etc.) without the permission of the originator of the copyrighted material.

2. Distribute copies of copyrighted work for public sale without the permission of the originator of the copyrighted material.

The copyright laws are complicated and our two sentence summary of the thousands of pages of the law obviously cannot cover the full intent of the laws. In reality, millions of people violate the strict rules of the copyright laws daily. Anybody who copies a page out of a copyrighted book — without the permission of the holder of the copyright — has in principle, violated the copyright laws. However, the real intents of the copyright laws are to protect the originator of the work from financial damages should anyone exploit their work. The real teeth in the law protects you against someone stealing your copyrighted work and reselling it for profit. The typical materials that can be copyrighted are listed as follows:

1. Literary, dramatic, and musical works.
2. Motion pictures and other audiovisual works.
3. Sound recordings.
4. Computer software.
5. Graphics, pictorial images, sculptural works, and maps.

Items that, in general, are not eligible for copyright protection include works consisting entirely of information that is common knowledge, and contains no original authorship. Examples would include a standard calorie, or archaeology chart.

APPLYING FOR A COPYRIGHT

Any citizen of the United States can apply for a U.S. copyright. The procedures for copyright registration are very simple. In most cases, you fill out a single page form and mail it along with a copy of your work to the following address:

Copyright Office
Library of Congress
101 Independence Avenue, SE
Washington, DC 20559
(202) 287-5000

Upon request, the Copyright Office will send you the forms and all of the information you need to prepare a copyright application. Unlike patent applications, copyright applications are relatively easy to prepare and submit. If your employees are working for you on copyrightable material, then you are considered the author under the copyright "working for hire" statute. This statute covers employers who hire employees to prepare copyrightable work for their companies.

SUBMISSION STEPS

There are four basic steps are required to submit an application for a copyright. We have summarized the requirements for each step in this section. The Copyright Office can provide you detailed instructions on how to complete the various steps in the application form.

1. Complete and sign the application form.
2. Include a check to cover the copyright fee (usually $10 per submission).
3. If the work is unpublished, include one complete copy of the work.
4. If the work has been published, include two complete copies of the work.

The copyright protection of your work goes into effect after your work is received and formally recorded by the copyright office. For this reason, you may want to send your material by registered mail. If your work is found to be acceptable as copyrighted work, an official copyright certificate will be sent to you. Depending on the copyright office backlog, it can take from two to four months before you will receive your certificate.

COPYRIGHT PROTECTION

The length of time that your copyright will be valid is once again subject to complex copyright laws. Most copyrighted work is protected from the time of its creation through the author's life, plus an additional 50 years after the death of the author. If the work was performed by more than one author, then the terms of the copyright last for 50 years after the last surviving author's death. For "works for hire," where the author was paid to write the material by a third party (e.g., company), the duration of the copyright is 75 years, in most cases.

TRADEMARKS

A trademark is a word, name, symbol, or combination thereof, that a company adopts and uses to distinguish its products, or services, from others. One of the primary purposes of a trademark, is to identify the origin of the product and to instill some positive image in the mind of customers. For example, the trademark name IBM, by itself, implies quality computers. Extensive advertising is used by businesses to develop desired trademark images.

The right to use a trademark is acquired through a combination of (a) the registration of the trademark and (b) the continued use of the trademark. If you register a trademark and do not practice the continued use of the trademark (e.g., display of trademark on product), you will lose your preserved rights to exclusively use the trademark.

REGISTERING TRADEMARKS

Applications for trademarks are submitted to the U.S. Patent Office and are relatively easy to prepare. Complex trademark applications may require the assistance of a trademark attorney. The basic application is submitted in three parts.

Written Application

The application must be written in English and state how the trademark will be used in connection with the goods and services of the business. You must also provide a brief description of each product or service that will use the trademark, and the date when it was, or will be first used.

Drawings

You must submit a drawing of the trademark on a sheet of 8 1/2 by 11 inch plain white paper. If the trademark is made-up of only words and numbers, the trademark can be typed in the center of the paper, which is referred to as a typed drawing. Special form drawings that conform to a particular style or design can be submitted for trademarks. All lines and letters in the drawing must be black, including any lines that are used in shading. You are allowed to submit a printer's proof, or a clear photocopy of the drawing. Photographs are not permitted.

Specimens

You are required to submit five specimens that show, by example, how the trademark will be used. The specimens may be all the same, or five different specimens. Examples of specimens would include actual trademark labels, containers, or tags that can be sent in a flat format, which meet a 8 1/2 by 13 inch size restriction. A 0 fee is charged for each class of goods or services covered in the application.

TRADEMARK RESTRICTIONS

Trademarks cannot be registered if they do not perform the function of identifying products or services as coming from a particular source, such as a company. They cannot be immoral, or falsely suggest a connection with people or institutions, where there is no association. In other words, trademarks cannot be deceptive. There are certain advantages for registering and protecting your company's trademark. First, it opens up your right to sue in Federal court for trademark infringement. You are allowed to recover damages to your business and attorney fees. A United States trademark registration can also be used as the basis for filing trademark applications in foreign countries.

PATENTS

Patents are protection grants issued by governments to inventors. The holder of the patent can exclude others from making, using, or selling their invention. In the United States, patents are granted through the Patent and Trademark Office and are good for 17 years from the issue date of the patent. Patents on ornamental designs are granted for 14 years. United States patents only grant protection throughout the United States and its territories. To obtain protection in foreign countries, you must file for a separate patent in each country where you want protection.

WHAT CAN BE PATENTED

Any person who invents or discovers a new and usable process, machine, manufacturing technique, or new composition of matter that shows useful improvements can apply for a patent. The composition of matter refers to chemical compositions, and may include chemical mixtures of ingredients. The Atomic Energy Act of 1954 excludes the patenting of nuclear and atomic weapons. The term "useful" means that the invention must have a useful purpose and be able to perform to this purpose.

Over the years, the courts have clarified what can and cannot be patented. For example, methods of doing business, such as total quality management (TQM), and printed matter cannot be patented. A mixture (e.g., composition of matter) cannot be patented unless it can be show that the combination of the components results in some greater benefit.

The statutes also state that the invention must be new before it can be patented. If the invention was known — or in use by others — it cannot be patented. If you demonstrate your invention to others, you have one year in which to file a patent, or your right to file a patent for the invention will be lost. Because of the demonstration or publication of the idea, if will no longer be considered new after one year from the demonstration or publication date.

To be eligible for a patent, the invention must be sufficiently different from similar inventions, and the differences must not be obvious. Small advances that would be considered obvious to anyone skilled in the applicable art would be considered obvious. For example, attempting to patent a device that is similar to an existing device but is composed of entirely different materials (e.g., plastic instead of metal) would probably be considered obvious and no patent would be issued.

PROTECTING YOUR IDEA

Protecting your idea before you formally apply for a patent is an important consideration for many inventors. The key to the protection process is your ability to provide evidence of the exact time you came up with the idea for your invention. This is important in the event that a dispute develops with others who may be working on the same idea. One of the best approaches for you to follow is to maintain a detailed and dated log book that covers the development of your invention. On a periodic basis, ask you trusted friends to witness and sign your notes as you progress.

You can file a disclosure document prior to the

submission of your patent application with the U.S. Patent and Trademark Office. On the form, you identify the basis of your invention and disclose your intent to file for a patent. This document will protect you for two years from the filing date. To learn more about the Disclosure Document Program, contact:

U.S. Department of Commerce
Patent and Trademark Office
Washington, DC 20231

APPLYING FOR A PATENT

Patent applications are submitted to the commissioner of patent and trademarks. They must be prepared in the English language on one-sided 8 1/2 by 11 paper, double spaced, with one inch margins on the left side and top of each page. Applications are assigned a serial number when they are received by the Patent Office. You will be notified of the serial number that is assigned to your application. You can use the number for reference when corresponding with the patent office. There are three primary sections in a patent application.

Specification

The specification section of the application begins with the title of your invention. The title appears in the heading and should be as short and specific as possible. It is followed by a written description of the invention that describes the exact process of making and using the invention. The features that clearly distinguish your invention from other similar inventions should be identified in terms that anyone familiar with the art of your invention can understand.

Drawings

Most patent applications include drawings that supplement the written description in the specification section. The drawings must show every feature of the invention, as it was described in the specification section. The Patent Office has established specifications for the size of the paper on which the drawing is made, the type of paper, margins, and other required specifications for drawings.

Declaration and Signature

You are required to sign a declaration stating that you believe you are the original and first inventor of the subject in the application. The basic cost for filing a patent application is $340. Additional charges can be added to the application fee for complex patents. If you are granted a patent, an issue fee of $560 is required. The Patent Office may reduce fees for independent inventors, nonprofit organization, and small businesses. You must submit a verification statement to petition for the lower fee.

PATENT SEARCHES

Before you can apply for a patent, you must first determine if you can establish "novelty" in your invention. Will it pass the novelty standards that have been established by the Patent Office? Does a patent on your invention already exist in the United States or a foreign country (i.e., search test)?

To pass the novelty test, the invention must be deemed new, useful, and a process that is not obvious, and results in a significant benefit or improvement. It cannot be an idea by itself, a method of doing business, or printed matter. The invention cannot be known through prior use or publication anywhere in the world.

The patent search involves searching historical patent records to ascertain if a patent has already been issued on your particular invention. If it has, you will not be eligible to receive a patent. The Scientific Library of the Patent and Trademark Office located at 2021 Jefferson Davis Highway, Arlington, VA is the national search library for U.S. patents granted since 1836. Patents are arranged according to a classification system, which includes over 300 subject classes and 65,000 subclasses. By conducting a search, you can determine if a patent has already been granted for the same or similar invention as yours. You can also obtain information about patents relating to any field that you desire.

You can hire the services of patent searchers to conduct a search for you, if you do not live in the Arlington area. Large metropolitan public libraries in most states have been equipped with patent search capabilities that will afford you the opportunity to conduct patent searches close to home.

PATENT MARKINGS

The protection afforded by a patent does not start until after a patent is granted, which can take several years. Once a patent is granted, you are required to mark the patented item with the word "patented" followed by the number of the patent. If you fail to comply with this statute, you may not recover damages from a patent infringer unless you can prove that you notified the infringer of the violation and they continued to trespass on your patent.

You are not allowed to mark your item with the word "patented" until after the patent has been granted. You can mark the item with the words "patent applied for," or "patent pending," as a means of warning potential infringers of your patent application. They can trespass on your patent pending process without concern for legal reprisal up to the point in time when you are granted a patent. Again, you are not protected by the patent laws until you have been granted a patent.

ADVANTAGES AND DISADVANTAGES OF PATENTS

In some respect, the disadvantages of obtaining a patent outweigh the advantages. The single most important advantage of obtaining a patent is that it affords you and your invention protection under the patent laws of the United States. As a result, many entrepreneurs believe that it is possible to make a fortune simply by having a patent granted to them for their original idea. Unfortunately, this may not be true for the following reasons:

- **Design options.** If your patent shows how to accomplish a certain task, chances are there are alternative ways to accomplish the same task. Someone else can study what you have done and develop an alternative approach without infringing on your patent.

- **Invalid patent.** A patent can be granted to you and later proven to be invalid. If you go to federal court to seek damages from an infringer and the infringer can find a flaw in your patent application, your patent could be ruled invalid by the court.
- **Costs.** Although it is possible to process your own patent application, most applications require the services of patent attorneys and patent searchers to successfully complete the patent application process. The cost for these services can amount to several thousands of dollars.
- **Court costs.** Federal court costs are an expensive proposition that many small business entrepreneurs cannot afford. Unfortunately, a large corporate patent infringer could bankrupt your business, by forcing you to incur more legal fees than you can afford to protect your patent.

SOURCES FOR ADDITIONAL INFORMATION

COPYRIGHT LAWS

Copyright Laws of the United States is a publication that is available upon request by contacting:

United States Copyright Office
Library of Congress
Washington, DC 20559

TRADEMARK INFORMATION

General Information Concerning Trademarks is a publication that is available upon request by contacting:

Superintendent of Documents
U.S. Government Patent Office
Washington, DC 20402

PATENT INFORMATION

General Information Concerning Patents is a publication that is available upon request by contacting:

Superintendent of Documents
U.S. Government Patent Office
Washington, DC 20402

Introduction to Patents is a publication that is available upon request by contacting:

Small Business Administration
P.O. Box 30
Denver, CO 80201-0030

PATENT ATTORNEYS AND AGENTS

Patent Attorneys and Agents Registered to Practice Before the U.S. Patent and Trademark Office is a listing that is available upon request by contacting:

Superintendent of Documents
U.S. Government Patent Office
Washington, DC 20402

17
Preparing a Business Plan

A sound business plan requires an investment of substantial time and resources to complete. To insure that your plan is effective in guiding your business and attracting investors, follow the suggestions offered in this chapter. If you intend to use your plan to attract capital, honestly ask yourself if you would invest in the business based on reading your plan. If you cannot answer yes, then your plan needs more work. This chapter will show you how to develop and write a business plan. A number of examples are included to help you get started.

WHAT IS A BUSINESS PLAN?

A business plan is a written statement that includes details about your business concepts, plans, goals, and objectives. It explains why, how, and when you plan to achieve strategic business goals. When you develop a business plan, you should have a clear understanding of what you want to accomplish. These are the basic questions that are addressed and answered in a business plan.

- What is your target market and who are your customers?
- What are your market strengths and weaknesses?
- Who are your competitors?
- What are your production and distribution plans?
- Who are your suppliers?
- How much money will you need to start the business and keep it running over the next several years?
- At what point in time will your business make a profit?

A solid plan is practical, pragmatic, and specific. It emphasizes implementation and the achievement of measurable objectives. A business plan is also a living document that over time, becomes marked up, modified, and relied upon to run your business. Do not fall into the trap of evaluating the adequacy of your business plan by its length. Ten to thirty pages should be sufficient for most plans, and each page must mean something to you. If it does not add value to your business, delete the page.

A well-written and thought out business plan is an essential tool for any business. The business plan brings together all the goals, plans, strategies, and resources of the business. A good plan can dramatically increase your chances of succeeding, and can be used to help you define your business concepts, evaluate the competition, estimate costs, predict sales, and control risks. It can be used to help launch new products and services, rejuvenate your business with new ideas, or analyze marketing opportunities. In addition, a business plan can do the following:

- It focuses your attention and ideas on the primary goals and objectives of the business.
- It creates a track for you to follow during the start-up stages of the business.
- It creates benchmarks against which you can measure business progress.
- It provides a vehicle for attracting capital to help finance the business.

LEARNING BUSINESS PLANNING BASICS

A business plan should reveal where your business stands at any moment in time, where it plans to go, and how you plan to get there. Progress is shown in the plan by comparing actual results to planned results. Financial projections are an essential component of the plan. Projections, and if they are available, actual results, should show in dollars and cents how well your business is going to accomplish the objectives in the plan. It therefore becomes a critical document to help prospective investors gauge your potential, to determine if they want to invest in your company.

Financial projections follow the same formats that we covered in the chapters on accounting and finance. Sales projections are reported along with supporting data that shows how you plan to meet your projections. Anybody reviewing your plan should be able to clearly understand how the numbers were derived, and if the numbers present a valid assessment of a company's growth potential.

To illustrate the importance of detailed revenue projections, let's assume that your company plans to sell $500,000 worth of products in its first year of operation. This lump-sum figure is all that is stated in the sales forecast section of your business plan, and it is hardly sufficient for planning the year's productions. The absence of quantitative information makes it impossible to rely on the projections. Prospective investors will lack the kind of solid information they need to make an intelligent business decision — and so will you.

All too often, sales forecasts are little more than theoretical projections, based on the total size of the market and the assumption that a business can command a certain percentage of the market. All revenue and cost projections must be substantiated in the business plan. Investors will want to know what evidence supports your market share predictions, and how solid is the company's market research data? Unless investors are confident in how your plan addresses these and other questions, you will not be able to qualify your company for a loan. If you cannot answer these questions to your satisfaction, you should seriously question the viability of the business that you are about to start.

For plan projections to serve their purpose, sales must be broken down into verifiable categories from which estimates can be drawn, market segments defined, and customer groups identified, as we have shown in Exhibit 17–1. Detailed revenue projections

Exhibit 17-1. Business Plan Sales Break-Down for First Year				
	Market Segment			
	North	**South**	**East**	**West**
Product A	$124,000	$80,000	$45,765	$33,896
Product B	$75,964	$56,985	$12,842	$88,444
Product C	$45,674	$97,755	$82,000	$55,432

Exhibit 17-2. Market Segmentation by Customer Type

	Market Segment			
	North	South	East	West
Customer Type A	$24,000	$180,020	$25,565	$53,896
Customer Type B	$55,960	$76,989	$32,742	$68,544
Customer Type C	$45,679	$87,750	$92,032	$55,400

are also used to accurately forecast your costs, based upon sales estimates. The interrelationships between sales and cost forecasts are a critical component of a good business plan.

MARKET SEGMENTATION

In every company, sales are made in different categories or segments. Similarly, revenue projections should be structured by first calculating the basic components of each segment, and then adding them together to reveal the company's sales forecast. Sales numbers can be segmented by a wide range of characteristics including product lines, geography, and customer profiles. The latter works best when the customer base falls into identifiable groups, such as retail and wholesale customers, as we have illustrated in Exhibit 17–2.

MARKET CHECKS

Do your market projections make sense? Review your numbers in the context of the projected time period. What percent of today's market do they cover? For example, if you are projecting 200 percent annual growth, is that feasible? Is your industry growing at a 200 percent annual rate? As a general rule, changes in sales levels should result in corresponding changes in profits. Test this assumption in your plan. What impact does a 5 percent increase in sales have on the profitability of your product lines? If profits increase markedly, chances are your cost estimates are out of line. Most likely, you have failed to capture the inter-relationship between sales and costs.

Shrewd investors are both wary and attracted by substantial revenue and profit projections in business plans. They are concerned when the reasoning and strategies that give rise to big numbers have not been thoroughly developed. Projecting revenues with supplemental detailed analysis demonstrates important insight into the financial performance of your business. This is critical to the credibility of your business plan, and will increase your chances of attracting partners and capital.

DESCRIBING THE PARTS OF THE PLAN

There are seven basic sections that make up a business plan. All plans start with an executive summary, and include financial projections that cover at least three to five years. Although no two business plans are alike, most of them follow a standard outline:

1. Executive summary. This one to two page summary covers the highlights of your business plan.

2. Company summary. This briefly describes your company and what it does.

3. Products and service analysis. This section begins with a brief description of your products and services. The analytical part of the section addresses why your products and services are better than your competitors.

4. Market analysis. In this section, you identify your target markets and show how you have segmented your market to achieve market penetration.

5. Strategic plan. The strategic plan is your action plan that explains how you will implement your overall business plan.

6. Management profile. A profile of the key employees, business associates, and the professional advisors that you plan to use to support your business is documented in this section.

7. Financial analysis. Financial statements and supporting accounting reports are presented in this section.

EXECUTIVE SUMMARY

The executive summary appears at the beginning of a business plan and summarizes the high points of everything in the plan. The purpose of the executive summary is to convince readers that your business has merit and encourages them to read the remaining sections of the plan. Executive summaries should be written in an enthusiastic, but realistic tone, in one or two pages, and should include:

- **Purpose.** Describe the intent of your business plan. If the purpose of the plan is to obtain financial backing, establish partnership interest, or whatever, make that statement in the executive summary.

- **Definition.** Define your business ideas clearly, in 30 words or less. Here's an excellent opportunity to see if you have a sharp focus on your concept.

- **Overview.** Cover the market potential for your business by summarizing who are the competitors and the customers.

- **Features.** Describe what makes your product or service unique and qualified to compete in the market.

- **Financial Requirements.** Quantify financially what it will take to put your business plan into action.

- **Growth.** Outline how your company will grow and show why it will continue to grow.

Make sure that your executive summary is as perfect as you can make it. The executive summary is sometimes all a potential investor or lender will read, so it must be written to capture their attention. An effective summary will properly position your company and help to distinguish your concepts from the competition. It must be concise and persuasive. If the executive summary fails to motivate the reader, then they will not read the rest of your plan. An example of an executive summary follows:

ExecutiveSummary for the ABC Company

ABC Company specializes in office automation. Although our product line includes computers, copiers, fax machines, and other office equipment, we specialize in the integration of these machines to create a completely automated office at an affordable price. All too often when a company is automating its office, it does so a piece at a time and usually ends up with unrelated and incompatible hardware and software. We sell office systems with the customer's future in mind.

COMPANY SUMMARY

The first question the company summary section of the business plan addresses is who you are and what are your qualifications? This section assumes that the reader knows nothing about you or your company. Company summaries tell the reader who the company is and where it is going. It also includes a brief statement about the people who run the company. Write this section as if you were writing the words for a brochure that would briefly describe your company. The questions addressed in the company summary section include:

- **Names.** The name of the business, the owner's name, and the names of key employees.

- **Background.** A brief background of the owner and key employees as it relates to the business.

- **History.** A short history of the industry showing how your company got started and where it is going.

- **Goals.** Business goals and objectives should be identified.

CompanySummary for the ABC Company

The ABC Company was founded last year to develop, produce, and market integrated automated office systems and to provide related support services. A brief outline of our key management team follows. The company has designed two advanced office systems units and has received letters of interest from two major corporations and the largest specialty department store chain in the state. The goal of the company is to go public in two years.

PRODUCT AND SERVICE ANALYSIS

The product and service section should describe in detail the products or service you intend to offer. The goal here is to differentiate yourself from your competitors. Start with a summary paragraph that clearly describes your products or services. Emphasize the following points:

- Benefits. Show why your products and services are unique, distinct, or of considerably better quality than what is available.

- Costs. Identify all expenses including the costs for raw materials, component parts, equipment, labor, and overhead. Explain where you plan to get your materials. If you are a service company, how much will it cost to fulfill your service obligations?

- Location. Provide details showing where your business will be located and why you choose that particular location. What are the costs of your facilities?

- Technology. If your product or service is based on a unique technology, show why it is unique and important to your business. Is it protected by a patent, copyright, or trademark laws?

- Future. If you have a family of products or services to offer at a future date, what are they? Investors are particularly interested in entrepreneurs who understand that long-term success more often favors businesses with several related products, rather than those with a single offering.

The product and service section of the business plan relies on information that you have collected and incorporated into your marketing and financial plans. An abbreviated summary of a product and service analysis follows:

Product and service analysis
for the ABC Company

ABC Company has defined its niche in the office automation market. Our products include personal and lap-top computers, copiers, fax machines, and other office equipment. Hardware is only half of the office automation solution. For this reason, the company also distributes office automation software including accounting, desktop publishing, data base, word processing, and spreadsheet applications. Our complete line of hardware and software products are fully integrated. Our support services include comprehensive client training on how to use everything we sell.

MARKET ANALYSIS

Many businesses fail because they do not perform an in-depth market analysis. In this section of your business plan, identify who your target market is and show how you have segmented the market. As with all sections in your plan, start with a summary paragraph, so your readers will know what the section covers. Then make sure to include the following points:

- Industry analysis. Present highlights of your industry. Is it growing or declining? What have been the historic business cycles? Is the industry seasonal and how long will the market need your products or service?

- Competitors. List all of your known competitors. Are they big companies with massive budgets, or small companies? What is their market share and are they profitable? What advantages and disadvantages do they have over your business? How do you plan to leverage your advantages and neutralize your disadvantages?

- Customers. Identify your most likely customers. How many are there? Is it a highly targeted market? What common traits do your customers share?

- Market Fit. Describe how you will fit into the market. How does your products or service meet market needs? How do you compare with the competition in terms of features, location, distribution, price, quality, and other factors?

Market analysis for the ABC Company

ABC Company operates six offices in the southwestern states, one of the fastest growing sections in the United States. As more and more companies enter into the advancing age of office automation, they are constantly increasing their demands for office automation products and services. Most companies would prefer to consolidate their orders so that they would have only one company to deal with to simplify the hardware, software, and service integration process. ABC Company is the only company that can provide a total solution to the office automation market.

STRATEGY

The strategic plan section is where you lay out your business plan of action. It shows how you plan to implement your strategies, based upon the information presented in the previous sections. Important points to cover are summarized as follows:

- **Marketing.** Identify the major parts of your marketing program and how they all fit together.

- **Pricing.** Summarize your pricing rationale, showing how it was developed and why it will work.

- **Distribution.** Describe the distribution channels that you plan to use. Many small businesses fail because they have not established adequate distribution channels.

- **Sales.** Outline how you plan to sell your products or services. Will you have a sales force, or use contract representatives?

- **Promotion.** Show how you plan to promote your business? What free publicity is available to you? How will you advertise and what will it cost?

- **Forecast.** Develop charts showing estimated sales for the next three to five years.

Segment your sales by the product and service lines of the business. Separate your total sales into

Exhibit 17-3. Projected Sales by Product Line

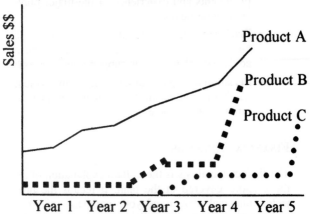

categories and show subtotals on a monthly basis in dollars and units, if applicable. Charting sales by product lines will often highlight trends, such as seasonal variations, as we have show in Exhibit 17-3.

You can also project the seasonal fluctuation in one product line, while planning for more steady growth across the rest of your business in another product line. Geographic regions could be the basis for segregating sales. The use of a computer database system, or a spreadsheet program to record sales by major customers, can be helpful in preparing sales projections. Once you know how you want to segment your sales, you can design an information system to capture this information on an ongoing basis.

MANAGEMENT PROFILE

The backgrounds of the company's management team are covered in the management profile section of the plan. This section is often supplemented with an attachment that includes resumes of each person featured in the profile. The management profile section should include the following components:

- **Organizational.** Include an organizational chart showing who reports to whom and what function they perform.

- **Resumes.** Resumes should list the accomplishments and experience of the major players in your business.

- **Professionals.** Include attorneys, accountants, business advisers, or industry experts whose advice you plan to use to support your business.

- **Personnel.** Explain in detail the employment needs of your business and how you plan to hire the right people.

FINANCIAL ANALYSIS

The financial analysis is the dollars explanation of all the sections covered in the plan. It recaps the projected financial growth of your company, and explains where the money will come from to run the business. Projections for everything from accounts receivable to expenses are included in this section. You should also include a break-even analysis to show how much you will spend before you become profitable.

- **Balance sheet.** This report projects business assets, liabilities, and owner's equity over a minimum of three years.

- **Income statement.** Project the net profits or losses of the business over a 3 to 5 year time period.

- **Cash flow schedule.** Show where and when cash will be spent and collected over the next three years. Project how much you will owe, and when each installment will be paid over the next three years.

- **Break-even analysis.** Show the point in time when your business will begin to make a profit. The break-even point is reached when total costs equal total sales. You will start making a profit when total sales is greater than total costs.

PUTTING THE PLAN TOGETHER

Writing a business plan is much easier if you conquer and divide all the elements by sections. Critique your plan carefully to determine if it is a true representation of the facts as you know them. And most important, is this the business you want to commit your time and resources to for the next several years? Before drafting your final version, show your plan to trusted colleagues and ask for their opinions. Incorporate valid suggestions into your final draft.

When creating a document as important as a business plan, you want it to look as professional as possible. The quality of the paper you choose can dramatically affect the look of your document. Produce the final draft of your plan on high-quality paper. Include a cover, table of contents, headers, and footers in your plan. A table of contents allows the reader to easily move around the document. Headers and footers help the reader find the sections that they are interested in and shows them that this is a carefully constructed and complete plan. Headers and footers should appear the same throughout, as should the use of indents, tabs, and headings. A consistent business plan shows that you are building a consistent and reliable business.

To make your plan more readable, format important text with bold, underline, italics, or different font sizes. Add borders around key paragraphs to break up text from financial charts, graphs, and illustrations. Use bullets and numbered lists when appropriate. Any good word processor can be used to handle the formatting and style recommendations that we have covered to give your plan a professional look. If you do not have access to the appropriate software, consider buying a desktop-publishing program, or have a professional desktop publisher produce the final draft for you. The final draft should be printed on an ink jet or laser printer. Even though dot-matrix printer output has improved dramatically, it can not match the print quality of these printers.

If you do not have an appropriate printer, find an office supply or computer store that will rent you one. Once you have a master copy, you can make duplicates on high-quality paper. Always retain an extra copy for your files and record the name of anyone who has a copy of the plan. Insert the final draft in a high quality binder. In addition to keeping your copy clean, binders will give your plan extra weight and presence.

SOURCES FOR ADDITIONAL INFORMATION

A business plan is an invaluable tool. It helps you understand where you are and where you want to go. It can be revised whenever you want to re-evaluate your business options, add a partner, or introduce a new product. However, putting it all together can be a headache. Major corporations often hire expensive consultants to help with this process. Small business owners can get some of the same advice from relatively inexpensive software packages. Two of the most popular are BizPlan Builder from Jan Software and Business Plan Toolkit from Palo Alto Software. Both were created by experienced business planning consultants and offer guidelines to write a business plan.

The software programs work under the assumption that it is easier to edit existing text than to write new text from scratch, and they provide a series of boiler plate text templates for the business plan sections that we have covered. Some of the business planning software packages include spreadsheet templates and charting options to facilitate the presentation of financial and marketing information. Most will accept text files as input from word processors.

Many of the planning software packages include helpful sample phrases you can use to fill in the blanks. Worksheets also use a fill-in-the-blank approach. For example, when preparing the sales forecast, you can enter your first month's projected sales and an annual growth rate or a flat monthly increment. The planning software then generates the sales data by month and year. Some of the better programs will generate graphics and charts from your data.

18
Managing Your Business

Ed Rye once said that "the highest art of professional management requires the literal ability to smell a real fact and to have the temerity, intellectual curiosity, guts, and if necessary, the impoliteness to be sure that what you have is indeed an unshakable fact. No matter what you may think, try shaking the facts to make sure they are facts." The successful management of any business is based upon understanding the facts, and initiating the appropriate management action to take advantage of the facts as you know them.

MANAGING BY OBJECTIVES

The philosophy of managing by objectives (MOB) may be old, but it still works today. It relies on the identification of specific and quantifiable performance goals that are considered critical to the company. All of the people who can contribute to the achievement of the MBO goals are identified, and in the pre-planning process, agree that they can meet the established goals. There are a number of advantages to using MBO.

1. Everybody who is involved in the process knows what is expected of them to help the MBO team reach its goal.

2. The employees feel like they are a part of your company, rather than just working for it.

3. The MBO process opens up ideas that can be shared between team participants to determine the best solution to problems.

4. MBO shows the importance of planning to everybody in the organization.

MBO is a rational system that is relatively easy for everyone in the organization to understand. It offers the added benefit of linking actual job performance to the objectives of the company. If properly used, MBO can be used to motivate your employees to do what you need them to do.

MANAGING BY MOTIVATION

Motivation is an important management component in the MBO process. Highly motivated employees will learn to do their jobs faster and more efficiently. How do your employees really feel about their jobs? Do they like working for your company, or are they biding their time until a better opportunity comes along? How much does employee morale matter to the overall success of your business? These are just a few of the question that you should ask yourself from time to time. The following guidelines will help you maintain a high level of employee morale within your company:

MOTIVATIONAL GUIDELINES

1. Care about the people, contractors, and suppliers who work for you. Recognize them as friends of your business and treat them accordingly.

2. If you make a mistake, admit the mistake and don't try to blame someone else for your actions.

3. Be tactful when dealing with people and always remember that they have feelings.

4. Give praise when a job is well done and never be afraid to use the work "thank you."

5. Be willing to learn as much as you can from other people, even if it means learning how not to do something.

6. Always demonstrate enthusiasm and confidence even in strained situations. Most people will follow your lead.

7. Maintain an open line of communications with your employees and other people who may need to talk to you. Always be prepared to offer help and advice whenever you can.

8. Set standards for yourself and your business. Follow your own standards if you expect others to follow them.

9. Always keep the people who are associated with your business informed as to where the

business is going. Do not let them try to guess what is happening.

10. Be flexible in everything you do. Just because you have always done something one way does not mean that it is the right way.

MANAGING BY OBSERVATION

Since entrepreneurs are motivated by a need for personal achievement, they often have little interest in the organizational structure of their own companies. Entrepreneurs who tend to focus on their own achievements, as opposed to the achievements of the people that work for them, incur a high failure rate. They overlook the fact that many of the people who work for them also want to become entrepreneurs. Management by observation is a simple process that allows managers to know their people by walking around. The process requires that you periodically observe what your employees are doing for the company and engage in personal conversation with your employees. This becomes an important employee motivator.

OBSERVATION GUIDELINES

1. Make daily tours of your business to check on the appearance of your facilities, the attitudes of your employees, and the presentation of your products.

2. Constantly make contact with your customers. Observe them as they shop, talk with them, and ask them questions. Review all customer complaints to assure that your business is initiating preventive action.

3. Try out every product and service that you sell to make sure that you would buy it over the competitive offerings, if you were the customer.

4. Spend consistent time with your employees. Get to know them and learn to understand their problems. Solicit their advice and ideas on improving your business.

5. Always look for additional ways to improve upon the overall efficiency of your business.

PROBLEM SOLVING STRATEGIES

What do you do if your business is floundering? Sometimes entrepreneurs are to busy building their business to see the larger picture. A major problem may suddenly erupt that they are not prepared to handle. The following guidelines should help you develop a rational approach to solving your business problems:

PROBLEM SOLVING GUIDELINES

1. State the problem in as many different ways as possible to make sure you understand the problem. A problem that is understood is half-solved.

2. Get the facts to determine what is known and what information is needed.

3. Analyze what the situation is all about and review the assumptions to determine if they are valid.

4. Based on what you now know, restate the problem and begin to develop alternative solutions.

5. Review the alternative solutions individually and select the alternative that best solves the problem.

RECORDS MANAGEMENT

Some of the most important information you may need to mange your business is not found in the library, or on a computer data base, but in your brain. Vital dates, records of important conversations, commitments, and verbal agreements are usually lost unless they are recorded in a retrievable form. The easiest way to establish a running record is to obtain a combination notebook and calendar that can be kept in a handy location. Day-Timers, Inc. (One Day-

Timer Plaza, Allentown, PA 18195-1551, (215) 395-5884) offers a variety of notebook-calendars that are designed for this purpose. Write and ask them to send you their comprehensive catalog.

MANAGING NEW PRODUCTS AND SERVICES

The effective management of introducing new products and services into your business is absolutely essential for the growth of the business. All products and services go through a life cycle — introduction, growth, maturity, and decline. Unfortunately, eight out of ten new products and service introductions fail because of poor management planning. Although the introduction of new business offerings is essential to the growth of your business, there could be a number of other compelling business reasons to either change, or introduce a new product and services mix, such as the following:

1. Your offerings are no longer competitive with the offerings of your competitors (i.e., price, quality, etc.).

2. The use for which your product was created has been eliminated. For example, when buggies became obsolete, there was no longer a need for buggy whips.

3. Your service was related to some phase of the economy. For example, when interest rates are increasing, a service that sells certificates of deposits may do well. When interest rates fall, certificates of deposits are very difficult to sell.

4. You may have excess capacity in the business such as floor space, and it may make sense to expand into another product or service to fully utilize the capacity of your business.

5. You may have surplus capital that would earn a higher rate of return if you invested it in the growth of your business as opposed to outside investment options, such as stocks and bonds.

6. The by-products from your business, such as scrap materials, could be used to make other products, or sold to obtain additional income.

7. By adding another product or service to your offerings, your sales force could be more effectively utilized if the same customer who buys product A, would also be interested in buying the new product B.

8. Your current products and services sales are dependent upon the seasons. You may want to add products and services that are popular in the off-season.

As an astute business person and entrepreneur, you should always be looking for new products and services to offer. In the process, look for improvements that you can make to your existing offerings that will extend their life cycle, and gain you an advantage over the competition.

SOURCES FOR NEW PRODUCTS

There are literally thousands of sources for new products and services. Many of these sources can be used to help you generate your own ideas for new offerings. We have listed several sources to help you get started.

- **Existing products and services.** Success follows success. If you are already enjoying the sales for highly successful products, now may be the time to consider the options you could implement to further improve upon your successes. Your improvements will make it more difficult for your competitors to copy what you are doing. For example, by the time they start selling the current product, your new and improved product is already announced.

- **Competitive products and services.** Monitor the activities of your competitors closely. If they offer a product or service line that you don't have, and you suddenly see a proliferation of ads appearing in the local media covering their unique offerings, it may be an indication that your competitors are doing well. If the advertising campaigns continue, you could assume that they would not continue to advertise if they were not doing well with the new product or service lines. Consider adding those same product and service lines to your business's offerings.

- **Inventor's shows.** The annual inventors' show features hundreds of new products that inventors would like to license to businesses who are interested in manufacturing their products. Many are willing to sell their inventions. For further information about the inventors' shows, contact the Office of Inventions and Innovations, National Bureau of Standards, Washington, DC 20234.

- **Newspapers and trade magazines.** Newspapers and trade magazines will often feature articles in their business section about individuals who have developed new products and services. Many of these periodicals include business opportunity advertising sections that cover new product and service opportunities. You may even choose to place your own ad in one of these periodicals.

- **Foreign product shows.** There are thousands of foreign products available for the offering if you know where to look. The U.S. Department of Commerce publishes a weekly magazine entitled Commerce Magazine Weekly that contains a listing of foreign products that are available for licensing. The American Register of Exporters and Importers, 38 Park Row, New York, NY 10038 is another excellent import directory. Check your local library for other popular directories and sources of foreign products.

- **Patent office gazette.** The U.S. Patent Office publishes The Official Gazette, a weekly publication that lists the patents granted by the patent office. The gazette includes a section on patents that are available for sale. Annual subscriptions are available from the Superintendent of Documents, Government Printing Office, Washington, DC 20402.

- **Trade shows.** Hundreds of trade shows tour the country annually and feature thousands of new product and service ideas. To find out more about trade shows, contact your local library and ask them for a copy of the Directory of the United States Trade Shows. The directory includes an index of trade shows, including types, dates, and locations of the various shows.

- **Other manufacturers.** If you are looking for a particular product from another manufacturer to add to your business offerings, consult the *Thomas Register of American Manufacturers*. This publication is available in a good public library; it lists manufacturers of all types of items made in the United States.

MANAGING YOUR BOTTOM LINE

There are hundreds of ideas and ways that you can use to directly, or indirectly improve upon the profitability, or bottom line of your business. In this section, we have listed several ideas that will help you get started.

- Know how to describe your business in 25 great words or less. Then, when someone asks you about your business, you will know exactly what to say without drowning them in a detailed explanation.

- Allocate a certain amount of your time to promote your business by whatever means you consider appropriate, such as direct mail and telephone calls.

- If appropriate, print more than one business card. For example, one card could be used to promote the service aspects of your business, while the other could promote the product aspects of the business.

- Seek recognition and awards for your business whenever you can. Recognition may come from speeches that you make, while awards may come from a trade association.

- Find sales representative and distributors who already know the clients that will buy your products.

- Contact your customers and find out how they discovered your business. Ask them what they like and do not like about your business, so that you can improve your operation.

- Use bold-face print in the important parts of your advertisements, such as the telephone number to call to attract attention.

- Use discounts to attract first time customers to your business.

- Offer special services, such as pickup and delivery, to differentiate your business from the competition.

- Consider swapping strategic business information, such as monthly expenses and salary information, with other business people that you trust to monitor the competitiveness of your business.

- Develop a set of customer testimonials that you can use in your sales presentations and brochures.

- Always send thank you cards and letters to anyone who has helped your business.

- Seek out advice and consult your friends to determine what you can do the improve you business.

- Develop your expert status within the industry that you are serving by making presentations and writing articles for the local papers or trade journals.

- People in your business community may be written up in the local newspaper for an award or promotion. Build your contact list by sending them a note of congratulations.

- Develop relationships with other people in your business field to build a source of expert advice.

- Always pass out additional business cards to anybody who can refer business to you.

- Get to know everything you can about your target customers.

- Hold sales in your slowest seasonal periods.

- Use your fax machine to promote your business by sending company brochures by fax.

- Deposit surplus business funds in interest bearing accounts, as opposed to letting the funds remain on deposit in a checking account.

- Keep records of every tax deductible expense.

- Depreciate your equipment, and take the depreciation expense tax deduction as quickly as possible if you need a tax shelter in the start-up years of your business.

- If you use a car more than 50 percent for business purposes, you may be eligible to take the more lucrative depreciation write-offs, instead of just mileage.

- If you have a limited background in accounting and taxes, hire a good accountant to do your books at least once. The added cost could save you many more dollars in the long run.

- If you are getting a refund from the IRS, file electronically to get your money sooner.

- Deposit as much money as you can afford, and are allowed, in tax sheltered retirement plans.

SELLING YOUR BUSINESS

At some point in your personal business cycle, you may decide to sell your business. Business owners have different ideas about how they should go about selling their businesses, and what their role should be once the sale is consummated. Every entrepreneur wants the highest price possible. However, there are a number of factors that may affect the final offer. The following are three ways of selling a business:

- **Cashout.** A straight cash sale is called a "cashout." This is the easiest and simplest way to sell a business. Once the price has been agreed upon between the buyer and seller, then the remaining details can follow. For example, will the buyer want the seller to leave the business immediately after the transfer of ownership, or stay on for a period of time? If there are some compelling reasons for the seller to remain with the business, a higher purchase price may be demanded.

- **Earnout.** An "earnout" is another type of sale where the seller remains with the business and shares in the profits.

- **Stock swap.** In a "stock swap" sales transaction, the seller may receive stock instead of cash. The selling price of this type of arrangement is usually than in a "cashout" transaction, since the seller is usually prohibited from selling the stock for some stated period of time.

Whatever the arrangement may be, the smart seller will consult with his or her lawyer and accountant before signing a contract of sale. The tax implications of a given sales offer could prove to be disastrous or advantageous, depending upon how the transaction is arranged.

SOURCES FOR ADDITIONAL INFORMATION

ASSOCIATIONS

The standard reference work for locating the names of associations and societies is *Gale's Encyclopedia of Associations*. Both the *World Almanac* and the *Information Please Almanac* contain short listings of associations and societies. These comprehensive directories are available in most public libraries, and will enable you to find associations by name or subject.

BETTER BUSINESS BUREAUS

The first Better Business Bureau was established in 1914 as a movement to enable business leaders to set standards for national advertising, and to eliminate selling abuses. Today's Better Business Bureaus help protect both the public and business from questionable business practices, false representation, abusive, and dishonest business practices. Further information about the organization, as well as how to start a local bureau, may be obtained by contacting:

Council of Better Business Bureaus
1515 Wilson Boulevard
Arlington, VA 22209
(703) 276-0100

SMALL BUSINESS VOICE

National Small Business United is an association that has been looking out for the interest of small businesses since 1937. The association has initiated and helped enact numerous pieces of favorable federal legislation for small businesses. For more information contact:

National Small Business United
1155 15th Street, NW
Washington, DC 20005
(202) 293-8830

EXECUTIVE SUPPORT

Many retired executives serve under SCORE (Service Corps of Retired Executives), an organization sponsored by the Small Business Administration (SBA). These men and women volunteer their services to small businesses that seek management assistance. SCORE volunteers work in the Small Business Administration's district offices and their services are free. For more information, contact your local SBA office or the national office.

Small Business Administration
1441 L. Street, NW
Washington, DC 20416
(202) 653-6365

MINORITY BUSINESS DEVELOPMENT

The minority business development program was created in 1968. As a result, the Minority Business Development Agency was created to assist minority businesses in achieving effective and equitable participation in the American free enterprise system. Management and technical assistance are provided to minority firms on request, through a network of minority business development centers. For more information contact:

Office of Public Affairs
Minority Business Development Agency
Department of Commerce
Washington, DC 20230
(202) 377-1936

FAMILY BUSINESSES

The Center for Family Business is an organization that serves the family interest of business owners. The principle activity of the center is to hold family seminars on topics such as "Managing Success Without Conflict," and "Planning for the Future as a Business Family." For further information, contact:

The Center for Family Business
P.O. Box 24268
Cleveland, OH 44124
(216) 442-0800

WOMEN IN BUSINESS

The American Business Women's Association is a membership of women from diverse backgrounds and professions. There are numerous local chapters throughout the United States. For further information, contact:

American Business Women's Association
9100 Ward Parkway
Kansas City, MO 64114-0728
(816) 361-6621

Appendix A _____
Glossary of Business Terms

Balance of Payments. A record of all financial transactions which take place between the United States and the rest of the world. It covers payments and receipts for private and governmental transactions. A country has a balance-of-payments deficit when its international payments are greater than its international receipts, and a favorable balance of payments when the reverse is true.

Bear Market. A period of time when prices on the stock exchange are falling.

Bull Market. A period of time when prices on the stock exchange are rising.

Business Cycles. Swings in business activity from peak periods, which bring prosperity, to lows, which accompany depressions.

Capital. A term meaning wealth (excepting land), which produces more wealth. Most of the assets used in a business are considered capital because they generate wealth. Money that people save is capital if it is invested to earn interest or dividends.

Capital Gains. Profits resulting from the sale of capital investments such as stocks and bonds, real estate, business enterprises, etc.

Capitalism. An economic system in which the means of production and the distribution of goods are mostly privately owned and operated for private profit. A capitalist, therefore, is an owner of capital, or one who has a large amount of money invested in a business.

Cartel. An association of independent financial, or industrial companies in the same business, or similar fields, formed to influence the market by regulating competition. It is regulated competition rather than free competition.

Competition. The rivalry found in business between individuals and/or companies trying to win the same markets. The old saying: "Competition is the life of trade" infers that each company must do its best in order to win and keep customers for its goods or services.

Conglomerate. A term coined during the 1960s to describe the giant enterprises created by business mergers when many corporations purchased a number of additional companies which had no relation to each other. The reason behind the wave of mergers was the desire to diversify, and hopefully acquire, companies whose operations would add to the parent corporation's profits.

Consumerism. A fairly new word coined to describe what has been called a consumer revolution. The old motto "Let the buyer beware" became "Let the seller beware." Although many states had bureaus offering consumer protection, the federal government took the lead in passing legislation to help protect consumers.

Credit Crunch. A credit crunch occurs when credit is not available to many businesses and individuals, as has been the case in the past.

Currency. Our current medium of exchange that consists of both paper bills and metal coins. The amount of currency in circulation varies, depending on how much the public requires. When money is not needed, it flows back into the banks in the form of deposits.

Deficit Financing. This term refers to a government's practice of borrowing money required to pay for goods and services for which no cash is available in the treasury.

Deflation. Deflation is the opposite of inflation and usually results when industry cannot sell its goods profitably. Business activity declines, workers are laid off, and a dollar buys more goods and services, as prices fall rapidly. When a period of deflation becomes severe, it is called a recession — or depression.

Demand Deposits. These are deposits of money in a bank account which the depositor may withdraw without giving advance notice.

Discretionary Income. The income remaining after an individual or family has provided for food, clothing and shelter.

Economic Indicators. The financial sections of some newspapers report the latest trends, as shown by many economic indicators. These consist of special price indexes and reports, the following being among the most important: business failures, business inventories, consumer credit reports, consumer price index, Dow Jones industrial average, gross national products, money in circulation, personal income, and retail trade.

Entrepreneur. A person who decides to start a business, expand a company, buy an existing firm, or perhaps borrow money, to manufacture a new product or offer a new service. He or she is the most important person in our free enterprise system, because the entrepreneur is the manager and the risk taker.

Excise Tax. A tax imposed on the manufacture or sale of various commodities such as liquor, tobacco, automobiles, safe deposit box rents, electrical energy, and so forth.

Fair Return. The profits which a public utility may earn. The law has established the principle that a public utility may charge a rate, which is sufficient to earn a reasonable return on the money it has prudently invested in the company, provided the utility is operated in a proper manner. At the same time the rate charged must be reasonable.

Fiscal Policy. The manner in which our federal government levies and collects taxes, purchases its goods and services, spends its funds and manages the national debt.

Fixed Capital. Fixed capital refers to things like airplanes, trucks, machinery, power plants and buildings, which are used to create more wealth by producing products or services.

Free Enterprise. An economic system based on the private ownership and operation of business with a minimum of governmental control. Free enterprise, also known as private enterprise, assumes that individuals own and control their own goals and labor, operate in a free market and have competition. In this system there is no place for cartels, monopolies, or government regulation.

Free Trade. International trade which is free of government regulations as well as import or export duties.

Fringe Benefits. Benefits an employer gives his workers in addition to wages. These may include paid holidays; paid vacations; pensions; life, accident and health insurance; medical examinations; free lunches and/or coffee breaks; tuition for evening courses; free transportation in the company's buses, trains, or planes; discounts on purchases of company products; free uniforms; bonuses; profit sharing; stock purchase plans; incentive pay plans; and travel time.

Gross National Product. This term is used to measure the total value of all the goods and services produced in the country during the year. The official statistics of the federal government divide the GNP into four parts. Consumer Purchases, Business Investor Purchases, Government Purchases and Net Exports of Goods and Services. Each of these classifications is broken down into numerous subdivisions, making it possible to find out how much consumers and government spend on various goods and services.

Guaranteed Annual Wage. An agreement wherein an employer promises to pay his workers all or part of their regular wages, even if the plant is closed. This term should not be confused with the term "guaranteed income," which refers to one possible solution to the poverty problem. Guaranteed income would give unemployed, part-time workers, or those paid sub-standard wages, a minimum income-floor for every family.

Holding Company. A company that owns enough stock of another company to control its policies and operations. Corporations so owned and controlled are called subsidiaries. If a company gains control of two or more holding companies, the practice is called "pyramiding." This type of organization has been

popular among public utilities, banks, and some manufacturing concerns.

Inflation. A period of time when prices climb because the supply of goods is not large enough to satisfy the public's purchasing power or demand. As
prices rise during an inflationary period, money loses
its value, companies may expand to earn larger profits, and some people may have extra cash to spend.
At the same time, workers demand higher and higher
wages to keep up with inflated living costs. The increased wages, however, only add to the worker's
purchasing power — and raise prices again, thus creating an inflationary "wage-price spiral." Deflation is
the opposite of inflation and usually results when industry cannot sell its goods profitably. Business activity declines, workers are laid off, and the dollar buys
more goods and services, while prices fall rapidly.

Interest. The price a lender charges for the use of
money. It is based on the idea that a person who lends
money to another is entitled to profit for the use of his
money. Interest is calculated as part of a percentage
of the whole amount of money to be borrowed, and is
always expressed in percentages. Interest rates are determined primarily by the law of supply and demand.
When money is scarce, interest rates rise — and decline when money is plentiful.

Multiplier Principle. The word multiplier refers to
the spending that is stimulated when a company has
money to invest in capital improvements. When a
company adds a new wing to a factory, in addition to
buying building supplies and machinery, management
will also pay wages to the construction workers. It is
assumed that they will in turn, spend the money they
receive and the money will spread out thereafter in
lesser and lesser amounts as it changes hands.

NASDAQ Composite Index. The National Association of Securities Dealers publishes eight indexes
each day to assist investors in evaluating the large
over-the-counter market. The NASDAQ Composite
Index is a daily index of the performance of over
3,000 stocks, the majority of which are over-the-
counter issues.

Partnership. Two or more individuals who have
agreed to pool their capital, work together, and share

the profits and risks of conducting a business, constitute a partnership. Most partnerships are formed by brokers, lawyers, architects and other professional men and women.

Private Sector. Consumers and private producers who operate in the free markets, as contrasted to the public sector, where government agencies decide what goods (such as surplus foods) and services (such as bank deposit insurance, or old-age pensions) will be provided, and who may buy them.

Proprietorship. A business owned and controlled by a single individual. Regardless of size, if there is only one owner, the company is known as a proprietorship.

Prospectus. Before a public offering of stock can be made, a company must file a detailed "Registration Statement" with the SEC. Incorporated in the Registration Statement is a section called the Prospectus. This is a report prepared for distribution to the public, and it contains all the data an investor would need to help him other decide whether or not to purchase the stock.

Right-to-Work Laws. Those who object to compulsory unionism believe it is contrary to our American way of life to force a person to join any kind of organization and contribute to its financial support, in order to obtain employment. A union that represents a majority of a company's employees understandably feels it is not fair for non-members to share in all the wage increases and other benefits which it has spent money to win. A partial solution is the "agency shop," devised to obtain financial aid from non-union members. A union, however, would naturally prefer a closed shop where it could represent every employee. Many states have enacted right-to-work laws, which effectively bar the closed, or union shop from preferential hiring and maintenance of membership agreements between employers and unions.

Subsidy. This term refers to a grant of money given by a government or private enterprise for the benefit of the public. Today the federal government makes grants for broad categories which include agriculture, business, labor, and homeowners and tenants. Actually many other subsidy programs exist for the needy such as school lunch programs, hospital operation, medical care, etc.

Supply and Demand. Supply is the total amount of goods or commodities which are available for purchase at a given price. Demand is not necessarily what people want to buy, but the amount of goods that people are willing and able to purchase, at a certain price.

Tight Money Condition. A period of time when the supply of credit shrinks and people find it difficult to obtain money at any price. In 1966 the Federal Reserve Board tried to halt inflation by stopping credit growth. The Board kept money scarce for about six months, creating a shortage of money which was called a "credit crunch." The Federal Reserve Board can create a tight-money condition by selling government securities, by raising the discount rate" (interest which the Federal Reserve charges commercial banks for borrowing money), or by raising the amount of "demand deposits" member banks must keep in the nearest Federal Reserve Bank.

Wholesale Price Index. This index shows changes in prices of approximately 2,400 commodities such as chemicals, farm products, leather, lumber, machinery, metals, paper, rubber, and textile products, which are brought by wholesale businesses. It measures prices against a base year of 1967 in the same way that the Consumer Price Index does. The Wholesale Price Index is also known as the Producer Price Index.

Working Capital. Money required to buy the materials needed to turn out goods and services — such as purchases and supplies. Although these things by themselves do not produce wealth, they enable the fixed capital to do so. In accounting terms, working capital refers to the excess of quickly convertible assets over current liabilities. Fixed capital, on the other hand, refers to things like airplanes, trucks, machinery, power plants and buildings, which are used to create more wealth by producing goods or services.

Appendix B
Selected List of Associations

Appendix B contains a selected list of associations and federal government agencies. These associations were chosen because they represent some of the principal areas of interest to the average business. Associations can provide you with a wealth of information about marketing, cost management, government regulation, and a variety of other relevant subjects. Address your request for general information to the public relations department of the respective association or agency. A comprehensive directory of domestic and international associations is available in *The Encyclopedia of Associations,* which is published by Gale Research. The encyclopedia is available in most public libraries.

Abrasives

Abrasive Engineering Society
1700 Painters Run Road
Pittsburgh, PA 15243

Aerospace

American Institute of Aeronautics and Astronauts
1633 Broadway
New York, NY 10019

Aerospace Industries

Aerospace Industries Association of America
1725 De Sales Street, NW
Washington, DC 20036

Agriculture

American Farm Bureau Federation
225 Touhy Avenue
Park Ridge, IL 60068

U.S. Department of Agriculture
Washington, DC 20250

Air Conditioning

Air Conditioning and Refrigeration Institute
1501 Wilson Boulevard
Arlington, VA 22209

Air Force

U.S. Department of the Air Force
The Pentagon
Washington, DC 20330

Air Freight

Air Freight Association of America
1730 Rhode Island Avenue, NW
Washington, DC 20036

Air Pollution

Air Pollution Control Association
PO Box 2861
Pittsburgh, PA 15230

U.S. Environmental Protection Agency
Washington, DC 20460

Air Taxis

National Air Transportation Association
4226 King Street
Alexandria, VA 22302

Air Transportation

Air Transport Association of America
1709 New York Avenue, NW
Washington, DC 20006

Airports

Airport Operators Council International
1700 K Street, NW
Washington, DC 20006

Aluminum

The Aluminum Association
818 Connecticut Avenue, NW
Washington, DC 20006

American Legion

American Legion
P.O. Box 1055
Indianapolis, IN 46206

Appliances

Association of Home Appliances Manufacturers
20 North Wacker Drive
Chicago, IL 60606

Appraising (Property)

American Society of Appraisers
11800 Sunrise Valley Drive
Reston, VA 22091

Architecture

American Institute of Architects
1735 New York Avenue, NW
Washington, DC 20006

Army

U.S. Department of the Army
The Pentagon
Washington, DC 20310

Art

American Federation of the Arts
41 East 65 Street
New York, NY 10021

Arthritis

The Arthritis Foundation
1314 Spring Street, NW
Atlanta, GA 30309

Asphalt

Asphalt Institute
1314 Spring Street
College Park, MD 20740

Audio-Visual Equipment

International Communications Industries Association
3150 Spring Street
Fairfax, VA 22031

Automobiles

Motor Vehicle Manufacrturers Association
300 New Center Building
Detroit, MI 48202

Aviation

U.S. Federal Aviation Administration
Washington, DC 20591

Banking

American Bankers Association
1120 Connecticut Avenue, NW
Washington, DC 20036

Beverages

National Soft-Drink Association
1101-16 Street, NW
Washington, DC 20036

Biological Sciences

American Institute of Biological Sciences
14-1 Wilson Boulevard
Arlington, VA 10011

Blindness

American Foundation for the Blind
15 West 16th Street
New York, NY 10011

Book Publishing

Association of American Publishers
1 Park Avenue
New York, NY 10016

Bookselling

American Booksellers Association
122 East 42 Street
New York, NY 10168

Broadcasting

National Association of Broadcasters
1771 N Street, NW
Washington, DC 20036

Business Aircraft

National Association of Business Aircraft
1634 I Street, NW
Washington, DC 20004

Business Counselors

Institute of Certified Business Counselors
3301 Vincent Road
Pleasant Hill, CA 94523

Cancer

American Cancer Society
90 Park Avenue
New York, NY 10017

Cement

Portland Cement Association
Old Orchard Road
Skokie, IL 60076

Ceramics

American Ceramic Association
65 Ceramic Drive
Columbus, OH 43214

Chemistry

American Chemistry Society
1155-16 Street, NW
Washington, DC 20036

Chiropractic

American Chiropractors Association
1916 Wilson Boulevard
Arlington, VA 22201

Civil Liberties

American Civil Liberties Union
132 West 43 Street
New York, NY 10036

Civil Rights

Civil Rights Division
U.S. Department of Justice
New York, NY 20530

Coast Guard

U.S. Coast Guard
Washington, DC 20590

Communications

U.S. Federal Communications Commission
Washington, DC 20554

Conservation

National Wildlife Federation
1412-16 Street, NW
Washington, DC 20036

U.S. Fish and Wildlife Service
Washington, DC 20204

Construction

Associated Builders and Contractors of America
1957 E Street, NW
Washington, DC 20005

Cystic Fibrosis

Cystic Fibrosis Foundation
6000 Executive Boulevard
Rockville, MD 20852

Dentistry

American Dental Association
211 East Chicago Avenue
Chicago, IL 60611

Diabetes

American Diabetes Association
1600 Duke Street
Alexandria, VA 22314

Direct Mail

Direct Mail Association
6 East 43rd Street
New York, NY 10017

Economics

American Economic Association
1313-21 Avenue South
Nashville, TN 37212

Electric Power

Bureau of Reclamation
U.S. Department of the Interior
Washington, DC 20240

Edison Electric Institute
1111-19 Street, NW
Washington, DC 20036

U.S. Department of Energy
Washington, DC 20585

U.S. Rural Electrification Administration
U.S. Department of Agriculture
Washington, DC 20250

U.S. Nuclear Regulatory Commission
Washington, DC 20555

Electric Utilities

Edison Electric Institute
1111-19 Street, NW
Washington, DC 20036

Electrical Manufacturing

National Electrical Manufacturers Association
2101 L Street, NW
Washington, DC 20007

Electronics

Electronics Industries Association
2001 Eye Street, NW
Washington, DC 20006

Engineering–Chemical

American Institute of Chemical Engineers
345 East 47th Street
New York, NY 10017

Engineering–Civil

American Society of Civil Engineers
345 East 47th Street
New York, NY 10017

Engineering–Industrial

Institute of Industrial Engineers
25 Technology Park
Atlanta, GA 30092

Engineering–Mechanical

American Society of Mechanical Engineers
345 East 47th Street
New York, NY 10017

Engineering–Mining

American Institute of Mining
Metallurgical and Petroleum Engineers
345 East 47th Street
New York, NY 10017

Engineering–Plastics

Society of Plastic Engineers
14 Fairfield Drive
Brookfield, CT 06805

Engineering–Professional

National Association of Professional Engineers
1420 King Street
Alexandria, VA 22314

Engineering Societies

American Association of Engineering Societies
345 East 47th Street
New York, NY 10017

Farming

U.S. Department of Agriculture
Washington, DC 20250

Federal Reserve

Federal Reserve System
Washington, DC 20551

Firearms

National Rifle Association
1600 Rhode Island Avenue, NW
Washington, DC 20036

Foreign Trade

U.S. Tariff Commission
Washington, DC 20436

Forestry

U.S. Forest Service
U.S. Department of Agriculture
Washington, DC 20013

Graphic Arts

Graphic Arts Technical Foundation
4615 Forbes Avenue
Pittsburgh, PA 15213

History

American Association for State and Local History
708 Berry Road
Nashville, TN 37204

House Organs

International Association of Business
  Communicators
870 Market Street
San Francisco, CA 94102

Housing

U.S. Department of Housing and Urban
  Development
Washington, DC 20410

Illumination

Illumination Engineering Society
345 East 47th Street
New York, NY 10017

Immigration

U.S. Immigration and Naturalization Service
Washington, DC 20538

Insulation

National Insulation Contractors Association
1025 Vermont Avenue, NW
Washington, DC 20523

Libraries

American Library Association
50 East Huron Street
Chicago, IL 60611

Machine Tools

National Machine Tool Builders
7901 Westpark Drive
McLean, VA 22102

Tool and Dye Institute
777 Busse Highway
Park Ridge, IL 60068

Manufacturers

National Association of Manufacturers
1776 F Street, NW
Washington, DC 20006

Mapping

American Congress of Surveying and Mapping
210 Little Falls
Falls Church, VA 22046

Marine Corps

U.S. Marine Corps
The Pentagon
Washington, DC 20390

Material Handling

International Material Management Society
650 East Higgins Road
Schaumburg, IL 60195

Medical

American Medical Association
535 North Dearborn Street
Chicago, IL 60610

Medicare

U.S. Department of Health, Education,
 and Welfare
Washington, DC 20210

Mental Health

National Association of Mental Health
1021 Prince Street
Alexandria, VA 22314

Monopoly

U.S. Federal Trade Commission
Washington, DC 20580

Motor Carriers

U.S. Interstate Commerce
Washington, DC 20580

Motors and Equipment

Motor & Equipment Manufacturers Association
222 Cedar Lane
Teaneck, NJ 07666

Multiple Sclerosis

National Multiple Sclerosis Society
205 East 42nd Street
New York, NY 10017

Muscular Dystrophy

Muscular Dystrophy Association of America
810 7th Avenue
New York, NY 10019

Natural Gas

U.S. Department of Energy
Washington, DC 20585

Navy

U.S. Department of the Navy
The Pentagon
Washington, DC 20350

Nuclear Energy

American Nuclear Energy Society
555 North Kensington Avenue
LaGrange, IL 06625

U.S. Regulatory Commission
Washington, DC 20555

Nursing

National League of Nursing
10 Columbus Circle
New York, NY 10019

Oil Pipe Lines

Association of Oil Pipe Lines
1725 K Street, NW
Washington, DC 20006

Optics

Optical Society of America
1816 Jefferson Place, NW
Washington, DC 20036

Optometry

American Optometric Association
243 North Lindbergh Boulevard
St. Louis, MO 63141

Osteopathy

American Osteopathic Association
212 East Ohio Street
Chicago, IL 60611

Paper

American Paper Institute
260 Madison Avenue
New York, NY 10016

Pension Plans

Association of Private Pension and Welfare Plans
1331 Pennsylvania Avenue
Washington, DC 20001

Planning

American Planning Association
1776 Massachusetts Avenue, NW
Washington, DC 20036

Podiatry

American Podiatric Medical Association
20 Chevy Chase Circle
Washington, DC 20015

Political Science

American Academy of Political and Social Science
3937 Chestnut Street
Philadelphia, PA 19104

Population

Population Association of America
806 15th Street, NW
Washington, DC 20005

Psychology

American Psychology Association
1200 17th Street, NW
Washington, DC 20036

Public Accounts

American Institute of Certified Public Accountants
1211 Avenue of Americas
New York, NY 10036

Public Health

American Public Health Association
1015 15th Street, NW
Washington, DC 20005

U.S. Public Health Service
Washington, DC 20201

Race Relations

National Association for the Advancement
  of Colored People
186 Remsen Street
Brooklyn, NY 11202

Railroads

Association of American Railroads
50 F Street, NW
Washington, DC 20001

Real Estate

National Association of Realtors
430 North Michigan Avenue
Chicago, IL 60611

Red Cross

American Red Cross
17 and D Streets, NW
Washington, DC 20006

Rehabilitation

National Rehabilitation Association
633 South Washington Street
Alexandria, VA 22314

Retailing

American Retail Federation
1616 H Street, NW
Washington, DC 20006

Rubber

Rubber Manufacturers Association
1400 K Street, NW
Washington, DC 20005

Savings Banks

National Council of Savings Institutions
1101 15th Street, NW
Washington, DC 20005

Securities Regulations

U.S. Securities and Exchange Commission
Washington, DC 20549

Selling

Sales and Marketing Executives International
6151 Wilson Mills Road
Cleveland, OH 44143

Shipping

American Bureau of Shipping
45 Eisenhower Drive
Paramus, NJ 07652

U.S. Maritime Commission
Washington, DC 20573

Soap

The Soap and Detergent Association
475 Park Avenue South
New York, NY 10016

Social Science

American Academy of Political and Social Science
3937 Chestnut Street
Philadelphia, PA 19104

Soil Conservation

Soil Science Society of America
677 South Segoe Road
Madison, WI 53711

U.S. Soil Conservation Service
U.S. Department of Agriculture
Washington, DC 20013

Tariffs

U.S. Tariff Commission
Washington, DC 20436

Taxes

Tax Foundation
1 Thomas Circle, NW
Washington, DC 20005

Technical Schools

National Association of Technical
   and Trade Schools
2021 K Street, NW
Washington, DC 20006

Textiles

American Textile Manufacturers Institute
1101 Connecticut Avenue, NW
Washington, DC 20036

Water Pollution

U.S. Environmental Protection Agency
Washington, DC 20460

Waterworks

American Waterworks Association
6666 West Quincy Avenue
Denver, CO 80235

Welding

American Welding Association
550 NW LeJeune Road
Miami, FL 33126

Wool

The Wool Bureau
360 Lexington Avenue
New York, NY 10017

Appendix C
State Sales and Use Tax Agencies

Alabama

Department of Revenue
Sales and Use Taxes
Montgomery, Alabama 36130

Alaska

Department of Revenue
Pouch S
Juneau, Alaska 99801

Arizona

Sales Tax Division
Phoenix, Arizona 85007

Arkansas

Sales and Use Tax Division
Department of Finance and Administration
Little Rock, Arkansas 72201

California

Department of Business Taxes
State Board of Equalization
P.O. Box 1799
Sacramento, California 95808

Colorado

Department of Revenue
State Capital Annex
Denver, Colorado 80203

Connecticut

Sales, Use, and Excise Tax Division
Hartford, Connecticut 06115

Delaware

State Division of Revenue
Wilmington, Delaware 19801

District of Columbia

Department of Finance and Revenue
300 Indiana Avenue, N.W.
Washington, DC 20001

Florida

Sales Tax Bureau
Department of Revenue
Tallahassee, Florida 32304

Georgia

Sales and Use Tax Unit
Department of Revenue
Atlanta, Georgia 30334

Hawaii

Department of Taxation
State Tax Office Building
425 Queen Street
Honolulu, Hawaii 96813

Idaho

Sales Tax Division
State Tax Commission
Boise, Idaho 83707

Illinois

Department of Revenue
Springfield, Illinois 62706

Indiana

Sales Tax Division
Department of Revenue
100 N. Senate Avenue
Indianapolis, Indiana 46204

Iowa

Division of Retail and Use Tax
Department of Revenue
Lucas State Office Building
Des Moines, Iowa 50319

Kansas

Sales and Condensation Tax Division
State Revenue Building
Department of Revenue
Topeka, Kansas 66612

Kentucky

Sales Tax Division
Department of Revenue
Frankfort, Kentucky 40601

Louisiana

Collector of Revenue
Baton Rouge, Louisiana 70821

Maine

Sales Tax Division
Bureau of Taxation
Augusta, Maine 04330

Maryland

Retail Sales Tax Division
Treasury Department
301 West Preston Street
Baltimore, Maryland 21201

Massachusetts

Sales and Use Taxes
Department of Corporations
Boston, Massachusetts 02133

Michigan

Sales and Use Taxes
Department of Treasury
Revenue Division
Treasury Building
Lansing, Michigan 48922

Minnesota

Sales and Use Tax Division
Department of Taxation
Centennial Office Building
St. Paul, Minnesota 55101

Mississippi

Sales and Use Tax Division
State Tax Commission
Jackson, Mississippi 39205

Missouri

Sales and Use Tax Unit
P.O. Box 840
Jefferson City, Missouri 65102

Nebraska

Sales and Use Tax Unit
Department of Revenue
Box 4818, State Capitol
Lincoln, Nebraska 65809

Nevada

Nevada Tax Commission
Carson City, Nevada 89701

New Jersey

Division of Taxation
Department of Treasury
Trenton, New Jersey 08625

New Mexico

Bureau of Revenue
Santa Fe, New Mexico 87501

New York

Sales Tax Bureau
Department of Taxation and Finance
Tax and Finance Building
State Campus
Albany, New York

North Carolina

Sales Tax
State Capitol Building
Revenue Building — Main Office
Raleigh, North Carolina 27611

North Dakota

Sales Tax
State Capitol Building
Bismarck, North Dakota 58501

Ohio

Sales and Excise Division
Department of Taxation
68 East Gay Street
Columbus, Ohio 43151

Oklahoma

Sales and Use Taxes
Oklahoma Tax Commission
2101 Lincoln Boulevard
Oklahoma City, Oklahoma 73105

Pennsylvania

Bureau of Taxes for Education
Department of Revenue
Harrisburg, Pennsylvania 17128

Rhode Island

Department of Administration
49 Westminister Street
Providence, Rhode Island 02903

South Carolina

Sales and Use Tax Division
South Carolina Tax Commission
Columbia, South Carolina 29201

South Dakota

Sales and Use Tax Division
Department of Revenue
Pierre, South Dakota 57501

Tennessee

Sales and Use Tax Division
Department of Revenue
War Memorial Building
Nashville, Tennessee 37219

Texas

Comptroller of Public Accounts
Austin, Texas 78711

Utah

Sales Tax
State Tax Commission
201 State Office Building
Salt Lake City, Utah 84114

Vermont

Department of Taxes
State of Vermont
P.O. Box 547
Montpelier, Vermont 05602

Virginia

Sales and Use Tax Division
Department of Taxation
P.O. Box 6L
Richmond, Virginia 23215

Washington

Department of Revenue
Olympia, Washington 98501

Index